MODERN LEGAL STUDIES

LOCAL GOVERNMENT IN THE MODERN STATE

AUSTRALIA AND NEW ZEALAND
The Law Book Company Ltd.
Sydney : Melbourne : Perth

CANADA AND U.S.A.
The Carswell Company Ltd.
Agincourt, Ontario

INDIA
N. M. Tripathi Private Ltd.
Bombay
and
Eastern Law House Private Ltd.
Calcutta and Delhi
M.P.P. House
Bangalore

ISRAEL
Steimatzky's Agency Ltd
Jerusalem : Tel Aviv : Haifa

MAYLAYSIA : SINGAPORE : BRUNEI
Malayan Law Journal (Pte.) Ltd.
Singapore and Kuala Lumpur

PAKISTAN
Pakistan Law House
Karachi

MODERN LEGAL STUDIES

LOCAL GOVERNMENT IN THE MODERN STATE

by

MARTIN LOUGHLIN
Lecturer in Law,
London School of Economics
and Political Science

LONDON
SWEET & MAXWELL
1986

Published in 1986 by
Sweet & Maxwell Limited of
11 New Fetter Lane, London.
Computerset by Burgess & Son (Abingdon) Limited.
Printed in Great Britain by
Page Bros. (Norwich) Limited.

British Library Cataloguing in Publication Data
Loughlin, Martin
    Local government in the modern state.—
    (Modern legal studies)
    1. Local government—Great Britain
    I. Title   II. Series
    352.041 JS3111

    ISBN 0-421-338601
    ISBN 0-421-338709 Pbk

PREFACE

My primary aim in writing this book has been to examine recent developments affecting the status of local government. Many of the traditional assumptions about the role of local government have been progressively challenged during the last decade or so. The Thatcher administrations of the 1980s have articulated a view of the role of local government which has been highly contentious. But they have also, to an unprecedented degree, used the legal power of the State in an attempt to convert that vision into a reality. It is because of the centrality of law as an instrument in the pursuit of this objective that I feel justified in examining these broad developments from a legal point of view.

Consequently, my approach had been to examine the nature and significance of legal and administrative developments rather than to produce a detailed exposition of the law relating to local government. The latter approach, that adopted by the standard legal texts, tends to focus on the relationships between individuals and local government. My concern, however, has been to examine, through the medium of law, the role of local government within the broader system of government. This means that I am concerned as much with central government as local government. It also means that decision-making within local government is analysed only to the extent that it reflects on the status of local government within that broader system. In so doing I hope to provide an insight into the role of local government in the modern state. Having said that, I must add one qualification. Strictly speaking, I do not examine local government in the British state; I deal in detail only with the law relating to England and Wales. While the pattern of developments in Scotland is similar I have been unable to examine specifically the law applicable in Scotland; although such comparison, particularly with respect to financial arrangements, could prove illuminating. The situation in Northern Ireland is such as to defy simple comparison.

Finally, I have adopted this approach because I believe that, provided they discard some of their heavier ideological baggage, lawyers and social scientists can learn from each other. Lawyers should realise that an understanding of the nature, functions and purposes of public law must be rooted in economics, political science and social theory. Social scientists, on the other hand, might benefit from being required to examine in detail the precise forms which governmental decision-making takes. I have therefore tried to be sensitive to social, economic and political developments in writing this text and have sought to integrate some of those perspectives, especially through the referencing system. I should add that the referencing style I have used was intended to eliminate the distraction of footnotes; the enactment of the consolidatory Housing Act 1985, however, frustrated the realisation of this object with respect to Chapter 4.

I am very grateful to the following who have kindly given me permission to reproduce copyright material: R.J. Bennett and the Syndics of Cambridge University Press for Fig. 1.1; the Association of County Councils for Fig. 2.1; the Audit Commission and the Controller of Her Majesty's Stationary Office for Figures 2.2, 2.3, 2.6 and 2.7; and the Editors of Political Quarterly for Fig. 4.1. The Editors of Public Money have given me permission to reproduce Figures 2.4, 2.5 and Table 4.1. They require me to tell my readers that Public Money is available on subscription from the publishers: The Chartered Institute of Public Finance and Accountancy, 3, Robert Street, London WC2N 6BH. This book in some respects builds on *Local Government, the Law and the Constitution,* a study produced for the Local Government Legal Society in 1983. I am grateful to them for permission to draw from this work. Finally I should like to thank the following people who, in a variety of ways and at different stages of the work, have provided valuable assistance: Malcolm Grant, Patrick McAuslan, Maureen McGuinness, Gill Morris, Doreen Murphy, Martin Pilgrim, Stewart Ranson and Kieron Walsh. Thanks to the flexibility of Sweet & Maxwell I have been able to incorporate developments up to the end of March 1986.

April 1, 1986   Martin Loughlin

OTHER BOOKS IN THE SERIES

Anatomy of International Law (Second Edition), by J. G. Merrills
Compensation and Government Torts, by C. Harlow
Confessions, by Peter Mirfield.
Constructive Trusts, by A. J. Oakley
Council Housing (Second Edition), by D. C. Hoath
Court of Justice of the European Communities (Second Edition),
   by L. N. Brown and F. G. Jacobs
Development Control, by J. Alder
Emergency Powers in Peacetime, by David Bonner
Exclusion Clauses in Contracts (Second Edition), by David Yates
The Family Home, by W. T. Murphy and H. Clark
The Governance of Police, by Laurence Lustgarten
Grievances, Remedies and the State, by Patrick Birkinshaw
Homelessness, by David Hoath
Human Rights and Europe (Second Edition), by Ralph Beddard
Immigration Law (Second Edition), by John Evans
International Dispute Settlement, by J. G. Merrills
Law, Legitimacy and the Constitution, by McAuslan and
   McEldowney
Law of the Common Agricultural Policy, by Francis G. Snyder
Natural Justice (Second Edition), by Paul Jackson
Registered Land (Third Edition), by David J. Hayton
Remedies for Breach of Contract, by Hugh Beale
Security of Tenure under the Rent Act, by Jill E. Martin
Small Businesses (Second Edition), by Michael Chesterman
Strict and Vicarious Liability, by L. H. Leigh
Taxation and Trusts, by G. W. Thomas

CONTENTS

Contents

Contents

TABLE OF CASES

Table of Cases

Table of Cases

Table of Cases

TABLE OF STATUTES

Table of Statutes

Table of Statutes

Table of Statutes

Table of Statutes

Table of Statutes

ABBREVIATIONS

A.E.G.	Aggregate Exchequer Grant
A.M.A.	Association of Metropolitan Authorities
B.A.	Base Amount
B.R.B	British Railways Board
B.T.C.	British Transport Commission
C.D.P	Community Development Project
D.E.S.	Department of Education and Science
DoE	Department of the Environment
DoT	Department of Transport
D.L.G.	Derelict Land Grant
D.L.O.	Direct Labour Organisation
F.I.G.	Financial Institutions Group
GLC	Greater London Council
G.N.P.	Gross National Product
G.R.E.	Grant-Related Expenditure
G.R.P.	Grant-Related Poundage
G.R.V.	Gross Rateable Value
H.C.D.	Housing Costs Differential
H.I.P.	Housing Investment Programme
H.M.I.	Her Majesty's Inspectors of Education
H.R.A.	Housing Revenue Account
ILEA	Inner London Education Authority
L.B.C.	London Borough Council
L.C.C.	London County Council
L.C.D.	Local Contribution Differential
L.E.A.	Local Education Authority
L.G.P.L.A.	Local Government, Planning and Land Act 1980
L.I.T.	Local Income Tax
L.R.T.	London Regional Transport
L.T.B.	London Transport Board
L.T.E.	London Transport Executive
M.C.C.	Metropolitan County Council
M.S.C.	Manpower Services Commission
N.A.F.E.	Non-Advanced Further Education
N.B.C.	National Bus Company
OPEC	Organisation of Petroleum-Exporting Countries
P.E.L.	Protected Expenditure Level

Abbreviations

P.E.S.C.	Public Expenditure Survey Committee
P.P.V.A.	Public Passenger Vehicles Act 1981
P.S.V.	Public Service Vehicle
P.T.E.	Passenger Transport Executive
P.T.P.	Public Passenger Transport Plan
P.W.L.B.	Public Works Loans Board
R.S.G.	Rate Support Grant
T.E.	Total Expenditure
T.H.C.	Transport Holding Company
T.P.P.	Transport Policies and Programmes
T.S.G.	Transport Supplementary Grant
T.V.E.I.	Technical and Vocational Educational Initiative
U.D.A.G.	Urban Development Action Grant
U.D.C.	Urban Development Corporation
U.D.G.	Urban Development Grant
U.D.P.	Unitary Development Plan
Y.T.S.	Youth Training Scheme

Chapter 1

LOCAL GOVERNMENT IN THE MODERN STATE

1.1 Introduction

Continuous functional differentiation and increasing centralisation
are two important, though not always harmonious, trends in the
modern state. Both trends, however, seem to challenge the idea of
local government as a general and relatively autonomous institution. Furthermore, the resulting tensions are especially highlighted
in a unitary state underpinned by the sovereignty concept, since
local government is not accorded any protected status and is
generally assumed to derive its authority from the centre. The task
of evaluating the position of local government in the modern state is
therefore one of some complexity. Undertaking this task from a
legal perspective is not made any easier by the fact that the idea of
government is essentially a concept of political science and is not
easily accommodated in law.

A range of theories on the position of local government in the
modern state could be fashioned. Unfortunately there has been a
dearth of theorisation about local government. One reason for this
is that over the last 100 years local authorities have in fact
undertaken important governmental tasks and the value of the
institution therefore went largely unquestioned. The traditionalist
view of local government thus merely suggests that, since the
institutions of local government have existed for as long as those of
central government, local government provides its own justification.
Alternatively it could be argued that local government is essential
because the scale and complexity of tasks in the modern state
requires the use of a variety of institutions; in effect, that functional
differentiation strengthens local government. Again, since centralisation of power heightens the danger of tyranny, a healthy local
government system reflects a necessary pluralism in a modern
democratic state; that is, that local government is an essential
bulwark against over-centralisation.

Most theoretical discussion, however, has attempted to identify
local government along an autonomy-agency axis. Certain aspects
of a functionalist approach to local government, which expresses
the view that local government is an agency of the central state,
seem undeniable. In law, local authorities are statutory corporations

which are dependent on powers given to them by statute for their ability to act; the doctrine of *ultra vires* exists to ensure that they keep within their statutory powers and are accountable to the courts; and central departments of state possess a range of powers enabling them to influence the manner in which local authorities conduct their affairs. Furthermore, as we shall see, local government structures and functions have been periodically altered to suit the requirements of central government.

That much seems undeniable. However, even if the essence of the functionalist approach is accepted, it must still be recognised that local authorities possess a significant potential for initiative and diversity. It is this potential which is emphasised by the autonomists. Thus, local government law is concerned primarily with *powers* rather than *duties* and many of these powers are drafted in wide discretionary terms which are capable of broad interpretation. Furthermore, local authorities use their powers in innovative ways; not merely by shifting expenditures but also by increasing the range and altering the nature of the services they provide. Autonomists therefore challenge the "top-down" orientation of the functionalist perspective. Indeed they argue that innovation originates at the local, rather than the central, level: local authority discretion provides the capacity for policy innovation; this leads to experimentation; this experience is recorded by the centre; and eventually the policies are adopted by the centre and filter back down to the local level through policy guidance or new legislation.

Consequently the autonomists highlight the fact that the local authority is a general organisation with responsibility for a multiplicity of functions; that it has a taxing power; that the scope of its powers provides it with a capacity for local choice transcending the mere routine administration of specific tasks; and that it derives political legitimacy from its status as an elected body. That is, that local authorities look beyond specific tasks and are concerned with general well-being of the communities they serve. In short, that they constitute a tier of *government*.

Autonomists thus generally characterise the relationship between central and local government as a form of "partnership." This idea is perhaps a simplification since the terms of this partnership are as ambiguous as the network of linkages is complex. Recent work has thus sought to refine conceptually our understanding of this central-local relationship by utilising notions of "structured bargaining" (Rhodes 1981) or "relational contract" (Elliott 1981). But much of this work is based on the notion that fundamentally central and local government have the same interest; to promote the public welfare. Consequently, although the relationship may be one of "competitive co-operation" (Sharpe 1970, p. 170), this work at some basic level rests on a view that central and local bodies share a common sense of purpose.

So long as the validity of the assumptions on which the post-war Welfare State were founded went unquestioned, these issues remained ambiguous and of peripheral importance. With the strains experienced since the mid-1970s, however, they assume new significance. Conflict in central-local government relations has become the norm. In the process the relationship has become both politicised and juridified (see Chap. 9). Politicisation occurs when the idea that central and local government have a basic mutuality of objective is widely questioned. Juridification results from the increased importance of investigating the legal limits of the powers of local authorities. The ambiguous issues thus become crucially significant. Is the discretion vested in local authorities an administrative or political phenomenon? Is discretion vested in local authorities to enable them to adapt centrally formulated services to specific local conditions and needs? Or is it to be viewed in terms of local representatives having the right to determine service levels, policies and priorities? And, if the latter, what limits are to be placed on the discretion of local representatives?

The process of juridification, therefore, is not without its complexities. The basic reason lies in the fact that the law in this area does not establish authoritative norms defining the respective spheres of responsibility of central departments and local authorities. Disputes were intended to be resolved through administrative processes rather than by recourse to the courts. Consequently, owing to the facilitative nature of much local government legislation, the *ultra vires* doctrine has not generally imposed a severe restraint on local authority action.

Contrary to some opinion, therefore, the *ultra vires* doctrine does not in itself render local authorities subordinate to central departments. But, given the realities of modern government, it does mean that in certain circumstances they are dependent on the central department's sanction. In the period of expansion and consensus the centre, despite particular disputes, was broadly supportive. With the emergence of a period of retrenchment, the notion of consensus has been strained as the centre has sought to impose its contentious view of the public good on local authorities. This has resulted ultimately in an attempt by the Government significantly to alter the legal framework in which local government operates.

The nature of legal relations in this period of retrenchment provides the primary focus of this book. It is during this period that the ambiguous issues assume novel significance, that claims concerning local government autonomy are highlighted and that the structural limitations to the adoption of the view of local authorities as instruments of central government are revealed. A study of relations during this period may therefore provide some acute insights into the role of local government in the modern state. In order to place these issues in context, however, the traditional status of local government through an examination of the key areas of *functions, structure* and *finance* must first be considered.

1.2 The Restructuring of Local Government Functions

At the start of the nineteenth century the functions of local government were undertaken by a variety of bodies such as the municipal corporations, the justices of the peace, the parishes and a range of special purpose authorities. But local government was not known as such. By the end of the century, however, and as a result of such reforms as the Municipal Corporations Act 1835, the extension of the principle of representative democracy to county councils in 1888 and the establishment of district councils in 1894 and the London boroughs in 1899, the framework of local government as we know it was more or less intact. This basic framework survived until the last 25 years.

These reforms were required because of the growth in local government functions in the nineteenth century. This was the result of social and economic change brought about by the forces of *industrialisation* and *urbanisation*. Collective action was needed for several reasons. First, on simple nuisance grounds: "it is unpleasant when a town of 2,000 inhabitants dumps raw sewage into the streets or local river; it is a major social and economic problem if this happens in a city of one million" (Dawson 1985, pp. 27–28). Secondly, the social conditions produced by urbanisation were breeding grounds for disease. This had tax consequences: "Filth caused epidemics, epidemics brought pauperisation of widows and orphans, and paupers meant increased taxation for poor relief" (Merrett 1979, p. 7). It also had an effect on labour productivity (Gauldie 1974, pp. 187–188). Thirdly, the social conditions were such that they caused concern about the dangers of social unrest:

4

"Some such measures are urgently called for," reported the Select Committee on the Health of Towns in 1840, "not less for the welfare of the poor than the safety of property and the security of the rich."

Collective action was required and local authorities seemed to be the most appropriate bodies to undertake the necessary action. Many of the services provided by local authorities were local *public goods*. That is, they were services which, although needed, either could not be provided by the market or could only be provided very inefficiently. The two standard characteristics of public goods are non-excludability and non-rivalness (Foster *et al.* 1980, pp. 40–42). Non-excludability means that it is almost impossible to charge consumers for the amount of the good they consume. Non-rivalness means that once a good is provided more of it can be consumed without generating additional costs. The provision of street-lighting is an example of a public good; it is extremely inefficient to attempt to charge consumers for the individual benefit they obtain and also, once street-lighting is provided in an area, the cost of the service does not increase when there is an increase in the numbers of consumers of the service. With such public goods it is much more efficient to provide them collectively and, since everyone benefits more or less equally, to finance the cost of provision through taxation. Many of the services pioneered by local authorities in the nineteenth century, such as highways, street-lighting, parks, public health, police and fire services, have the characteristics of public goods.

Local authorities were also significantly involved in the provision of certain types of *trading services*. These services could be provided by the market. However, because they were extremely capital intensive there was a tendency to monopoly in the provision of such goods. (Scott 1982, pp. 143–145). Consequently, "it was more efficient to provide these as local spatial monopolies, but to avoid monopoly profits it became common for these to be provided for by municipal enterprise." (Foster *et al.* 1980, p. 52). Thus, especially in the latter half of the century, there was a significant growth in municipal trading services such as markets, slaughterhouses, bathing establishments, refuse disposal, waterworks, gasworks, electricity works and street transport.

Finally, certain services were provided by local authorities which were *redistributive* in nature; the provision of these services benefited a particular social group. During the nineteenth century the main redistributive service was the provision of poor relief. After the Education Act 1870, however, education grew in

5

importance as a redistributive service and later, after the First World War, housing provision assumed this characteristic.

Throughout the nineteenth century local authorities increased the scope of their responsibilities. By the 1930s local government had reached the highpoint of its functional range. At this stage local government services were primarily public goods or trading services and were production orientated. In 1885, for example, redistributive services accounted for only 23 per cent. of local expenditure and in 1935, although the proportion had risen, it still constituted only 43 per cent. (Figures derived from Foster *et al.* 1980 pp. 103–112).

Since the 1930s local government functions have been radically restructured. Local authorities have been stripped of various responsibilities, including trunk roads in 1936, electricity in 1947, gas in 1948, water and sewerage in 1974, public assistance between 1934 and 1948, hospitals in 1946 and the remaining local health services in 1974. This has not necessarily resulted in a reduced status for local authorities, however, since they have both retained and assumed responsibility for many services which have grown in importance with the establishment of the welfare state; especially education, housing and personal social services. But what is significant is that there has been a disproportionate loss of production-orientated trading services and a growth in significance of consumption-orientated redistributive services. Local government is now largely concerned with the provision of redistributive services; in 1975, for example, 65 per cent. of local expenditure was devoted to redistributive services.

This restructuring of local government functions has had a significant impact on central-local government relations. It is a basic principle of public finance that there are severe limitations on a local authority's ability successfully to undertake independent policies of income redistribution. If a local authority sought to do so a more equal distribution of income might be achieved but "through the emigration of the rich and possibly also the immigration of the poor, a fall in average real income per head will occur." (Foster *et al.* 1980, p. 44). This would limit the authority's ability to continue the policy. Consequently, as a result of this restructuring of functions, central government may legitimately claim to take an active interest in the redistributive policies of local authorities in order to ensure a degree of co-ordination and effectiveness in service provision. This restructuring also has certain financial implications which are considered in section 1.4 below.

1.3 Local Government Reorganisation

Nineteenth–century local government reforms were incremental and pragmatic and led to the establishment of a local government structure which was divided along urban-rural lines. With continuing urban growth in the twentieth century, conflicts emerged between urban and rural authorities as the towns and cities grew beyond their administrative boundaries. These conflicts highlighted the need for reform and caused William Robson, writing in the 1930s, to predict that "unless a major adaptation of the structure is effected before we reach the second half of the twentieth century an alternative solution will be sought through the establishment of boards or commissions set up to conduct local services and entirely divorced from existing municipal institutions" (Robson 1935, p. 458).

As we have seen, this is precisely what happened after the Second World War with the establishment of public corporations to run the nationalised gas and electricity industries and with the creation of the national health service. Other pressures for centralisation existed at the time, such as the adoption of Keynesian macro-economic policies, the pursuit of equality through uniform and standardised service provision, the search for perceived economies of scale, and the centralisation tendencies of trade union bargaining arrangements. (Sharpe 1982, p. 154). Nevertheless, the inadequacy of the existing local government structure undoubtedly provided a further reason for nationalisation rather than municipalisation.

The urban-rural division, however, meant that local authorities "were locked into a conflict which was imposed by the structure and which acted as a major inhibitor of the structural change" (Alexander 1985, p.52). These conflicts ensured that there would never be unanimity amongst the various groups of local authorities over the need for, and certainly the form of, any reorganisation since they were engaged in a zero-sum game. Consequently, "the conflict that was built into the local government system in the nineteenth century created *immobilisme* in the twentieth." (*ibid.*). If central government were to intervene and impose reorganisation, however, that in itself would reinforce the sense of hierarchy in the central-local relationship. As a result, although the need for reorganisation was widely recognised by the 1930s, it was not until the 1960s that the process of reform was under way.

The institutional reforms proposed in the 1960s were part of a broader technocratic movement which viewed institutional modernisation as the key to the reversal of Britain's economic decline. During this period reports on local government staffing (Mallaby 1967), management (Maud 1967; Bains 1972) and structure (Herbert 1960; Redcliffe-Maud 1969) were commissioned. Local government in London was the first to be reformed. Local government in the metropolitan conurbation was comprehensively reorganised by the London Government Act 1963; around 100 local authorities were replaced by a two-tier system consisting of the Greater London Council (GLC), as the strategic authority, and 32 London borough councils together with the City of London Corporation as district-level authorities (see Alexander 1982. Chap. 2). The distribution of functions between the two tiers is illustrated in Table 1.1.

The London exercise demonstrated the feasibility of comprehensive reorganisation and in 1966 the Royal Commission on Local Government in England and Wales was established. The Commission (Redcliffe-Maud 1969, Vol. 1, para. 85) recognised that the failure of the existing local government structure "to recognise the interdependence of town and country" was its "most fatal defect" and recommended the establishment of larger, unitary authorities.

English and Welsh reorganisation followed. But the newly elected Conservative government opted for a two-tier system. Given the Conservatives' attachment to tradition and the fact that their power base lay in the counties (which were most threatened by urban-centred unitary structures) it is hardly surprising that reforms were constructed around the existing system. In the Local Government Act 1972 the number of local authorities in England and Wales was significantly reduced and the new system, consisting of 6 metropolitan counties, 47 non-metropolitan counties, and 369 district councils, was established. The primary significance of this distinction between metropolitan and non-metropolitan authorities relates to the distribution of functions. Allocation of functions between county and district in metropolitan and non-metropolitan areas is laid out in Table 1.1.

Consequently, by 1974 the local government system had been comprehensively reorganised with the establishment of larger authorities and the creation of a universal two-tier system. This two-tier structure was not without its critics. Alan Alexander considered that the structure ensured "that the new classes of authority would be as mutually antagonistic as the old ones" and consequently "it ensured that local government would be ill-equipped to resist the rapid increase in pressure for centralisation." (Alexander 1985,

Table 1.1 Allocation of Major Local Authority Functions.

	COUNTY COUNCIL	DISTRICT COUNCIL

NON-METROPOLITAN AREAS	Police
	Fire
	Consumer protection
	Highways, traffic and
	  transportation
	Structure plans
	Refuse disposal
	Education
	Social Services
		Housing
		Environmental health
		Development control
		Refuse collection
		Public transport
		  undertakings

METROPOLITAN AREAS	Police Fire Consumer protection Highways, traffic and transportation Refuse disposal Passenger transport	Housing Environmental health Development control Refuse collection Education Social services

LONDON	Fire
	Highways, traffic and
	  transportation
	Planning (strategic)
	Housing (strategic)
	Refuse disposal
	Education (inner London)
	Passenger transport
		Housing
		Environmental health
		Planning (local)
		Refuse collection
		Education (outer
		  London)
		Social services

p. 64). Indeed one could go further and suggest that the reforms which were enacted were not part of a programme of creating functionally effective units through which the trend towards centralisation could be reversed (*cf.* Ministry of Housing and Local Government 1970), but part of the centralisation process itself. This argument is based on the fact that the trends towards centralisation had placed a premium on reducing the number of local government units, since there were limits to the number of units the centre could co-ordinate in order to achieve its aims. This would suggest that, just as in the nineteenth century, the political will to reform local government structures arose only once the centre accepted that structural reform was a necessary precondition of efficient governmental action. But whereas the need in the nineteenth century was for local action, in the twentieth the impetus has moved to the centre.

1.4 The Financing of Local Government Expenditure

The scale of local government expenditure has increased significantly over the last 100 years. In 1885 local expenditure constituted around 4 per cent. of gross national product (G.N.P.); by 1975 its share of G.N.P. had increased to 18 per cent. Furthermore, despite losing certain functions, there has been a rapid increase in local expenditure since the Second World War. The period between 1965 and 1975 was particularly significant, since it was marked by a high rate of growth in local expenditure combined with an unprecedented increase in its share of G.N.P. By the mid-1970s local government was spending £15,000 million a year, was servicing a capital debt of £25,000 million and was employing 3 million people (Layfield 1976, pp. 13–14). Local government expenditure today amounts to about one-quarter, and is the biggest single item, of total public expenditure.

This growth in local expenditure has been largely the result of the growing importance of the social welfare services provided by local authorities. The growth in demand for these services results from various developments such as the nature of population changes (especially the increase in the numbers of elderly); rising relative costs (due primarily to the labour-intensive nature of these services); the impact of social change (indicated by such factors as structural unemployment and the growth in the numbers of one-parent families); and the fact that improvements in welfare generate their own dynamic for further improvements (*e.g.* improvements in secondary education result in a demand for the expansion of higher educational opportunities). (Gough 1979, Chap. 5). As a result, real increases in local expenditure have been required merely to maintain existing standards.

How was this growth in local expenditure financed? Local authorities receive revenue from three main sources: rates, central government grants, and fees and charges for the services they provide. The trend in the proportion of revenue met from these sources over the last century is illustrated in Figure 1.1. This shows that grants have steadily increased in importance as a source of revenue, while rates have significantly decreased. In fact the rates: fees: grant ratio has switched from 55 : 33 : 12 in 1885, to 34 : 38 : 28 in 1935 and 25 : 27 : 48 in 1975. Thus the dramatic increase in local expenditure which has occurred since the war has been financed mainly by central government grants, and the burden of domestic rates expressed as a proportion of personal disposable income has remained fairly constant. (Dunleavy 1980, p. 63).

Figure 1.1   Source of revenue on the current account of local authorities in England and Wales 1867 – 1980.

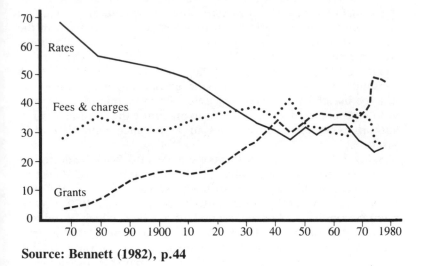

Source: Bennett (1982), p.44

The reasons for, and implications of, these trends are of some importance. There are two basic principles of taxation; the *benefit* principle and the *ability to pay* principle. The benefit principle implies that people are taxed in accordance with the benefits they derive from the expenditure financed through taxation, whereas the ability to pay principle is based on a judgement about desirable distribution of income or wealth. Since rates are regressive in effect and have not been fashioned in accordance with ability to pay, it could be argued that this tax reflects the benefit principle. Thus rates may have been an appropriate local tax in the nineteenth century when local government was primarily concerned with trading services or public goods provision, but with the growth in importance of redistributive services, rates became an inappropriate tax. Some alternative tax, such as local income tax, reflecting the ability to pay principle could have been fashioned, but this would have given local authorities a degree of independence which central government seems unprepared to countenance. Consequently, local expenditure growth has been financed by grants from central government.

This is not without its problems since a significant increase in proportion of local expenditure met by grants could undermine the autonomy of local authorities, especially if the grants are earmarked for specific services. In fact this is precisely what occurred in the early part of the post–war period and by 1957/58 specific grants were meeting the costs of 24 per cent. of total local expenditure (Bennett 1982, p. 55). However the Local Government Act 1958 consolidated many of these specific grants into a general grant, unhypothecated to specific services. This principle of grant provision has operated since and aims to maximise the freedom of local authorities to allocate revenues in accordance with their own priorities.

Since 1958 various modifications have also been made to the rating system to alleviate some of its limitations as a modern taxing mechanism for financing redistributive services. First, in the 1958 Act industry, which had been partially de-rated since 1928, was re-rated. Secondly, the Local Government Act 1966, which introduced the rate support grant (R.S.G.) as the basic form of the general grant, also included a "domestic element" as part of the R.S.G; in effect this was a discount on the rates payable by domestic ratepayers (or alternatively a form of super-rating on industrial and commercial ratepayers). Finally, the General Rate Act 1967 gave widespread rate relief, through a rate rebate system, to domestic ratepayers on low incomes. The effect of the first two measures was to reduce the proportion of rates paid by domestic ratepayers from around two-thirds before the war to 44 per cent. today (Jackman 1985, p. 156). The impact of the rate rebate scheme was even more significant; by 1981 30 per cent. of all householders were in receipt of rate rebates (*ibid.*). As a result of these measures, the regressive nature of domestic rates was modified and by the late 1970s domestic ratepayers were financing only about 15 per cent. of total local government expenditure.

These reforms have generated their own set of problems. Since the receipt of R.S.G. is tied to a local authority's aggregate expenditure, the regressive nature of the rating system in effect provided a restraint mechanism which bolstered the principle of local financial accountability. The rating reforms, however, have weakened this mechanism. As a result, the incentives on local authorities to increase their expenditure threatened to jeopardise the sophisticated system of public expenditure controls which the Treasury introduced through the P.E.S.C. system in the early 1960s. Indeed, local government expenditure could be viewed not only as the Achilles heel of the public expenditure control system but also, particularly because of the restructuring of functions, of the modern capitalist state (Saunders 1980, p. 551). Given central government's reluctance to reform comprehensively the system of local government finance, increased central controls seemed inevitable.

1.5 Retrenchment

The impetus for centralisation came with the era of retrenchment experienced in the last decade. Local expenditure growth came to an abrupt halt with the economic crisis of the mid-1970s. This crisis was sparked off by the increase in oil prices by OPEC in 1973 which provoked a major world slump in which Britain, as a weaker economy, suffered very severely. Production declined and inflation and unemployment rates soared. Cuts in public expenditure were imposed (Gough 1979, pp. 128–136). It became imperative for central government to find mechanisms for encouraging local expenditure restraint. The Layfield Committee (1976), which was set up to review the system of local government finance, should therefore be seen not as the final stage in the process of institutional modernisation, but rather as a response to the financial strains caused by the costs of local government reorganisation and public expenditure cutbacks resulting from the economic crisis.

The Labour Government 1974–1979 sought to achieve expenditure restraint within the existing legal framework, through a process of exhortation together with steady reductions in the proportion of local expenditure which the centre would finance through the R.S.G. system. New administrative mechanisms were devised. In 1975 the Consultative Council on Local Government Finance was established to act as a forum within which central and local government could meet to discuss financial matters (Taylor 1979;

Binder 1982). This forum enabled local expenditure to be brought into the P.E.S.C. system in a more coherent manner, and in 1977/78 cash limits were applied to central government grants (Bevan 1980). The result was that by 1979/80 the volume of grant support had fallen by 15 per cent. from the 1975/76 level and local government had largely complied with central government guidelines on expenditure (Greenwood 1981; 1982).

This strategy was therefore quite successful in encouraging restraint. In 1979, however, matters reached a new stage. The newly elected Conservative Government took the view that Britain's economic problems largely resulted from the level and nature of public expenditure and the lack of innovation and responsiveness of public bodies. Their aim has been not merely to reduce the level of public expenditure but also to restructure the Welfare State. This has had a profound impact on local government.

Key elements in this attempt to restructure the Welfare State have been attempts to reduce public sector employment, to shift expenditure priorities away from social welfare services and to reconstruct social policy on the principle of individualism rather than collectivism. Consequently the policies of the Conservative Government have for several reasons had a severe impact on local government: first because of the fact that, owing to the labour-intensive nature of their services and central government's lack of executant responsibility, local authorities employ more people than central government; secondly, because local government tradition-ally represents a commitment to the collective provision of services; thirdly, because, as a result of the restructuring functions, local government is heavily social-welfare orientated; and finally because central government has failed to devise a modern system of local finance which will protect the autonomy of local government. The result has been a period of serious conflict between central and local government. It is during this period that the ambiguities of the central-local relationship assume new significance.

The legal framework of local government was established primarily during the post–war period of economic growth and expansion of services. The Conservative Government took the view that this framework was quite inappropriate for the era of retrenchment. As a result, in the period since 1979 an unpreceden-ted volume of local government legislation has been enacted. Of greater significance than the volume, however, has been the nature of this legislation. Basically the Government have been attempting to alter the nature of the framework by imposing specific duties on local authorities, curtailing administrative discretion by imposing detailed statutory procedures on local decision-making and by centralising discretionary decision-making by vesting broad powers of intervention in the Secretary of State.

The attempt to do so provides the primary focus of this book. Conflicts over *finance* have been of central importance as the government have tried various mechanisms to encourage local authorities to reduce expenditure and have sought to instil new forms of financial discipline on them. These issues are dealt with in Chapters 2 and 7. The issue of local government *functions* is dealt with primarily by examining legal developments and legal disputes concerning certain redistributive services; public transport (Chap. 3), housing (Chap. 4) and education (Chap. 5). But Chapter 6 also deals with the relationship between local authorities and the production process. Reforms to the *structure* of local government are focussed on in Chapter 8. Finally, the impact of these changes on central-local government relations are examined in Chapter 9.

1.6 A Local Government Life Cycle?

Before examining legal developments in detail, an assessment of their potential significance might be attempted. One working hypothesis is that the Conservative Government, being unprepared to restore the financial independence of local government, are seeking to impose one particular type of financial discipline on local authorities by attempting to eliminate the redistributive dimension to local services. The most obvious way of doing this would be to convert redistributive services into trading services: for example, by eliminating revenue subsidies to local public transport and requiring transport services to operate on a commercial basis; by pushing up council house rents to economic levels; and by reorientating education away from a focus on personal development of pupils and towards training for their future employment roles.

Local authorities would therefore be responsible only for the provision of public goods and trading services. The question of why these services are provided by local authorities may then be raised. If trading services are operated on a commercial basis they might just as well be provided by private bodies. Even local public goods provision could be privatised through a tendering process in which the successful contractor is granted a local spatial monopoly, albeit subject to regulation and monitoring by the local authority. Thus it might be envisaged that local authorities will completely withdraw from collective service provision. The function of the local authority will be essentially that of a regulatory and monitoring agency with redistributive issues being dealt with by nationally established schemes for income transfers.

This view is necessarily speculative although it may prove a useful hypothesis against which to evaluate legal developments affecting local government. What may be termed a technocratic functionalist life cycle of local government (*cf.* Dawson 1985, pp. 32–33), identifying all critical stages in the rise and fall of local government, can then be postulated.

1. Parliament passes *permissive* legislation, enabling ad hoc local authorities to act in order to fill the gaps in service provision left by the private market.

2. Eventually, after experience is gained by the pioneering authorities, *compulsory* legislation, requiring local authorities to act, is enacted.

3. Responsibilities are transferred from ad hoc authorities to local government.

4. Thereafter central government is concerned with the uneveness of service provision and this leads to greater central control.

5. The search for economies of scale or the desire to achieve uniformity of service provision leads to the transfer of functions to central government.

6. The emergence of the welfare state results in the expansion of the social welfare services of local authorities which are used as agents for national policies of redistribution.

7. The structure of local government is reformed after concerns are expressed about the inefficiency of local government units along with the inability of the centre to co-ordinate adequately the activities of local authorities.

8. Retrenchment causes the centre to switch concern from minimum to maximum standards of service provision.

9. Local government functions are restructured along individualistic rather than collectivistic lines, the redistributive dimension to services is minimised and some functions are undertaken by private bodies.

10. Local government becomes essentially a regulatory and monitoring authority.

11. Problems requiring governmental initiatives are dealt with by special purpose authorities established and funded by central government.

This hypothesis is based on the view that local government has flourished during a particular phase in the development of capitalism in Britain and that its primary function has been to minimise the strains imposed by the transition from incipient to advanced capitalism. That is, its role has been to minimise the disruption caused between the decline of *rentier* landlordism and the growth of owner-occupation, to ensure the efficient provision of mass public transport until the rise of widespread ownership of the private motor car, and to maintain the infrastructure of the major industrial cities while they remained centres of production. This argument implies that there are links between industrialisation, urbanisation and the logic of collective action. Britain, at its particular stage of advanced capitalism, is undergoing the process of *deindustrialisation* (Fothergill and Gudgin 1982) and *deurbanisation* (Young and Mills 1982). These processes challenge the (capitalist) logic of collective action.

This functionalist hypothesis, however, underplays the fact that local authorities are large organisations which have a fair amount of autonomy and, as a tier of government, a degree of legitimacy which enables them to promote their own conception of public welfare. This ensures that central government will not easily be able to impose its will on uncooperative local authorities. This is especially the case with the local authorities based on the major industrial cities, which grew with industrialisation and urbanisation in the nineteenth century. These authorities are traditionally Labour controlled and have generally been in the vanguard of public service provision.

Thus an understanding of the economic, social and political developments affecting the major cities are important if recent legal developments affecting local government are to be understood (see section 9.2). While the impact of the Conservative Government's policies has been felt by all local authorities, those authorities based on the major industrial cities have, arguably, been most severely affected (Bramley 1984) and certainly have been most vociferous in their opposition. Consequently, these authorities figure prominently in legal disputes since many which have arisen are part of a broader ideological conflict between urban authorities pursuing the policies of municipal socialism and those interests most opposed to such

17

policies—ratepayers, Conservative controlled local authorities and the Government. While it seems unlikely that we will be able to determine conclusively the reality of any local government life cycle, the issues thrown up by such general speculation should be borne in mind when examining the nature of specific legal developments.

Chapter 2

LOCAL GOVERNMENT FINANCE

2.1 Introduction

Since the mid-1970s local government has been experiencing severe fiscal strain. On the one hand it has been faced with increasing costs for maintaining existing levels of services, while on the other it has encountered pressures which have resulted in a reduction in the resources available to it. The pressure for restraint has come mainly from central government who, since the mid-1970s, have steadily reduced the real value of central government grants. Local authorities wishing to protect service standards were therefore faced with three alternatives for increasing their income: raising income from rates; increasing fees and charges on services; or from increasing their indebtedness. None of these options seemed particularly attractive.

Rates are levied on occupiers of property. The rate is expressed as a rate of x pence in the £ (a rate poundage) and the amount payable depends on the rateable value of the property, based on a notional annual rental value of the property calculated by the Inland Revenue. The basic law of rating, which is contained mainly in the General Rate Act 1967, is not examined here (see Cross 1981, Chap. 8; Davies 1983, pp. 174–182), but it should be mentioned that one general rate is levied in each rating area by the rating authority (district councils and London borough councils). County authorities take a share of the income raised by the general rate by issuing precepts, which are then included as an element in the general rate.

Raising extra income by increasing rates is not a particularly attractive option for local authorities because the rates are generally regarded as an unpopular tax. One reason is that, notwithstanding the reforms mentioned in section 1.4, rates are generally regressive in effect. Perhaps of even greater significance, however, is the fact that rates are both highly visible and non-buoyant, *i.e.* people are more conscious of rates than other taxes and the rateable tax base does not automatically increase with a rise in the general price index.

The second alternative, that of increasing fees and charges, might be particularly unattractive to many local authorities as it could undermine the original redistributive objective of local authority service provision. Nevertheless, the Layfield Committee (1976, Chap. 9) felt that charges could play a larger part in the financing of local government and the Labour Government set in train a review of charging policies (DoE 1977, para. 6.25–6.26). The Conservative Government has instituted a variety of incentives designed to encourage local authorities to increase fees and charges (see section 7.3).

Finally, increasing indebtedness is not a viable option for local authorities, both because central government effectively controls the level of local authority borrowing and because local authorities cannot generally borrow for revenue purposes. A distinction between capital and revenue expenditure must be made. Capital expenditure is expenditure used to acquire assets such as land, buildings and machinery. Because these assets have a relatively long life they are financed by borrowing, spreading the cost of the assets through time and therefore across future ratepayers who are likely to receive their benefits. The debt charges incurred by borrowing thus constitutes an item of revenue expenditure. Revenue expenditure, then, is expenditure which meets the current cost of providing services; such as debt charges, wages, heating and fuel costs, and the purchase of goods which are consumed quickly. Although local authority debt has steadily increased since the mid-1970s (Newton 1981, pp. 195–196) increasing indebtedness is hardly a solution to a local authority's financial problems.

Since local authorities are faced with a range of unsuitable alternatives for financing their expenditures, grant allocation gives central government a potentially powerful control mechanism. In this chapter, therefore, the reforms which have been made to the system of local government finance by the Conservative Government in an attempt to ensure that the local government expenditure complies with central government's plans are examined. But before examining these reforms in detail we must first evaluate the Government's argument that they need to control aggregate local authority expenditure in order to protect their legitimate macro-economic policy objectives.

2.2 The Economic Rationale for Expenditure Control

According to the Conservative Government, the level of public expenditure lay at the heart of Britain's economic difficulties and therefore had to be reduced. Since local government expenditure is a major item of public expenditure and was not falling as rapidly as the Government wished, a priority has been to reform the system of local government finance in order to ensure that local government spending falls in line with the Government's plans. These reforms have therefore been justified as a necessary consequence of the Government's economic policies.

There does not, however, appear to be any technical reason why monetarist economic policies are more concerned with aggregate local expenditure. In fact the Treasury appears to have adopted monetarist policies since 1976 and the effect of the election of a Conservative Government has been merely to make this more explicit. Certainly the level of local authority borrowing becomes a key variable. But central government has always possessed sufficient powers to control borrowing levels. Local expenditure financed by tax income, however, has no effect on the P.S.B.R., money supply, aggregate demand in the economy or the rate of inflation (Barlow 1981; Jackson 1982; Jackman 1982). That is, local government is a largely self-regulating sector of the economy.

The Government have argued, however, that they have a legitimate concern with the total tax burden because this may discourage effort and thus have an effect on economic growth. Also, they are particularly concerned about the burden on industry, whose profits have been squeezed by the economic recession (Brittan 1982; Department of the Environment (DoE) 1983, Chap. 1). The strength of these more general economic arguments also seem debatable. Since the mid-1970s local government expenditure has not increased as rapidly as central government expenditure. Furthermore, although the value of central grants has been diminishing, rates have not increased as steeply as the growth in central taxes (Travers and Burgess 1983, p. 13). The local contribution to the total tax burden does not therefore seem in need of particular control. Nor has the government justified its assertion that the local tax burden creates a disincentive effect; the research evidence is equivocal and indeed may even show that it stimulates greater earning efforts (*ibid.* pp. 14–15).

The Government's argument about the effect of taxation on industry is also difficult to sustain. Non-domestic rates constitute roughly 60 per cent. of total rates. But industry contributes only one-quarter of the non-domestic rate bill. Furthermore, rates constitute only about two per cent. of manufacturing industry's total costs and three per cent. for private business as a whole and during the late 1970s rates bills rose less than any other major cost on industry and commerce (Bramley 1983, pp. 11–14). Consequently rates seem a relatively unimportant aspect of industry's costs. Arguments that rates as a proportion of profits have increased, therefore, merely reflect the fact that rates are difficult to avoid and that industry's profitability has declined significantly in recent years; they do not provide conclusive evidence of a causal connection.

This analysis suggests that the general economic arguments relating to the Government's need to manage the economy do not provide a sound basis for engaging in detailed control of total local expenditure. Certainly the Government has a legitimate interest in regulating the general economic environment, but the traditional instruments enabling it to control the level of grants to local government and the level of local authority borrowing seem quite effective for macro-economic management purposes.

Consequently it is suggested that the Government's attempts to obtain detailed control of local expenditure are part of a more explicitly political strategy. The economic arguments make sense only within the framework of a contentious political ideology such as a theological belief in the virtues of a minimalist or non-interventionist government. So while the argument that the size of the public sector "crowds out" investment opportunities for the productive sector (Bacon and Eltis 1976) does not seem to have much technical or empirical support (Barlow 1981, pp. 8–10), it has been adopted by the Government as an article of faith. In essence it stems from a belief that the growth of the public sector has distorted the formation of market relations throughout the economy. The Government's objective has been to expand the sphere of society subject to market disciplines. This has resulted in an attempt fundamentally to restructure the Welfare State. Detailed controls over local government finance are an essential part of this restructuring. The immediate priority was to reform the grant system, since that framework was never designed as a control mechanism. But individualised expenditure controls were almost inevitable since the control of each local authority's aggregate expenditure was required, not to protect the Government's macro-economic policies, but to enable it to achieve its contentious market-based and individualistic social policies. Without individualised controls local authorities opposed to the Government's social policies might frustrate their realisation.

2.3 Reform of the Grant System

2.3.1 Introduction. The Conservative Government on assuming office immediately set about the task of reforming the grant system. The basic grant, known as the rate support grant (R.S.G.), provided general financial support to local authorities and accounted for about 85 per cent. of central government grant aid. The R.S.G. system, which had been introduced in the Local Government Act 1974, was to be left intact by the Conservative Government, whose objective was essentially to change the principles on which the R.S.G. was distributed. This new grant distribution mechanism was enacted in Part VI of the Local Government, Planning and Land Act 1980.

Although the R.S.G. is extremely complicated in its details the objectives of the grant are relatively straightforward; the basic objective is to achieve some degree of equalisation of both financial resources and expenditure needs of local authorities. Some local authorities are much more wealthy than others. This may be expressed in terms of the gross rateable value (G.R.V.) of their area. The standard measure of wealth is the G.R.V. per head of population; that of Westminster London Borough Council, for example, is almost ten times that of Wandsworth London Borough Council. One objective of the R.S.G. is to compensate authorities for disparities in wealth. Also, some local authorities have greater spending needs than others. If, for example, a local education authority has a higher than average number of schoolchildren per head of population then, other things being equal, it would have greater spending needs. Another objective of the R.S.G., therefore, is to compensate authorities for differences in spending needs. In theory the ultimate objective of the R.S.G. is to compensate authorities for disparities in both resources and needs so as to enable them all to provide similar standards of services for a similar rate in the pound.

Before the 1980 Act this was achieved by dividing the R.S.G. into three elements. The *domestic element* was introduced in effect to subsidise the rate bills of domestic ratepayers (Bennett 1982, pp. 78–82). The *resources element* aimed to redress differences in the tax bases of authorities. It did so by setting a national standard rateable value per head. The resources element made up the deficiency to that standard for all local authorities below it. The standard was set quite high and most authorities received some resources element. The *needs element* compensated an authority for differences in expenditure needs per head of population due to variations in the cost of providing a given standard of service.

Various difficulties existed with this system. For example, since the resources and needs elements were calculated separately equalisation could not fully be achieved; local authorities with both high spending needs and high rateable values still received the needs element. Also, ascertainment of spending need proved difficult. Basically, certain factors (such as the numbers of schoolchildren or old people, or the road mileage) that were felt to have a systematic influence on spending need were identified. By a process known as stepwise multiple regression analysis, these key factors were used to determine differences in expenditure needs. This method was therefore based on the assumption "that differences in needs are systematically and consistently related to various types of local authority characteristics—demographic, geographical, socio-economic—and that other influences on local authority spending (levels of beneficial services, operating efficiency, etc.) are not systematically related to these services." (Foster *et al.* 1980, p. 254). This meant that if local authorities with similar characteristics and expenditures *all* increased service levels they could influence the needs formula and receive more.

The Conservatives, in introducing a new mechanism for distributing R.S.G., argued that it would deal with these difficulties by enabling a greater degree of equalisation to take place and by eliminating the incentives within the grant system for higher spending. These, however, were not the only difficulties. Multiple regression analysis proved rather volatile. This had led to the introduction in 1975/76 of *damping* and in 1978/79 of *safety nets.* Damping had the effect of making only part of the needs element distributed in any particular year dependent on the formula used for that year. Safety nets limited the loss which an authority could incur in its needs element in any year. The result, however, was a system of great complexity with little principled division between centrally and locally determined services. The new mechanism, it was claimed, would not only be easier to understand but would also lead to the restoration of a principled system and therefore would increase local accountability.

This new mechanism, which was based on a combination of the needs and resources elements, is called the block grant. Its history can be traced to the *combined grant* proposal of the DoE in its evidence to the Layfield Committee (1976, App. 7) and which was favourably considered by the Labour Government as a *unitary* grant (DoE 1977, Chap. 3). Cynics may suggest that by changing the name of what is essentially the same proposal Labour and Conservative, in switching roles as Government and Opposition, were able to reverse their positions on the desirability of the block grant proposal without too much embarrassment.

2.3.2 The Grant Distribution System. Central government, as part of its public expenditure planning process, makes projections concerning aggregate local government expenditure. A primary method of seeking to ensure that these projections are met is through the system for grant distribution. The Consultative Council on Local Government Finance, which is chaired by the Secretary of State for Environment and consists of representatives of central departments and the local authority associations, is the main forum within which formal discussions concerning local expenditure and grants takes place. A considerable amount of detailed work is undertaken by working groups of the Consultative Council as can be seen from the diagrammatic outline of the administrative structure of the Consultative Council in Figure 2.1. These working groups undertake continuous review of the workings of the system. The starting point for each year's grant settlement, however, is the announcement by the government of the provisional figure for total local authority *relevant expenditure*. Relevant expenditure is the "expenditure for that year falling to be defrayed out of the rate fund of a local authority" (L.G.P.L.A. 1980, s. 54(5)). This figure appears to be derived from the projected expenditure on each local authority service laid out in the annual Public Expenditure White Paper. From this figure the Secretary of State determines the *aggregate exchequer grant* (A.E.G.). This is generally expressed as the percentage of relevant expenditure which central government is prepared to finance. In determining the A.E.G. the Secretary of State must take into account, *inter alia*, "the current level of prices, costs and remuneration and any future variation in that level" and "the need for developing those services and the extent to which, having regard to general economic conditions, it is reasonable to develop them" (s. 54(4)). Before determining the A.E.G., however, the Secretary of State "shall consult with such associations of local authorities as appear to him to be concerned and with any local authority with whom consultation appears to him to be desirable" (*ibid*.). The Consultative Council therefore provides an institutional framework for realising this statutory requirement for consultation.

Having determined the A.E.G. the Secretary of State then

Fig. 2.1 The R.S.G. Negotiating Machinery

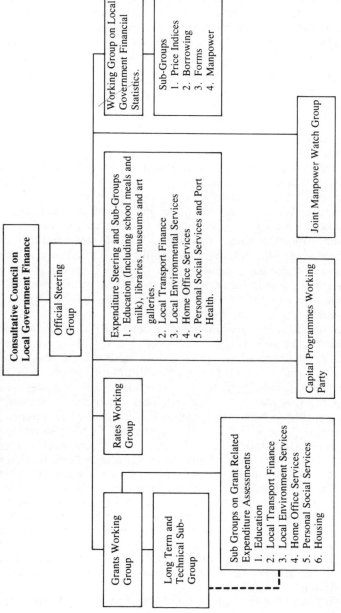

Source: Rate Support Grant (England) 1984/85 Published by Association of County Councils *et al.* (April 1984)

allocates portions of the A.E.G. to particular categories of grants. First, he deducts "the portion of the amount which he estimates will be allocated to grants in respect of specific services" (s. 54(2)(*d*)). These *specific grants* include grants in respect of police, magistrates' courts, probation services, Commonwealth immigrants, the urban programme, civil defence, improvement grants and slum clearance. Next, he determines "the aggregate amount of supplementary grants" (s. 54(2)(*b*)(*c*)). *Supplementary grants* are payable in respect of transport and national parks. Specific and supplementary grants together absorb about 15–20 per cent. of the A.E.G. The remainder constitutes "the aggregate amount of the rate support grants for that year" (s. 54(3)).

From the total amount of the *rate support grants* the Secretary of State deducts the amount of the *domestic rate relief grant* (s. 55; Sched. 9.); this is basically the domestic element renamed. Thus "the amount of block grant for a year is the balance left after deducting the amount of domestic rate relief grant from the aggregate amount of the rate support grants." (s. 56(1)). The *block grant*, therefore, combines the needs and resources elements of the old system. It is by far the largest grant, taking 70–75 per cent. of the A.E.G.

Figure 2.2 contains an outline of the system for distributing grants, together with an approximate annual timescale on which the expenditure planning process is based. Clearly this is a complex process of forward planning which requires adjustments as actual (outturn) rather than proposed (budgeted) expenditure figures materialise. This is provided for in the 1980 Act. Each year the Secretary of State is required to make a Rate Support Grant Report (s. 60(2)). Before making the Report he must consult the local authority associations (s. 60(5)). Also, the Report requires the consent of the Treasury (s. 60(4)). This Report must specify all the determinations relating to the A.E.G. which the Act requires to be made and the considerations leading the Secretary of State to make any such determination (s. 60(6)). It must be laid before the House of Commons (generally in December) and no payments may be made until the Report is approved by a resolution of the House (s. 60(7)(8)).

Once the R.S.G. Report is approved the Secretary of State must, on the basis of information made available to him by local authorities (s. 65), "estimate and notify to each local authority the amounts of domestic rate relief grant and block grant which will become payable to the authority for a year" (s. 66(1)). Payments in

Figure 2.2   Outline of the System for Distributing Grants.

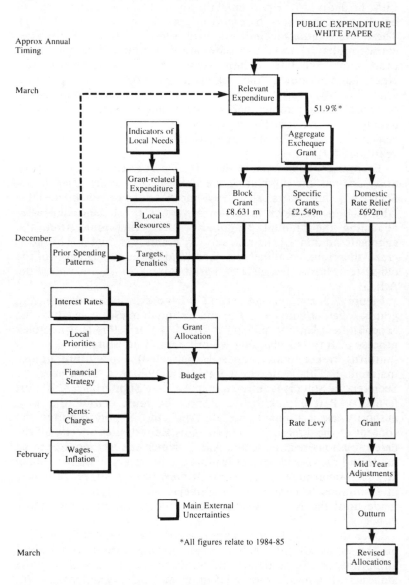

Source: Audit Commission (1984) p.11.

respect of rate support grants "shall be made to a local authority at such times as the Secretary of State may with the consent of the Treasury specify" (s. 53(8)).

In order to ensure "that the total amount paid in respect of block grant in any year is the same as the aggregate amount available for that grant in that year, the Secretary of State may adjust (whether by increasing or decreasing it) the amount payable to each local authority" (s. 62(1)). This process is generally known as *clawback*; while the Secretary of State may for this purpose "make a fresh calculation of the entitlement of each local authority to block grant" (s. 62(3)), the adjustment shall be in the same ratio as that applicable to all local authorities (s. 62(2)).

For such purposes, and to adjust for outturn expenditures (s. 66(2)), the Secretary of State may, "at such time or times as he thinks fit, make one or more supplementary reports for that year" (s. 61(1)). Such reports are subject to the same procedures as apply to the R.S.G. Report (s. 61(2)). They may "specify fresh determinations" (s. 61(3)), but this power "shall be exerciseable only in accordance with principles applicable to all local authorities and specified in the supplementary report" (s. 61(5)). The effect of this complex process of adjustment may be to vary the block grant entitlements of a local authority through the financial year. Finally, if sums in excess of entitlement are paid to a local authority, the Secretary of State "may recover that sum by deduction from any amount due to that authority in respect of those grants, whether for the year or for any subsequent year, or by issuing a demand for it to the authority" (s. 66(4)).

2.3.3 The Principles of the Block Grant System. The block grant combines the needs and resources elements into a single grant, the objective of which is to enable local authorities to provide a common standard of service at an equal rate poundage cost to their ratepayers. Clearly the system requires some concept of the assessment of spending need. This is derived not by stepwise multiple regression analysis, as under the old system, but from a formula which is compiled from over 60 statistical indicators of need. These indicators are based on the factors most likely to affect spending need on each service. The factors are then given a set of weights which express their relative importance. These indicators and the weights given to them, being considerations leading the Secretary of State to make a determination of a local authority's grant entitlement, must be specified in the R.S.G. Report (s. 60(6)).

The formula is then used to apportion the national total of grant for each service to individual local authorities. These service apportionments to individual local authorities are then aggregated. This aggregate constitutes that local authority's *grant-related expenditure* (G.R.E.).

Behind this relatively straightforward explanation of G.R.E.s lies a detailed and complicated process of analysis and bargaining over their compilation (see Bramley *et al.* 1983). This is undertaken by the Grants Working Group of the Consultative Council (see Figure 2.1 above). Virtually none of this is incorporated in statutory form. Section 56(8) of the 1980 Act merely defines G.R.E. "in relation to each local authority to whom block grant is payable for any year" as "the aggregate for the year of their notional expenditure having regard to their functions." A fuller explanation is that G.R.E. is the notional cost to a local authority of providing the services for which it is responsible "on the assumption that all local authorities provide services to the same standard and with the same efficiency, consistent with central government plans for the aggregate expenditure of all local authorities." (*R.* v. *Secretary of State for the Environment, ex p. Hackney London Borough Council* (1984) 148 L.G.Rev. 691,692 (D.C.)).

The G.R.E. is therefore an assessment of spending need. The actual amount of block grant payable to a local authority is dependent on the following formula, contained in section 56(6) of the 1980 Act.

$$\text{Block grant} = \text{T.E.} - (\text{G.R.P.} \times \text{G.R.V.} \times \text{M.}).$$

T.E. is the local authority's *total expenditure*. Total expenditure basically is the local authority's relevant expenditure less the specific and supplementary grants it receives (s. 56(8)).

G.R.V. means *gross rateable value* or "the aggregate of the rateable values of the hereditaments in their area" (s. 56(8)).

G.R.P. means *grant-related poundage*. Leaving to one side M., a *multiplier*, for a moment, G.R.P. provides the key to the formula.

G.R.P. is defined in section 56(8) as a poundage related to a given ratio between the local authority's total expenditure and their G.R.E., or a poundage related to a given difference between their total expenditure divided by their population and their G.R.E. so divided. This does not make much sense unless we first appreciate the function of the G.R.P. If all local authorities provide a common standard of services with the same degree of efficiency, the ratepoundage they have to charge ratepayers will differ because their G.R.V.s are different. The function of the G.R.P. is to iron out these differences; that is, to equalise notional rate poundages for spending at G.R.E. despite differences in G.R.V.s. The G.R.P. schedule is thus set at a certain level for spending at G.R.E. (130.00p for 1984/85) and is reduced or increased by a certain amount (0.6p in 1984/85) for each £1 per head of population which the authority spends below or above G.R.E. (reducing the G.R.P. has the effect of increasing grant entitlement). This is provided for in section 58 of the 1980 Act.

However, in addition to enabling greater equalisation to take place, the block grant system aimed to discourage high levels of expenditure. This is achieved by incorporating a tapering provision into the G.R.P. schedule. Section 58(3) thus empowers the Secretary of State to increase the G.R.P. schedule above G.R.E. which has the effect of requiring a larger local contribution towards marginal expenditure above G.R.E. In practice, since the introduction of the block grant system the Secretary of State has permitted a degree of tolerance, known as the *threshold* and set at 10 per cent. of the national average G.R.E. per head of population (DoE 1980a. para. 33), before increasing the G.R.P. schedule.

Finally, the Secretary of State is empowered by section 59 to modify the basic grant formula by applying a multiplier to the prescribed G.R.P.s. A multiplier of greater than unity has the effect of reducing an authority's entitlement to grant. Since this power otherwise would enable the Secretary of State to alter the grant entitlements of individual local authorities quite arbitrarily, certain limitations are placed on the use of multipliers. First, the power may generally be exercised only in accordance with principles to be applied to all local authorities, or all local authorities belonging to the appropriate class (s. 59(5)). These principles must be specified in the R.S.G. Report (s. 59(8)). Secondly, subject to one exception, multipliers may be used only to *increase* the amount of grant payable to an authority (s. 59(2)). Section 59(3) provides that the power may be used to decrease the amount of grant only "if the Secretary of State is satisfied that there will be an unreasonable increase, unless he exercises the power, in the amount of block grant payable to the authority for a year, compared with the amount payable to them for the previous year." Multipliers are therefore intended to be used primarily to introduce the damping and safety nets mechanisms used in the distribution of the needs element under the old system.

Since this is a rather complex system it may be useful to illustrate its operation by way of an example. The Audit Commission (1984, pp. 67–68) provides the example of an imaginary metropolitan district council with a population of 250,000 and a G.R.V. of £25 million. Its G.R.E. has been assessed at £100 million and its G.R.P. for spending at G.R.E., expressed as G.R.P.*, is 130.00p. In accordance with the G.R.P. schedule, 0.6p is added to or subtracted from G.R.P.* for each £1 per head of expenditure above or below G.R.E. respectively. Finally, a multiplier of 0.985000 applies.

Under these circumstances, if a local authority budgets to spend £104,500,000 we can calculate its block grant entitlement. First it is necessary to determine the relevant G.R.P. This is calculated as follows (see s. 56(8)):

$$G.R.P. = G.R.P.* + 0.6 \frac{(T.E. - G.R.E.)}{\text{population}}$$

$$= 130 + \frac{[0.6\,(104,500,000 - 100,000,000)]}{250,000}$$

$$= 130 + 10.8$$
$$= 140.8$$

Thus the authority's G.R.P. for spending at £104.5 million is 140.8. The authority's entitlement to block grant can now be calculated (s. 56(6)):

$$\begin{aligned}
\text{Block grant} &= T.E. - (G.R.V. \times G.R.P. \times M) \\
&= £104,500,000 - (25,000,000 \times 140.8 \times 0.985000) \\
&= £104,500,000 - 34,672,000 \\
&= £69,828,000
\end{aligned}$$

Thus for spending at £104.5 million the authority would receive £69.8 million in grant and would therefore have to raise £34.7 million in rates.

However, it should be recalled that section 58(3) empowers the setting of a greater G.R.P. for expenditure above G.R.E. In practice this has been used only after a degree of tolerance above G.R.E. called the threshold, which on average is set at 10 per cent. above G.R.E. If the authority were budgeting to spend above the threshold, therefore, a new formula for calculating the G.R.P. would apply. Where the threshold is the amount, expressed in £ per head by which the threshold exceeds G.R.E.; and where 0.75p for each £1 per head is the extra by which the G.R.P. is increased for expenditure above the threshold:

$$G.R.P. = G.R.P.^* + 0.6 \times \text{threshold} + 0.75 \, \frac{(T.E. - G.R.E. - \text{threshold})}{\text{population.}}$$

It is clear, therefore, that the concepts of G.R.E. and G.R.P. and the relationship between the two lie at the heart of the block grant system. The calculation of a local authority's G.R.E. and G.R.P. is made by the Secretary of State, albeit in accordance with principles applied to all local authorities. (s. 57(1)). The principles on which G.R.E.s are determined must be specified in the R.S.G. Report (s. 57(2)), although those used in determining G.R.P.s need not (s. 57(3)). The expenditure-grant relationship for each authority is therefore quite different and depends on the authority's responsibilities and expenditure needs (G.R.E.); its tax base (affecting G.R.V. in the grant formula); its grant volatility (which may cause a multiplier to be used); and the level of its expenditure (which may result in the use of the tapering provision in the G.R.P.). A simplified example is given in Figure 2.3 of three authorities (A, B and C) having the same G.R.E. but different profiles. Authority C has low spending needs and high rateable resources; grant increases slowly up to the threshold and decreases thereafter. Authority B is a typical metropolitan authority; grant continues to increase above the threshold, although at a lower marginal rate. Authority A has

Figure 2.3 Expenditure-Grant Profiles of Hypothetical Authorities.

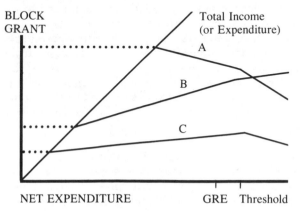

Source: Audit Commission (1984) p.68.

both high spending needs and high rateable resources; grant entitlement declines throughout the relevant expenditure profile (because of the wealth of its rateable resources) and the effect of the threshold is to increase the rate of marginal grant loss.

Having examined the principles underlying the block grant system it remains to evaluate the system in terms of its objectives. The objectives of the block grant system seem to have been to achieve greater *equalisation* and greater *simplification* of the system along with *fairer marginal grant adjustments* within a *controlled total expenditure*, while at the same time promoting greater *local accountability*. These objectives will be examined in turn.

First, the combination of the needs and resources elements in the block grant system has enabled a greater degree of equalisation to be achieved. The major impediments to equalisation under the old system were the wide disparity in tax bases and the fact that an authority with high needs and high resources would still receive the needs element. The block grant is able to take this coincidence into account and therefore achieve equalisation at a lower total grant level than the old R.S.G. system.

Secondly, it was argued that block grant would simplify the R.S.G. system by replacing the complexities of stepwise multiple regression analysis with a series of simple methods. Few would argue that this has been achieved. The block grant system is no easier to understand than the old system:

> "Compared with the previous system it is fair to say that the formula for the block grant has added very significantly to, rather than diminished, the complexity of need assessment. For the English counties, which are a level of authority permitting comparison, the number of need indicators has increased from 22 in 1980/81 to 52 in 1981/82. For Outer London the equivalent increase is from 30 to 49; and for Inner London (excluding ILEA) the increase is from 26 to 39. Contrary to its aims, therefore, G.R.E. has tended to increase the complexity of needs assessment" (Bennett 1982, p. 106).

Thirdly, the block grant system was advocated on the grounds that it enabled fairer marginal adjustments to grant distribution to take place since it uses a less blunt method of financial control than clawback of the resources element. This may in fact be true, but it could be argued that the old R.S.G. system was necessarily crude because it was essentially a procedure based on the need to retain a fair degree of local autonomy. Therefore this advantage may not be without its costs.

Fourthly, it was suggested that the new system would provide a more effective mechanism for enabling central government to control the total of local government expenditure. It has already been argued (section 2.2) that this is a political rather than a "technical" economic objective. Whether it has been successful is evaluated in section 2.3.5 below.

Finally, the block grant system was championed as promoting local accountability. The theory is that expenditure above G.R.E. is, by definition, not the result of the authority's need to provide a common standard of service. The expenditure is either the result of the authority's decision to provide services of a quality higher than the national standard, or is the result of the authority's inefficiency in providing services. In either case the Government argues that the local authority must be responsible to the local electorate; increasing the marginal cost of expenditure above the threshold which must be financed from the rates is an important means of promoting local accountability. Whether this has in fact been achieved is examined below. However, the validity of this argument is founded on the objectivity of the G.R.E. as a mechanism for determining expenditure need. Foster *et al.* (1980, p. 437) refer to the difficulties in accurately assessing spending need as "substantial and insuperable," while Bennett (1982, p. 127) considers that the block grant assessments are "largely political choices by the Secretary of State for which few objective criteria are available." Substantial doubts therefore exist concerning the objectivity of the G.R.E. mechanism.

2.3.4 The Transitional Arrangements. The block grant system was introduced with effect from the financial year commencing in April 1981. Sections 48–50 of the 1980 Act, however, made certain interim amendments to the old system in relation to 1980/81. The objective of these transitional arrangements was, so far as possible, to place the grant distribution arrangements for that year on a similar basis to a fully operative block grant system. Since the old system did not incorporate the use of centrally determined assessments of spending need for each authority, there would inevitably be a certain degree of rough justice in the arrangements.

The key to these arrangements lay in the power vested in the Secretary of State to reduce the amount of R.S.G. payable to a local authority for 1980/81 if its rate exceeds the "notional uniform rate" (s. 48(1)). This notional uniform rate is the rate which the Secretary of State considers an authority needs to levy "in order to finance the spending needs of the authority and of all authorities with power to issue precepts to the authority" (s. 48(2)). This power would be effected by multipliers which would be used to reduce the amount of the resources element payable to a local authority (s. 49) or, in the case of certain London authorities which did not receive the resources element, by reducing the needs element (s. 50). These multipliers must be applied to authorities in accordance with the same principles (ss. 49(5), 50(4)).

In December 1979 the notional uniform rate was set at 119p but the Secretary of State stated that there would be a threshold above this level before grant abatement would apply. However, it was announced that it would be impossible to determine the precise level at which grant abatement would operate until after the start of the 1980/81 financial year, when local authorities had fixed their rates and detailed information on their budgets had been received. Eventually, in September 1980, after calling for revised budgets because of what were considered to be excessive expenditure plans, the Secretary of State announced that he proposed to set the threshold level at which grant abatement would apply at 155p. Fourteen authorities were vulnerable.

The transitional arrangements became effective on November 13, 1980 when the 1980 Act received the Royal Assent. On December 16 the R.S.G. (Principles for Multipliers) Order 1980, containing the grant abatement measures, was laid before the House of Commons and was scheduled for debate on January 14, 1981. Meanwhile some authorities had made adjustments to their expenditure plans and on December 19 the eight authorities still vulnerable wrote to the Secretary of State asking him to meet a delegation in order to avoid the possibility of any misunderstanding. The Secretary of State refused since he did not believe that such a meeting would have any practical effect. The order was duly confirmed and the grants of the eight authorities were abated in accordance with the principles laid down in the order.

The six London boroughs affected thereupon applied for orders of certiorari to quash the Secretary of State's decisions. The three principal grounds on which relief was sought were that: (1) the order which provided the formula for grant abatement was *ultra vires*; (2) the decision to abate was a decision which no reasonable Secretary of State could have reached; and (3) the Secretary of State, in refusing to consider representations from the applicants, fettered his discretion and acted in breach of the rules of natural justice.

In *R. v. Secretary of State for the Environment, ex p. Brent L.B.C* [1982] 2 W.L.R. 693, the Divisional Court rejected the substantive challenges but quashed the Secretary of State's decision on procedural grounds. On the first ground of challenge the applicants had argued that the order had not specified the principles on which multipliers are determined as required by sections 49(4) and 50(2) of the 1980 Act. However, Ackner L.J. held that, while the order merely prescribed how the multipliers were to be ascertained and did not disclose the rationale or justification for the multipliers, the underlying principles could be discerned from the specification of the multipliers by an "instructed reader" (p. 724). The attempt to challenge the Secretary of State's decisions on *Wednesbury* principles of unreasonableness (see section 9.4.3) was fairly summarily dismissed by the court. But on the procedural issue the court held that "since the decision to reduce the applicants' rate support grants adversely affected not merely an expectation but a right to substantial sums of money" the applicants had a right to be heard (p. 731). Consequently, in refusing to listen to new representations after he obtained the statutory power under the 1980 Act, the Secretary of State was in breach of his duty of fairness to the affected authorities.

In certain respects the success of the applicant authorities was largely symbolic since the Divisional Court recognised that it would be open to the Secretary of State "after considering the applicants' respresentations, now fully documented, to reach any decision he considered right and which is within the terms of the Act of 1980 and the Multipliers Order" (p. 735). In fact the Secretary of State did consider the applicants' representations, did not view them sufficient to justify modifying his position and in February 1982 informed the applicants that he had decided to abate the grants to the same extent as before.

However, this is not the whole story. One effect of the *Brent* decision was that the grant abatement provisions were eventually calculated by reference to outturn rather than budgeted expenditure; this enabled Hackney L.B.C. to avoid grant abatement and resulted in their saving almost £1million in grant. The decision also clarified the basic legal principles concerning consultations and representations between central departments and local authorities. These have been used as a guide to appropriate practice since. Finally, the *Brent* case marks most clearly the commencement of a new era in legal relations between central departments and local authorities (see section 9.4). This is illustrated by the fact that the

Secretary of State's decision to maintain abatement was also challenged, albeit unsuccessfully, in the courts: see *R.* v. *Secretary of State for the Environment, ex p. Hackney L.B.C.* [1983] 1 W.L.R. 524. The *Brent* and *Hackney* cases are thus indicative of the new approach in the era of retrenchment; disputes between central departments and local authorities will not merely be dealt with administratively through the traditional channels, but the nature and limits of powers will also be tested in the courts.

2.3.5 Manipulation of the Grant System. The block grant system became fully operational in 1981/82. When the Government received the estimates of local authority expenditure for that year, however, they found that authorities were proposing to spend 5.3 per cent. above the Government's projection of aggregate local government expenditure. Local authorities, when faced with the incentive to reduce service levels provided by the tapering mechanisms of the block grant, had nonetheless opted to attempt to maintain service levels and to raise the required additional revenues from the rates.

The Secretary of State responded to these estimates by announcing a new expenditure target for local authorities, based not on G.R.E. but on past expenditure. It required all local authorities in 1981/82 to make a 5.6 per cent. reduction in the volume of their revenue expenditure as compared with their outturn revenue expenditure for 1978/79. Any authority not complying with this target was to be subject to a new system of penalties. This system of expenditure targets and penalties became known as the *holdback* system.

This system was very controversial. Since there was no clear reason for using the 1978/79 base many argued that it was arbitrary (*e.g.* Travers 1981). Being based on historic spending, these targets were generally set below G.R.E. for non-metropolitan authorities (which were more likely to be low-spenders and Conservative-controlled) and above G.R.E. for London and metropolitan authorities (generally high-spenders and Labour-controlled). In September 1981 the Secretary of State therefore announced that the penalty system would not apply to any authority which, although exceeding this target, was spending below its G.R.E. This led to a further criticism of the holdback system—namely that is was politically biased.

Perhaps of greater significance for our purposes was the fact that the holdback system appeared to lack any statutory foundation.

The most obvious course of action would be for the Secretary of State to apply a multiplier to the grant entitlement of any local authority not complying with this expenditure target. This, however, would be contrary to the protections in section 59(3) of the 1980 Act governing the use of multipliers. Instead, the Secretary of State proposed to increase the G.R.P. schedules across the board (which had the effect of reducing the amount of grant payable to each authority) and to use multipliers to *increase* the amount of grant payable to those authorities which complied with the target (Heseltine 1981). This seemed contrary to the spirit, if not the letter, of the 1980 Act. The adjustments to the R.S.G. required by this holdback system were expected to be introduced in a supplementary report during 1981/82. This report did not materialise. Rather, the Secretary of State, on the advice of Government lawyers (presumably by now accommodated to the post-*Brent* situation), announced that retroactive powers would be sought to legitimate the use of targets from 1981/82.

The Local Government Finance Bill, which was published in November 1981, was therefore the product of the Government's dissatisfaction with the ability of the block grant system to achieve expected expenditure reductions. The Bill, in addition to legitimating the holdback system (cl. 12), sought two new powers to constrain the budgetary autonomy of local authorities. First, it proposed that a local authority could only levy a rate or precept which was within a ceiling determined in accordance with a method specified by the Secretary of State (cll. 1,2,4). This constituted a direct attack on the local authority's power to determine the level of its expenditure. But one outlet was provided: a supplementary rate could be levied if the authority gained the consent of their electorate in a poll (cl. 3). The burden of any supplementary rate, however, would be weighted more heavily on domestic ratepayers (cl. 5). Secondly, it was proposed that the Secretary of State have the power to reduce a local authority's grant during the current financial year (cl. 12(4)). This power, known as superholdback, when read in conjunction with the proposed controls over rates would effectively give the Secretary of State the power to determine a local authority's total expenditure.

These aspects of the Bill generated a great deal of controversy and, after a threatened revolt by Conservative backbenchers concerned in particular about the challenge to the principle of representative democracy posed by the referendum proposals, the Government decided not to proceed with the Bill. Instead, in

January 1982 it introduced the Local Government Finance (No. 2) Bill. This retained the proposals on holdback and superholdback but withdrew the proposed powers over rates. This was replaced with a proposal to abolish altogether the power to levy supplementary rates. During the passage of this Bill, and as a result of further pressure, the Government accepted an amendment effectively abolishing the power of superholdback (see Local Government Finance Act 1982, s. 8(6), (8), (9)). This was achieved, however, only after the DoE won a battle with the Treasury. The Treasury's concern arose from the fact that, given the exemption from holdback penalties for authorities which spent with their G.R.E., if all authorities spent up to their relevant targets in 1982/83 they could overspend on the Government's target for aggregate local authority expenditure by £790 million, or 4.3 per cent., without being subject to penalties.

The Local Government Finance Act 1982 therefore reformed the finance system primarily by abolishing the power to levy supplementary rates or issue supplementary precepts (ss. 1,2) and providing a firm statutory foundation for the holdback system (s. 8). This foundation was achieved by amending section 59 of the Local Government Planning and Land Act 1980. Subsections 59(2) and (3), providing protection against the use of multipliers to decrease the amount of grant payable to an authority, were repealed and a new paragraph added to subsection (6) which now reads:

"59(6)The purposes . . . [for which multipliers may be exercised] . . . are

(*cc*) making, in the amount of block grant payable to an authority, adjustments by reference to guidance issued by the Secretary of State and designed to achieve any reduction in the level of local authority expenditure (or any restriction or increases in that level) which he thinks necessary having regard to general economic conditions."

Finally, although the holdback system had been operating administratively in financial years 1981/82 and 1982/83 no grant penalties had actually been levied. Section 8(10) of the Local Government Finance Act 1982, however, validated the holdback system with effect from the start of financial year 1981/82. Consequently, after the 1982 Act received the Royal Assent on July 13, 1982, the Secretary of State abated the grant of those authorities which had incurred penalties under the holdback system since April 1981.

Figure 2.4   High Resource Authority, G.R.E. Above Target.

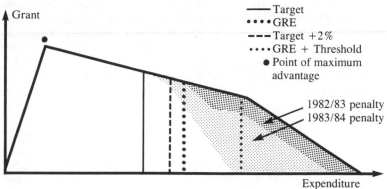

Source: Smith (1983a) p.48.

Figure 2.5   Low Resource Authority, G.R.E. Above Target

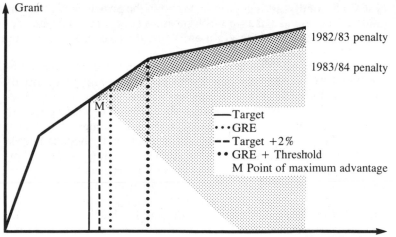

Source: Smith (1983a) p.48.

41

As a result of these developments the operation of the block grant system has been entirely obscured. While G.R.E.s and the threshold tapering mechanism affects the general profile of grant entitlement (shown by the broad outer line in the illustrative expenditure-grant graphs in Figures 2.4 and 2.5), the targets and their penalties became the key variables in local authority budgeting. The holdback system provided a much greater incentive for expenditure reductions than did the block grant mechanism; this is shown in Figures 2.4 and 2.5 which illustrate grant expenditure options for authorities similar to A and B in Figure 2.3. But a further complexity has arisen from the fact that the system of targets and penalties has been altered in every year since 1981/82 (for details see Smith 1983a).

The most basic change, however, occurred between 1982/83 and 1983/84. In 1981/82 and 1982/83 the holdback system operated effectively as a fine or tax on expenditure above the target and the result was to lower the grant curve: see 1982/83 penalty in Figures 2.4 and 2.5. From 1983/84, however, the Government, having acquired the holdback power, made two basic changes. First, presumably as a result of the Treasury's arguments on the need for a superholdback power, no concession was made for authorities spending within their G.R.E.s. (This is illustrated in Figures 2.4 and 2.5 by the fact that for 1983/84 grant abatement commences below G.R.E.) Secondly, as the figures also show, the principle of using the holdback system as a taxing mechanism, by lowering the height but not the basic shape of the grant entitlement curve, was altered and no ceiling was placed on grant penalties.

Furthermore, as Table 2.1 demonstrates, since the introduction of the holdback system its penalty rates have been progressively tightened. Basically, the Government's view is that the penalties must become increasingly severe because otherwise, once an authority has incurred a penalty, it will be built into its financial system. This means that, if the penalties were not tightened, it could maintain its expenditure level without increasing its rate. This tendency is known as the "ratchet effect." It is perhaps largely as a consequence of this that, although the then Secretary of State in 1983 referred to the target system as "emergency regulations" and expressed the hope that after 1983/84 the holdback system would be abolished (King 1983; see also DoE 1983, para. 3.8), this did not prove to be the case (but see section 2.6).

Finally, the severity of the holdback penalties were such that it could be argued that any local authority incurring them must be in

Table 2.1 Penalties Imposed. Rate Poundage Effect (pence/£)

Expenditure above target

Year	1%	2%	5%	10%	15%
1980/81	–	–	–	–	–
1981/82	2	2	9	9	9
1982/83	3	6	15	15	15
1983/84	1	2	17	42	67
1984/85	2	6	32	77	122
1985/86	7	15	42	87	132

Sources: 1980/81–1984/85: Audit Commission (1983 Table 9)
1985/86: *Hansard* H.C. Deb Vol. 64, col. 829
(24 July, 1984).

breach of its fiduciary duty to its ratepayers. This concept of fiduciary duty in 1981 had received the imprimatur of the House of Lords in *Bromley L.B.C.* v. *Greater London Council* (see section 3.4.1 below). If applied strictly by the courts it could conceivably have been used to convert targets into expenditure ceilings. However, the courts refused to do so; see *e.g. R.* v. *Greater London Council, ex p. Royal Borough of Kensington and Chelsea* (1982) *The Times*, April 7; *R.* v. *Greenwich L.B.C., ex p. Cedar Transport Group Ltd.* (1983) *The Times*, August 3; section 9.4.3.

However, the severity of the penalties also led to a different type of legal action. In 1984 Hackney L.B.C. challenged the legality of its 1984/85 target primarily on the ground that the target must incorporate some concept of attainability, and more specifically, that it must be attainable without requiring the authority to act in breach of their statutory duties. In *R.* v. *Secretary of State for the Environment, ex p. Hackney L.B.C.* (1984) 148 L.G. Rev. 691 the Divisional Court rejected the application; this decision was upheld by the Court of Appeal: (1985) *The Times* May 11. There were three main reasons for this decision.

First, it was held that the question of whether a given expenditure

**Figure 2.6   Local Authority Current Expenditure in Cash —
England and Wales.**

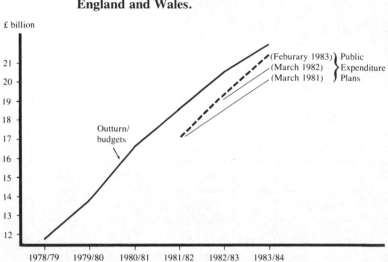

Source: DoE (1983) p.7.

level must inevitably cause a local authority to be in breach of its
statutory duties could not be a matter of pure fact. Given the nature
of a local authority's statutory responsibilities this question inevitably is a value judgment and therefore a question of policy with
which the courts could not interfere. Furthermore, the court was
simply not equipped to evaluate the mass of evidence which it
would be necessary to assemble in order to test the validity of a
judgment of this nature.

Secondly, there was nothing in the 1982 Act which required
targets to be set at a level which would allow local authorities to
meet them without detriment to the performance of their statutory
functions; since grant is only one of the sources from which local
authorities can defray expenditure, any shortfall in grant may be
made up by levying a larger rate.

Finally, the only constraint which prevented the Secretary of
State from producing wholly arbitrary targets was the requirement
in section 59(5)(a) of Local Government, Planning and Land Act
1980 that the power be exercised in accordance with principles to be

**Table 2.2   Domestic Rate Increases in England
1980/81 – 1985/86.** (%)

1980/81	1981/82	1982/83	1983/84	1984/85	1985/86
27	19.4	15.4	7.3	6.7	9.5

Source: C.I.P.F.A. Financial and General Statistics
1980/81 – 1985/86.

applied to all local authorities. On this point *Hackney* resurrected the argument, unsuccessfully used in the *Brent* case (section 2.3.4.), that the term "principles" required the Secretary of State to disclose the philosophy behind the guidance, or at least its rationale, in the R.S.G. Report and that this had not been done. The courts rejected this argument and held that in this context a principle meant merely a self-sufficient proposition intended to be applied to a set of relevant circumstances and that the Act merely required the Secretary of State to specify simply the mathematical principles (*i.e.* the formula or formulae) on which the targets were based. Furthermore, in *R* v. *Secretary of State for the Environment*, ex p. *Nottinghamshire C.C.* [1986] 2 W.L.R. 1 the House of Lords rejected the argument that the requirement in section 59(11A) that expenditure guidance must be framed by reference "to principles applicable to all authorities" meant that the Secretary of State was unable to differentiate between authorities by reference to past expenditure. Consequently references to the need for principles governing action under this Part of the Act do little to circumscribe the Secretary of State's power to set discriminatory targets.

2.3.6 Evaluation. Since the Conservative Government came to power in 1979, it has made great efforts to restrain local expenditure through a series of reforms and modifications to the grant system. How successful have they been? As Figure 2.6 shows, despite these changes local expenditure levels have not been adjusted in accordance with the Government's plans. In fact "public expenditure plans have been adjusted to conform with what local authorities are actually spending, rather than local authorities adjusting their expenditure to take account of government spending plans." (Jackman 1984 p. 166). It is on the basis of these trends that the Government justified its proposals to take direct control over the

Figure 2.7   Net Contributions to Special Funds 1975/76 – 1982/83.

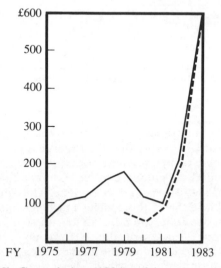

FY   1975   1977   1979   1981   1983

Source: Audit Commission (1984) p.26.

level of a local authority's rate. But, even accepting the logic of the Government's political-economic strategy, are the local authorities at fault?

It is clear that the Government never permitted the block grant system to operate. Instead of attempting to deal with high expenditure levels by tightening the tapering mechanism of the block grant system, they immediately introduced a new system of targets based on quite different principles. This not only complicated the grant system but, since targets are based on historic expenditure, also created incentives to maintain or increase expenditure levels. This came about because of the ratchet effect of the holdback system and the consequent need for local authorities to maintain expenditure to protect their base spending levels for future years. The result, as Table 2.2 shows, has been, at least in the three years between 1980/81 and 1982/83, fairly high rate increases. Part of the reason for this has been the need for local authorities to protect themselves against the uncertainties of future grant settlements. The main indicator would be increased contributions to rate fund balances and special funds. That this was occurring is vividly illustrated by the challenge to the legality of the establishment by the GLC of a "special contingency balance" for 1982/83; *R. v. GLC, ex p. Royal Borough of Kensington and Chelsea* (1982) *The Times,* April 7. But Figure 2.7 provides more objective evidence of this effect.

Consequently much of the "excess" expenditure may be because of, rather than in spite of, government policies. That is, local authorities have reacted to government policies by sound financial planning; either by boosting expenditure or, if above target, by such accounting devices as rescheduling debt repayments and capitalising expenditure formerly funded out of revenue. Thus, in the words of the Audit Commission (1984, p. 23) "local authorities have responded rapidly, predictably and (from their point of view) sensibly to the pressures induced by the uncertainties."

Indeed some commentators have gone further and accused the Government of incompetence in its handling of the grant system. This argument goes as follows. If aggregate expenditure control is the objective there is a standard mechanism for achieving this which is well known both to civil servants (Pliatsky 1982, pp. 117–118) and ministers (Barnett 1982, pp. 75–76). This mechanism simply involves reducing the proportion of local expenditure which central government will support. However, this mechanism was not used by the Government; "the three post-block grant rate support grant settlements for 1981/82, 1982/83 and 1983/84 could be all described as inappropriate, or 'soft' or ridiculous" (Gibson 1983, p. 19). Although the Government set reduced expenditure targets for individual authorities, the authorities were then given a variety of, often conflicting, incentives to meet them. In 1981/82, for example, to have met the Government's targets, local authorities on average should have *reduced* their rates by 10 per cent. in real terms (*ibid.* p. 20). Jackman (1984 pp. 167–8) supports this analysis: "In 1980/81 and in 1981/82 the rate support grant was higher both in real terms and as a proportion of local government spending than the grant the Conservatives 'inherited' for 1979/80." Thus, according to Gibson, "it is difficult to describe the full ineptness of the Government's mishandling of the system."

This analysis has been challenged by a DoE economist on the ground that it fails to account for the fact that there are a plurality of objectives within the block grant system (Heigham 1984). That is, the Government were not looking for expenditure cuts regardless of the effect on rates and services, but were attempting to restructure the system. Heigham asks whether it is unreasonable to suppose that local authorities might choose "the combination of a progressive improvement in value for money, lower rates, and a low but still reasonable provision of services." Maybe not. But in this context it does seem unreasonable for local authorities which decide not to opt for that particular package to be branded "overspenders" and threatened with severe restraints on their financial powers.

Nevertheless Heigham is correct in pointing to the plurality of objectives of the system. In fact, in a review of the system by the Audit Commission it was suggested that this has been its undoing. The Audit Commission (1984, pp. 1–2) felt that the grant system was being used to achieve at least four different objectives which were not mutually compatible: "to distribute grant in a way some of which reflects local needs and resources, to control aggregate local government expenditure, to ensure that individual authorities do not exceed their spending targets *and* to limit rate increases from year to year for individual authorities." It is essentially because of these conflicting objectives that problems have arisen. The Audit Commission's report is scathing. It is found that:

1. There are too many unnecessary uncertainties in the grant system. This encourages the build up of reserves and inhibits forward planning.

2. Serious distortions exist in the grant system because the information used to compile G.R.E.s is often inadequate or out of date.

3. The holdback system has created the perverse incentive for some authorities to increase expenditure.

4. Managerial accountability for local services has not been strengthened, local understanding of the system has not been furthered and central control has not been reduced.

5. The system provides few incentives for local authorities to improve their efficiency and effectiveness.

There thus seems a broad spectrum of opinion that the Government have displayed a great deal of ineptness in their handling of the grant system (see also National Audit Office 1985). It is only by 1983/84 that the Government incentives appear to limit rate increases (see Table 2.2). This is largely because of the steepening of holdback penalties (see Table 2.1) used in combination with the traditional method of significant reductions in the proportion of aggregate local expenditure which central government will support (see Table 2.3).

Table 2.3 Central support for local government relevant expenditure (%).

1980/81	1981/82	1982/83	1983/84	1984/85	1985/86
60	59.14	56.12	52.82	51.88	48.8

By this stage, however, the Government is in the position of applying the brakes to a system which is unstable, distorted and confused. And for this state of affairs the Government must bear primary responsibility. However, by 1983/84 two authorities, the GLC and the ILEA, accounted for 52 per cent. of "overspending." But, since these two authorities (having profiles similar to Authority A in Figure 2.3) did not receive any R.S.G., the grant mechanisms could not be used to control their spending. Partly as a result of this, and certainly as a result of the politicisation of the entire question of spending need, the logic of the Government's approach led them to propose taking direct control over the rates.

2.4. Rate Control

2.4.1 Political Background. One reason for the "soft" grant settlements in the early years of the first Thatcher government may have been that in their 1979 election manifesto the Conservatives had pledged to do something about domestic rates. If they had sharply cut central support for local expenditure, total local expenditure would probably have fallen, but only after significant rate rises. This may have seemed politically unacceptable to the Government. In furtherance of their election pledge the Government in 1981 published *Alternatives to Domestic Rates* (DoE 1981). This Green Paper was criticised generally on the ground that it is difficult to examine seriously the question of domestic rates without also examining the entire system of local government finance. But it was also criticised specifically because of the predominance given to the administrative difficulties with any reform measure (Jones and Stewart 1982).

The House of Commons Environment Committee in 1982 examined local government finance in the light of the Green Paper. After reviewing the alternatives—local sales tax, poll tax, assigned revenues, central financing of education and local income tax (L.I.T.)—they took the view that L.I.T. was the most suitable alternative since it would provide a substantial yield and ensure local accountability. They therefore recommended that the Government should give early consideration to L.I.T. by conducting a detailed examination of methods of implementation and administration (House of Commons 1982). By this stage, however, the Conservative Government seemed to be more concerned with short-term strategies and included in their 1983 election manifesto a proposal to cap the rates of "overspenders."

In August 1983 the second Thatcher government issued their *Rates* White Paper (DoE 1983). This reviewed the economic reasons why central government needed to control local expenditure, the recent history of central-local government financial relations and alternatives to domestic rates. The first two issues have already been examined (see sections 2.2 and 2.3.6). On the issue of domestic rates the Government took the view that, since there was no consensus on an alternative local tax to replace domestic rates, the rates should for the foreseeable future remain the main source of local revenue for local government. The Government then argued that since local authorities had refused to tailor their expenditure in recent years and had, as a result, placed a great burden on ratepayers, they saw no alternative but to promote a measure to control the rates levied by local authorities. Although this highly controversial proposal was much criticised, the Bill was published in December 1983 and enacted in June 1984.

2.4.2 Rates Act 1984. The Rates Act 1984 confers powers on the Secretary of State to limit the level of the rate or precept of local authorities. Two schemes for rate limitation are contained in the Act. The selective scheme in Part I empowers the Secretary of State to limit the rates of certain designated authorities. The general scheme in Part II, when operating, would empower the Secretary of State to control the rates of all local authorities.

Under the selective scheme the Secretary of State is empowered to designate, in a report laid before the House of Commons in the preceding financial year, the authorities selected for rate limitation (s. 2(1)). These authorities must be notified of that decision (*ibid.*). An authority may be designated for rate limitation only if its total expenditure exceeds £10 million (s. 2(2)(*a*)). The ostensible objective of this expenditure threshold is to exclude a large number of authorities which have a small expenditure and whose expenditure is likely to have a marginal impact on aggregate local government expenditure. The Government have estimated, for example, that the 296 non-metropolitan district councils in England account for only 7 per cent. of total local government expenditure, and that the expenditure threshold would remove 275 of them from the selective scheme (DoE 1983, para. 3.7). This expenditure threshold may be adjusted by statutory instrument in proportion to the change in the total of relevant local government expenditure from one year to the next (s. 2(3), (4)).

If an authority's expenditure exceeds this threshold it may be designated for rate limitation if it appears to the Secretary of State "from the best information available to him that its total expenditure in that year is likely—(a) to exceed its grant-related expenditure for that year . . . and (b) to be excessive having regard to general economic conditions" (s. 2(2)). The power to designate an authority must be exercised in accordance with principles determined by the Secretary of State. The principles must either be the same for all authorities within the relevant class (s. 2(6)) or for all of them within the appropriate class which respectively have or have not been designated in the previous year (s. 2(5)). The report designating these authorities must contain a statement of these principles (s. 2(7)).

Once an authority has been designated, the Secretary of State, for the purposes of prescribing a maximum rate, determines "a level for its total expenditure in the financial year for which the maximum is to have effect." (s. 3(1)). This maximum expenditure level must be determined in accordance with principles similar to those in section 2(5) (s. 3(2)). The maximum expenditure level is a notional figure since it does not constitute a legally enforceable expenditure ceiling. Its significance is that it forms the basis for calculating the maximum rate once the grant entitlement of the authority is determined in the R.S.G. settlement.

The maximum expenditure level must be notified to each designated authority (s. 3(3)). The authority then may, within a period specified in the notice, apply to the Secretary of State for a re-determination of the maximum expenditure level (s. 3(4)). This procedure is generally known as derogation (DoE 1983, para. 3.11). Any application for derogation must be accompanied by such information in such form as the Secretary of State may require (s. 3(4)). The Secretary of State may then either confirm his original determination or re-determine the level at a greater or smaller amount and, in doing so, may depart from the principles applied to authorities in the relevant class. If the Secretary of State re-determines a level at a greater amount he may impose on the authority "such requirements relating to its expenditure or financial management as he thinks appropriate" (s. 3(6)). The authority will then be under a duty "to comply with any such requirements and to report to the Secretary of State whenever he so directs on the extent to which those requirements have been complied with." (s. 3(6)). These duties are enforceable at the suit of the Secretary of State and, if an authority fails to comply with any such duty, it may be designated for rate limitation in the subsequent financial year without regard to the general requirements of section 2(2).

The final stage in the process is the translation of the maximum expenditure level into a maximum rate. The Secretary of State must notify each designated authority of its maximum rate as soon as practicable after the R.S.G. Report for any financial year has been laid before Parliament (s. 4(1)): see *R.* v. *Secretary of State for the Environment, ex p. Leicester City Council* (1985) *The Times*, February 1. In determining the maximum rate or precept the Secretary of State may take into account any financial reserves available to the authority (s. 4(2)). (On the legal obligations of the Secretary of State when setting a maximum rate or precept see: *R.* v. *Secretary of State for the Environment, ex p. GLC and ILEA* (1985) April 3, Q.B.D.; unreported.) If the authority accepts the proposed maximum, or agrees with the Secretary of State a different maximum, the power of the Secretary of State to prescribe a maximum rate shall be exercised by specifying that maximum in a direction in writing served on the authority (s. 4(3)). In any other case the maximum, either equal to or greater than that stated in the notice, shall be specified by an order which has been laid before and approved by a resolution of the House of Commons (s. 4(4)–(6)).

If no maximum has been prescribed by February 15 of the preceding financial year in the case of precepting authorities, or March 1 in the case of rating authorities, the Secretary of State may prescribe an interim maximum which shall have effect until it is replaced by a final maximum (s. 5). If an authority makes a rate by reference to an interim maximum and the final maximum is higher it may make a substituted rate complying with the final maximum (s. 5(4)). The proper officer in the rating or precepting authority must certify that any rate or precept subject to a maximum rate under the Act complies with the maximum (s. 7) and any rate or precept which exceeds the maximum prescribed under the Act shall be invalid (s. 6).

The general limitation scheme in Part II of the 1984 Act comes into force only after a draft order to this effect has been laid before and approved by a resolution of each House of Parliament (s. 9).

Before making this order the Secretary of State must consult such associations of local authorities as appear to him to be concerned and any local authority with which consultation appears to him to be desirable. (s. 9(2)).

When the general limitation scheme comes into force section 2 of the 1984 Act, establishing the criteria for designating certain local authorities, will not apply and Part I shall have effect as if every local authority were a designated authority (s. 10(1)). There are, however, mechanisms for exempting certain authorities from the general limitation scheme. If in any financial year it appears to the Secretary of State, from the best information available to him, that an authority in each of the three preceding financial years has complied with targets and not exceed its G.R.E., has not been designated under the Act in any of these years, and is likely to comply with those criteria in that financial year, then the Secretary of State *must* exempt it from the general limitation scheme for the next financial year (s. 10).

In addition, by virtue of section 10(5), the Secretary of State *may* prescribe an expenditure figure by an order subject to annulment in pursuance of a resolution of the House of Commons. If, on the best information available to him, the total expenditure of an authority is not likely to exceed that amount he *may*, by a notice in writing served on that authority, exempt it from the general limitation scheme for the next financial year.

Under the general limitation scheme the Secretary of State must consult with such associations of local authorities as appear to him to be concerned before designating the maximum expenditure levels (s. 11(1)). Otherwise the procedure is similar to that under the selective limitation scheme. The only variation concerns the matter of a local authority which does not agree to the proposed maximum rate under section 4(3). In this case the Secretary of State fixes an interim maximum rate (s. 4(4)) while discussions continue. But section 5 will not apply. Instead, the Secretary of State has the power to *increase* the interim maximum by a direction in writing or alternatively to *reduce* the maximum by an order which has been laid before, and approved by, the House of Commons.

In reality, the difference between the selective and general schemes is of marginal significance since the criteria for designating authorities under the selective scheme is very broad. Consequently it seems unlikely that the general scheme will be made operative in the near future.

2.4.3 Evaluation The form of the Rates Act 1984 suggests that the Government has adjusted itself to the new legal relationship between central departments and local authorities quite successfully. From the Government's viewpoint a rational response would be to draft new legislation in such a way as to maximise the discretionary powers of the Secretary of State, to minimise the possibility of local authorities taking evasive action, and, in particular, to minimise the possibility of local authorities successfully seeking judicial review. There is some evidence to indicate that these considerations were taken into account in the drafting of the Act.

First, the authorities are designated for rate limitation by the Secretary of State without any prior consultation with the local authority associations.

Secondly, there is no requirement for anything other than a minimal rationality between means and ends. That is, the Secretary of State has very broad power to determine both the objectives of the Act and the restrictions on local authorities necessary to achieve them. In designating authorities and in determining maximum expenditure levels, the Secretary of State is required to do so in accordance with principles applicable to authorities in the relevant class. But, as we have seen in both the *Brent* and *Hackney* (1984) cases, this is not a rationality criterion. As a result, the Secretary of State has power to manipulate principles to catch the desired authorities. The Secretary of State himself recognised this during the Committee stages of the Bill by providing 10 illustrative designation lists which identified different authorities. (House of Commons 1984a). Furthermore, in the case of the principles for determining the maximum expenditure level (s. 3(2)) there is no obligation even to publish these principles, let alone justify the levels in relation to the objectives of the Act. And the process of converting this expenditure level to a maximum rate (s. 4(2)) seems to be a matter for discretionary action without reference to principles applicable to all designated authorities.

Thirdly, the use of G.R.E. as a basis for designation seems controversial since G.R.E. was not designed as a prescriptive target and the principles underlying G.R.E. arguably cannot suitably be adapted for this purpose (Bramley and Evans 1984).

Fourthly, the structure of the derogation procedure makes it highly unlikely that local authorities will use it. The powers of the Secretary of State under section 3(6) are such that, notwithstanding his assurances on the use of these powers (House of Commons 1984b), to apply for derogation is potentially to *invite* the Secretary of State to determine the expenditure policies and priorities of the authority. However, if local authorities refuse to use this procedure, although it will not act as a bar to judicial review, it may be a factor which the Court will take into account in deciding whether to grant an application for judicial review (Evans 1980, pp. 358–360).

Finally, the authority is invited to agree to the maximum rate. If it does this may be taken as evidence of acquiescence and may affect any subsequent attempt to challenge it in the courts. If the authority does not agree, the rate limit is fixed by statutory instrument which may be challenged only on limited grounds; *R. v. Secretary of State for the Environment, ex p. Brent London Borough Council* [1982] 2 W.L.R. 693.

The Rates Act received the Royal Assent on June 26, 1984. On July 24, 1984 the Rate Limitation Report, designating 18 local authorities for 1985/86, was laid before the House of Commons (House of Commons 1984c). The principles for designation were those authorities whose 1984/85 budgets were more than 4 per cent. above their targets and more than 20 per cent. above G.R.E. No distinctions were made between classes of authority. At the same time the Secretary of State announced their maximum expenditure levels; three authorities had their maximum expenditure levels set at $1\frac{1}{2}$ per cent. below their effective 1984/85 budgets and for the rest it was set at the same level in cash terms as their 1984/85 budgets (House of Commons 1984d). These expenditure levels may not seem too harsh provided budgets are a good indicator of actual expenditure. However, there is evidence to suggest that, owing to the use of creative accounting techniques, budgets significantly understate actual proposed expenditure and the expenditure levels therefore may be more severe than they appear.

Nevertheless all designated authorities refused to apply for derogation and only one authority accepted its maximum expenditure level. Furthermore, in furtherance of a strategy of non-compliance with the Act, nine of the eighteen rate-capped authorities commenced the 1985/86 financial year without having made a rate. This strategy is examined in section 7.2.3.

The Rates Act 1984 seems the inevitable result of the policies pursued by the Conservative Government towards local government finance since 1979. The Government itself has argued the need for this measure in terms of the need to control public expenditure. If this is correct then rate limitation must also contain its own ratchet effect; it must be applied to a fairly wide group of authorities since controlling the rates of 18 or so authorities will have a negligible impact on aggregate local a government expenditure (Hepworth 1984). Consequently the inexorable logic of the Government's policies is leading to an unprecedented degree of centralisation of local government finance.

If rate limitation is not applied to an ever-growing group of authorities this may indicate that it has been introduced primarily as a weapon in the ideological conflict between the Conservative Government and Labour local authorities. Several mechanisms have been introduced to encourage local authorities to organise service provision along individualistic lines (see section 7.3). Many local authorities have resisted and sought to maintain collectively-organised service provision (see section 9.2). Given the nature of these mechanisms this has placed a heavy financial burden on these authorities. Rate control may therefore be designed to ensure that these authorities have little option other than to introduce individualistically organised services.

2.5 Capital Expenditure Controls

Before 1981 local authority capital expenditure was controlled by central government controls over borrowing. All borrowing by local authorities required loan sanction from the sponsoring department. This system of control seemed to work reasonably well since aggregate local authority capital expenditure during the 1970s was very close to government estimates. Nevertheless, for various reasons this system was felt to be an inappropriate means of expenditure control. First, loan sanction was given for a particular project rather than authorising a level of expenditure over a particular period. This meant that the control mechanism was not very responsive since it tended to produce reduced capital spending only after a significant time lag. Secondly, during the late 1970s an increasing proportion of capital expenditure was being financed by methods other than borrowing. Consequently this was not subject to central control.

In Part VIII of the Local Government, Planning and Land Act 1980, therefore, new arrangements for central control of local authority capital expenditure were enacted. The new system is designed both to provide a more suitable mechanism for ensuring the achievement of the Government's macro-economic policy objectives while also allowing local authorities greater freedom to determine their own priorities for capital expenditure (DoE 1977, para. 5.1). This system is designed to control the local authority's capital programme for a particular year rather than maintaining control over individual projects.

The Act provides a basic definition of capital expenditure (Sched. 12, para. 1) which is subject to the controls under Part VIII:

(a) the acquisition of land, including buildings and structures on land;

(b) the acquisition of vehicles and vessels and of movable and immovable plant, machinery and apparatus;

(c) the reclamation, improvement or laying out of land;

(d) the construction, preparation, conversion, improvement, renewal or replacement of buildings and structures;

(e) the repair and maintenance—
 (i) of land (including dwelling-houses and other buildings held under Part V of the Housing Act 1957); and
 (ii) dwelling houses held otherwise than under that Part of that Act,
 to the extent that the expenditure is defrayed by borrowing;

(f) the renewal or replacement of vehicles and vessels and the installation, renewal or replacement of movable and immovable plant, machinery and apparatus; and

(g) the making of grants and advances of a capital nature other than grants and advances to local authorities or Passenger Transport Executives.

This is subject to a broad power to alter, or adjust the details of, this definition by regulations (Sched. 12, paras. 4,5).

Under this system expenditure allocations are made by the relevant central departments under five service blocks: housing, education, transport, social services and other services (which include town and country planning, refuse collection and disposal, libraries, etc.). Police, probation and magistrates' courts services are not covered by this system and for these the old loan sanction arrangements apply. Once authorities have received these allocations, however, they are able, at least in law, to aggregate these blocks and use the total capital sum for purposes determined in accordance with their own priorities (s. 72). This is subject only to the limitation that in the case of a project declared to be of national or regional importance the Minister may direct that a specified part of an authority's aggregate amount be spent on that project (s. 73).

Initially it was proposed that any spending above allocation would automatically be *ultra vires*. This position was modified. Section 78 empowers the Secretary of State to direct any authority whom he thinks has exceeded, or is likely to exceed, its allocation not to make any further capital payments or enter into new contracts without the consent of the appropriate minister. Only if a local authority ignores such a direction, or a direction under section 73, will expenditure be *ultra vires*.

Flexibility is built into the system in four main ways. First, since an authority could exceed its allocation quite innocently (if, for example, its building work progressed faster than anticipated) a tolerance of up to 10 per cent. of allocation is permitted (s. 73(3)(*b*)). This amount will then be deducted from the following year's allocation (s. 73(8)). Secondly, any authority not using the full amount of its allocation may enter into an agreement with other authorities under which the unspent amount may be transferred to their allocations (s. 77(3)). Thirdly, authorities may supplement their allocations with the profits from their trading undertakings (s 72(3)(*e*)). Finally, authorities are able to use their net capital receipts, or such proportion of those receipts as may be prescribed, to augment allocations (s. 72(3)(*d*); s. 75(5)). These capital receipts arise principally from the sale of assets. This provision thus ties in with the Government's policy of encouraging local authorities to sell assets (see sections 4.2, 6.2.3).

There has been some debate over the question of whether the new system is a centralising measure or one giving greater autonomy to local authorities. In fact it is both. It integrates local authority capital expenditure into the cash limits system (Bevan 1980) while giving greater flexibility to local authorities *within* the centrally-approved total. Much depends on how the system operates in practice. At the time of its introduction it was suggested that there were three key implementation problems (Loughlin 1981, p. 430). First, that the authority's freedom of virement within its total allocation was likely to prove more illusory than real as the block allocations, being based on central government's priorities, could in practice be ignored only at the risk of jeopardising future allocations. Secondly, that the Government may use its comprehensive powers over capital investment for short-term macro-economic policy purposes. If so, local authorities would be subject to "stop-go" policies which would be detrimental to proper expenditure planning. Thirdly, the freedom to use capital receipts could pose problems because if authorities were to use all their capital receipts to bolster allocations this would affect the government's capital expenditure projections. The experience may be evaluated in terms of these issues.

First, every local authority submits detailed capital expenditure plans to the relevant central department for each of the four specific service blocks (see, *e.g.* sections 3.2, 4.4). If central government were serious about freedom of virement, however, one might expect that they would regard local authorities as being better equipped to judge local priorities, in which case it could be argued that the practice of requiring authorities to submit detailed expenditure plans should be abandoned. This, however, seems unlikely to happen (*cf.* Layfield 1976, p. 250).

Secondly, if the new system is concerned with *control* rather than the *limiting* of spending, it has been argued that underspend is as great a challenge to the control mechanism as overspend (Watt 1982, p. 94). By this criterion the system has not been at all successful: "The new system for controlling capital expenditure does not seem to have been conspicuously successful either from the local authorities' or the government's point of view." (Audit Commission 1985, p. 6.). In October 1980 the Secretary of State, in response to trends which indicated that local authorities were overspending on their Housing Investment Programmes (H.I.P.s) announced a six-month *moratorium* on housing investment (DoE 1980b). This restraint mechanism was also applied late in 1981 with the announcement of a *moratorium* on new housing starts. This resulted in a considerable underspend in 1981/82. Consequently in March 1982 local authorities were being exhorted to spend extra on housing. This exhortation was repeated by the Government in the Queen's Speech in November 1982. Nevertheless local authorities also underspent their capital allocation in 1982/83.

There were several reasons, in addition to the *moratoria*, for this state of affairs:

(1) there were problems in adapting to the new system of controls;

(2) there was unwillingness to borrow in a period of historically high interest rates;

(3) there was unwillingness to spend on capital account because of its revenue implications and the possibility of grant penalties;

(4) administrative problems caused by the lateness of notification of allocations after the submission of expenditure programmes contributed to the problem; and

(5) there were difficulties in spending capital receipts in the same year as they arose because the sum was rather unpredictable.

The result was that the decline in capital spending was greater than the Government wanted. Consequently, capital expenditure in 1982/83 was just over half the level for 1978/79 and was only one-third of the levels operating in the late 1960s and early 1970s (Jackman 1983).

By 1983, however, local authorities were able to deal with some of the administrative problems and respond to exhortations. The result was that they turned a 1982/83 underspend into a 13 per cent. overspend in 1983/84. This trend continued into 1984/85 and thus posed a problem for the new control mechanism because, with the possible exception of Liverpool City Council, no authority seemed to be exceeding its allocation. The Secretary of State's power to issue a direction under section 78, therefore, could not be used. This brings us to the third issue because the reason for the overspend was that authorities were permitted to spend capital receipts they had accumulated from previous years. This meant that aggregate local authority capital expenditure could exceed the cash limit allowed for in the Public Expenditure White Paper without any individual authority exceeding its own permitted allocation. The Secretary of State's response in July 1984 was to call for a voluntary system of restraint; authorities were asked to limit their 1984/85 capital expenditure to their approved capital allocation plus the prescribed proportion of capital receipts arising in that year only. But behind this voluntary system of restraint lay the threat that the Secretary of State would have regard to the extent to which authorities had complied with this request in determining their 1985/86 allocations (Jenkin 1984).

In addition to taking this short-term expedient the Government also had to review the operation of the system itself. One response was the decision to reduce the proportion of capital receipts which could be reinvested from 40 to 20 per cent. for housing and from 50 to 30 per cent. ior other investment (S.I. 1985 No. 257). But there is also the possibility of more radical proposals materialising. The right to re-invest capital receipts could be further reduced or eliminated. This proposal could even be coupled with a new system under which authorities would be given external financing limits and would be placed on much the same footing as the nationalised industries. Indeed, there is some evidence that this system might be slowly emerging. Thus, in June 1982 the Chancellor of the Exchequer announced that he wished to reduce the dependence of local authorities on bank lending. Since then bank lending to local authorities has reduced and the amount borrowed from the Public Works Loan Board (P.W.L.B.) has significantly increased. There are advantages to the Government in such a change. Apparently, lending by the banks to local authorities helps to increase the M3 definition of money supply whereas lending by central government via the P.W.L.B. does not (Webster 1984). But this could also be one stage in the establishment of a unified borrowing system under which local authorities would be compelled to use the P.W.L.B. The P.W.L.B. could then use interest rates fixing as a policy tool, regardless of the rates being charged in the commercial money markets. This system would thus result in further centralisation of power but would require new legislation before it was introduced.

2.6 Conclusions

In 1979 the Conservative Government inherited a system of local government finance that was under considerable strain. Difficulties arose from the need to adapt a grant system designed for growth to a period of restraint. Also the rating system, being tied to a market rental value system which had completely disappeared in the domestic sector, was becoming increasingly hard to defend. Furthermore, the Layfield Committee in 1976 had suggested that effective control of local expenditure was possible only within a clearer structure of accountability.

The Government appeared initially to be concerned about these issues. They had pledged in their election manifesto to examine the rates problem and they immediately proposed to reform the grant system in order to deal with both the restraint and accountability issues. The subsequent history seems to indicate that these concerns have been jettisoned in the pursuit of a short-term strategy of controlling local expenditure. This strategy, however, has been pursued in a hyperactive fashion and with a fair degree of ineptness. As a result, the principles behind the block grant system have been buried beneath individual expenditure targets; the strains imposed on the rating system have been greater than ever; and local accountability, far from having been restored, has been almost destroyed as a result of grant penalties and rate-capping.

Whatever expenditure objectives have been achieved have been achieved only at the cost of a much greater degree of centralisation

of power. In a governmental system without a constitutional
demarcation of central and local government responsibilities and
with just about the narrowest and most inadequate local government financial base of any major advanced capitalist country
(Newton 1980), these developments are likely significantly to
weaken local government. Furthermore, the structural problems
remain. Thus, the Government continues to tinker with the grant
system; the Secretary of State, as a result of mounting criticism from
Conservative-controlled authorities, hass announced that the holdback system will be abandoned from 1986/87 (Jenkin 1985a). This
means essentially that the block grant mechanism and rate
limitation will be the primary control devices. Of potentially greater
significance is the fact that the Government, with an unpopular
rating revaluation long overdue, has once again turned its attention
to rates reform. Proposals include the nationalisation of the non-
domestic rate levy, which would then be recycled to local
authorities through the R.S.G. system, and the possible introduction of a poll tax which could then, because of its regressive nature,
be used as a breaking mechanism on local authority expenditure.
Possible reforms to the rating system along these lines were the
subject of a Green Paper published in January 1986 (D.O.E. 1986),
although the Government has indicated that legislation to reform
the rating system will not be introduced until after the next election.
Reforms along such lines, however, seem likely merely to weaken
further the autonomy of local government.

Chapter 3

PUBLIC TRANSPORT

3.1 The Development of Transport Policy

At the heart of the development of post-war transport policy lie the issues of public or private ownership, monopolistic or competitive service provision, and regulatory or market controls. The post-war Labour Government's policy was basically to nationalise the transport sector of the economy. This was achieved primarily by the Transport Act 1947 which established the British Transport Commission (B.T.C.). The B.T.C. brought into public ownership the main line railway companies, the private bus companies, London Transport, the road haulage sector and some docks and waterways. Its statutory duty was "to provide, secure or promote the provision of an efficient, adequate, economical and properly integrated system of public transport and port facilities for passengers and goods" (Transport Act 1947, s. 3(1)).

Subsequent Conservative governments modified this regime. During the 1950s the organisation of the railways was restructured, B.T.C.'s road haulage services were privatised and its power to acquire bus undertakings was removed. This general process of deregulation and commercialisation was taken further in the Transport Act 1962 which divided the B.T.C. into five autonomous bodies: British Railways Board (B.R.B.), British Waterways Board, London Transport Board (L.T.B.), British Transport Docks Board and the Transport Holding Company (T.H.C.). The Labour Government 1964–70 reorganised the bus industry in the Transport Act 1968 by forming the National Bus Company.

Nationalisation and denationalisation therefore seemed to be the key policies of governments in relation to transport. But local authorities have also played an important role in transport policy. Many local authorities are empowered under public and private Acts to operate transport undertakings (Cross 1981, pp. 344–345) and by the 1960s there were 80 municipal transport undertakings in operation (Starkie 1976, p, 25). Furthermore, local authorities are the principal bodies responsible for the discharge of traffic management functions and since the war have played an important role in the development of urban transport policies.

The major factor underpinning post-war urban transportation policy has been the growth in ownership of the motor car. This trend caused considerable problems in transportation planning since transport planners had consistently underestimated traffic growth in their forecasts, with the result that until the 1960s it was felt that the growth in the volume of traffic could be accommodated by a programme of new road construction. During the early 1960s, attention turned to traffic *management* policies; of seeking to devise techniques to increase the capacity of the existing road system. And during the late 1960s following the influential Buchanan Report (1963), the idea that traffic was self-regulating was rejected and concern switched to methods of traffic *regulation* (Ministry of Transport 1966, Pt. II). A key element of traffic restraint policies is the maintenance of an efficient urban public transport system (Ministry of Transport 1967). This responsibility rested primarily with local authorities. Given the bias towards private transport inherent in the system, some degree of financial support seemed inevitable.

During the 1960s, however, the structure of local government was inappropriate for this task; in the early 1960s there were over 800 highway authorities and nearly 400 traffic authorities. As a result, the reforms to the legal framework were rather incremental. With structural reorganisation in London the GLC became the strategic transport planning authority, the highway authority for metropolitan roads and the traffic authority for all roads except trunk roads (London Government Act 1963, Pts. II, III). But responsibility for London Transport was not transferred from the Minister of Transport to the GLC until the Transport (London) Act 1969. Outside London the Transport Act 1968 established Passenger Transport Areas covering four conurbations. In these areas Passenger Transport Authorities (P.T.A.s), consisting of representatives of the constituent local authorities, were formed with responsibility for developing public transport policy in these areas. These policies were to be carried out by the Passenger Transport Executives (P.T.E.s) which assumed ownership of the amalgamated municipal undertakings and were responsible for the management of the service. With local government reorganisation the six metropolitan county councils became P.T.A.s Two new P.T.E.s were therefore established and the P.T.As remained responsible for the administration of the undertakings.

After the 1974 reorganisation county councils in both metropolitan and non-metropolitan areas assumed primary responsibility for highways, street parking, traffic management and public transport policy (Local Government Act 1972, s. 186). All county councils became under a duty to promote public transport services which meet the needs of their areas (Transport Act 1968, s. 9(3); Transport (London) Act 1969 s. 1; Transport Act 1978, s. 1) and were empowered to provide grants to public transport operators (Transport Act 1968, ss. 13, 20; Transport (London) Act 1969, s. 3; Transport Act 1978, ss. 1(5), 3(1)) in order to achieve an efficient and integrated transport system.

3.2 Public Transport Planning in the 1970s

Local government reorganisation and the reforms of the Transport Acts of 1968 and 1969 established a modern legal framework for dealing with urban transport planning. But the system of central government grants in support of local public transport seemed inappropriate. The Transport Act 1968 had introduced a range of specific grants which were targeted primarily at capital expenditure. Specific grants seemed to discourage comprehensive local transport planning and the forms of grant-aid established a bias in favour of capital intensive solutions. By the early 1970s these distortions were widely recognised (House of Commons 1972) and the oil crisis of 1973 added urgency to the need for reform.

In the Local Government Act 1974 the grant system was reformed. Some specific grants were absorbed into the R.S.G. system and the remaining part is distributed through a Transport Supplementary Grant (T.S.G.). There are three main features of this grant system, First, the objective of this system was to absorb specific transport grants into a general grant system which covers both revenue and capital expenditure, and public transport as well as roads. Secondly, the T.S.G. system is based not on the approval of individual schemes but on a projected programme of expenditure for each authority for the following year. Thirdly, the system clarified the fact that local authorities bore the primary responsibility for local transport policies, since grants were payable to local authorities rather than directly to transport operators.

In order to strengthen comprehensive local transport planning and to encourage a corporate approach, a new planning mechanism was devised. Transport Policies and Programmes (T.P.P.s) provided the planning foundation to the submission of bids for T.S.G. The T.P.P. consists of "a series of inter-related proposals covering both capital and current expenditure over the whole transport field—

public transport, roads, parking, traffic management, pedestrians. It would need to contain some overall assessment of policy county-wide, including the allocation of expenditure between different parts of the county as well as between different types of expenditure." (DoE 1973, para. 2). The T.P.P. is not a statutory document although it was envisaged that it would relate to structure plans (section 6.2.2). T.P.P.s thus provide rolling 15-year transport projections together with a five-year programme of policies devised in the context of these projections and a detailed costing of the policies for the following 12 months. This costing forms the authority's bid for T.S.G.

On the basis of these bids central government accepts a certain amount of expenditure for each authority; this amount is known as "accepted expenditure." T.S.G. is then paid at a fixed rate on all accepted expenditure above a threshold. (Local Government Act 1974, s. 6). The threshold is normally set at a certain sum per head of population. Since T.P.P.s also cover capital expenditure plans, local authorities generally receive loan sanction details in respect of transport expenditure along with the notification of their award of T.S.G.

The T.P.P. initiative was thus an early example of a general movement in the 1970s towards expenditure-based central-local planning systems. In the context of the reduction in expenditure aspirations in the late 1970s the tendency has been for resource considerations "to dominate the planning process to the point where other considerations, such as needs or service development priorities, are ignored." (Hambleton 1983, p. 163). Within these constraints, however, the Labour Government found that their policy of seeking to maintain a basic nationwide network of bus services was not being supported by many non-metropolitan counties. It was largely as a result of this concern that the Transport Act 1978 was enacted. This Act imposes a duty on each non-metropolitan county council, in consultation with district councils and transport operators, "to develop policies which will promote the provision of a co-ordinated and efficient system of public passenger transport to meet the county's needs."(s. 1(1)). To facilitate this duty the county councils are required, by section 2, to prepare and publish public passenger transport plans (P.T.P.s). The P.T.P.s should contain a review of the county's needs in respect of public passenger transport services, a description of the council's policies and objectives, and estimates of the financial resources required for the realisation of those policies and objectives (s. 2(2)). In drawing up P.T.P.s, which take the form of annual five-year rolling plans, the county councils must consult with district councils and transport operators and also afford those bodies, together with trades unions and transport user organisations, an opportunity of making representations on the contents of the plan at the draft stage (s. 2(3), (4)).

These P.T.P.s are a development from T.P.P.s since they require more detailed planning, closer and more extensive consultation with the interests involved and must formally be published (DoT 1978). Furthermore, unlike T.P.P.s they are statutory plans. The P.T.P.s were largely a response by the Government to the fact that broader socio-economic trends were rendering many rural bus services unprofitable. They provided a mechanism through which the Government could encourage non-metropolitan county councils to provide financial support to transport operators in order to ensure the maintenance of a basic public transport network. The difficulty with this policy is that it seemed to require an ever-increasing volume of financial support for both urban and rural public transport services.

3.3 Issues in the Era of Retrenchment

The growing levels of private car ownership since the 1950s have made it very difficult to maintain an efficient and economic public transport system. Nevertheless, 39 per cent. of households in the country still do not have the regular use of a car and the people most dependent on local public transport are in less well paid jobs or are unemployed, women, pensioners or schoolchildren (Department of Transport (DoT) 1984, para.1.1). Until 20 years ago the regulatory licensing system (see section 3.7 below) was able to sustain comprehensive networks of services through the ability of operators to cross-subsidise between profitable and unprofitable routes. As a result, little direct subsidy was required. Since then, however, circumstances have significantly changed.

Since the 1950s bus miles have fallen by about 50 per cent. and bus share of the total travel has gone down from 42 per cent. to 8 per cent. During the same period operating costs have risen faster than the general level of inflation. This is largely because labour accounts for about 70 per cent. of costs and average earnings have risen faster than prices. As demand weakened and real costs rose, the ability to maintain a comprehensive public transport network through cross-subsidisation diminished. Direct public subsidies were required; initially in the urban areas which have the most adverse conditions in terms of congestion and peakiness of demand, but later also in respect of rural services. The scale of subsidy has progressively grown with revenue support increasing from £10 million in 1972 to £520 million in 1982, a thirteenfold increase in real terms. The nature of the problem is highlighted by the fact that during the same period the level of fares has increased 30 per cent. in real terms and the long-term trend of decline has not been halted (DoT 1984).

The problems facing the Conservative Government in respect of public transport policy were immense. The Government has accepted that the country needs good bus services (DoT 1984, para. 1.1), but it did not wish to see any growth in subsidy (H.M. Treasury 1980, Table 2.6). However, given general trends, even the maintenance of the then existing levels of revenue support would probably lead to increases in real fares and a fall in patronage. Their attention therefore turned to the nature of the public transport regulatory system. In effect they have argued that the nature of this system, together with the existence of public subsidies, has bred inefficiency in the form of higher unit costs and lower operating performances than could otherwise be achieved.

This argument is part of a broader re-examination of transport policy around the key issues of public or private ownership, monopolistic or competitive service provision and regulatory or market controls. Thus the National Freight Corporation (Transport Act 1980, Pt. II) and the British Transport Docks Board (Transport Act 1981, Pt. II) have been privatised; parts of B.R.B.'s undertaking have been privatised (Transport Act 1981, Pt. I); and the N.B.C. has been reorganised with a view to possible privatisation (Transport Act 1982, Pt. II; Transport Act 1985, Pt. III). However, the Government has moved more slowly in relation to local public transport policy.

3.4 Urban Transport Policies in the 1980s

In the metropolitan areas local authorities have been attracted to solutions which require increasing the level of revenue support for public transport. These policies were not supported by the Government which did not wish to see any increase in subsidy levels. Conflict thus seemed inevitable since, although London and the metropolitan areas contain 40 per cent. of the population, they account for over 80 per cent. of revenue support to bus services (DoT 1984, para. 1.10). Nevertheless, local authorities based on the major conurbations have argued that, by international standards, the level of subsidy to urban public transport in the United Kingdom is not high.

The antagonism between central and local government in respect of urban public transport policy was heightened by the fact that control of the GLC and the metropolitan county councils (M.C.C.s) of Merseyside and the West Midlands switched to Labour after the May 1981 elections. This meant that all the metropolitan county councils were subject to Labour control; and all seemed to be increasingly attracted to a cheap fares public transport policy.

3.4.1 The GLC's "Fares Fair" Policy. When Labour gained control of the GLC in May 1981 it was conscious of the fact that since the mid-1970s real fares on public transport in London had been increasing and patronage had been declining (House of Commons 1982b, App. B, para. 90). In order to deal with this situation they pledged in their election manifesto that within six months of winning the election they would cut fares on London Transport's buses and tubes by an average of 25 per cent. This was to be financed by issuing a supplementary precept.

Under the Transport (London) Act 1969 the GLC had been established as the strategic transport planning authority for Greater London. Its primary duty was "to develop policies and encourage, organise and, where appropriate, carry out measures which will promote the provision of integrated, efficient and economic transport facilities and services for Greater London." (s. 1). It was also required to prepare general transport plans for Greater London (s. 2). However, the GLC did not directly provide public transport services. The main provider of services in Greater London was the London Transport Executive (L.T.E.) which was responsible for 84 per cent. of the passenger miles travelled on public transport. Under the 1969 Act the L.T.E. was obliged to provide such services "as best meets the needs for the time being of Greater London" (s. 5). These services were to be provided "with due regard to efficiency, economy and safety of operation" (s. 5). Nevertheless, since the GLC was also responsible for appointing the members of the L.T.E. (s. 4), establishing its general policies (s. 5(1)), approving its budget and fares policy (s. 11(2)(*d*)) and, was empowered to give the L.T.E. subsidies for any purpose (s. 3) and directions on the performance of its functions (s. 11), it was clearly established as the strategic authority.

The proposed fares reduction was estimated to require an extra £30 million for revenue support in 1981/82. However, because of its high resource base the GLC was one of the few authorities which under the block grant system had negative marginal grant rates throughout the entire range of its feasible budgetary options (see A in Figure 2.3). This meant that a decision to increase its budget resulted in a reduction in its entitlement to block grant. As a result, the supplementary precept issued in furtherance of its public transport policy had to raise roughly twice the amount which was needed to finance the fares reduction.

This supplementary precept was challenged by Bromley London Borough Council which applied for judicial review by way of an order of certiorari to quash the precept, a declaration that the precept was *ultra vires* and an injunction to restrain the GLC and the L.T.E. from implementing the policy. The Divisional Court dismissed the application but this decision was overturned by the Court of Appeal. In *Bromley London Borough Council* v. *GLC.* [1983] 1 A.C. 768 the decision of the Court of Appeal was affirmed unanimously by the House of Lords.

The precise basis on which the supplementary precept was quashed is complicated by the fact that five separate speeches were delivered by the Law Lords. Bromley London Borough Council's challenge was based on arguments concerning both *excess* of power and *abuse* of power. The abuse of power argument revolved around the manner in which the decision to issue the precept was made. On this point a minority (Lords Diplock and Brandon) were of the view that the GLC, in deciding to proceed with the fares reduction after becoming aware of the consequent grant losses, had considered themselves to be irrevocably bound by their election manifesto and had therefore not lawfully exercised their discretion. Since this decision was taken only after full consideration by the appropriate committees which were in receipt of official advice, this finding seems controversial. Indeed it could be argued that this constitutes an attempt to place an inappropriate judicial curb on the functioning of the political process.

However, the arguments concerning the issue of excess of power were of greater significance. This issue hinged on the true interpretation of the statutory power of the GLC to provide, and the L.T.E. to receive, revenue support for public passenger transport services. Despite differences of nuance, the construction placed on the Transport (London) Act 1969 by Lords Wilberforce, Keith, Scarman and Brandon were similar. All agree that the nature of the financial duty imposed on the L.T.E. is such that "while permitting advance budgeting, it nevertheless requires the L.T.E. so to provide its services as to ensure, so far as practicable, that deficit is avoided" and therefore, although deficit budgeting is permitted, it is not permitted "as an object of social or transport policy, but as a course of action which it may not be practicable or possible to avoid" (pp. 845–846).

This construction is determinative of the issue on the question of excess of power. There is, however, a distinction in the routes which are taken to reach this result. Lords Wilberforce and Scarman interpret the Act in the context of a fiduciary duty which the local authority owes to its ratepayers. As a result they hold that, having regard to the term "economic" in sections 1 and 5 of the Act, the GLC are not empowered to adopt a fares policy which unduly benefits transport users at the expense of ratepayers. Lords Keith and Brandon, however, interpret the Act in the context of a general legal principle that statutory transport undertakings, unless a contrary intention is clearly demonstrated, should run their services on ordinary business principles. Consequently, they focus their attention directly on the duties of the L.T.E. In particular, they construed section 7(3), which appeared to be a technical accounting provision prohibiting the L.T.E. from cumulatively building up deficits, as imposing on the L.T.E. a duty to break even so far as practicable. The difference between these two routes is that the fiduciary duty concept circumscribes the powers of the GLC whereas the business operation principle defines the duties of the L.T.E. As the powers of the GLC and the duties of the L.T.E. are interlinked the result is the same.

There is another connection between the two routes since the primary authority for both lines of reasoning rests on the Court of Appeal's decision in *Prescott* v. *Birmingham Corporation* [1955] Ch. 210; in this case the defendants, who were empowered to run a transport undertaking charging such fares as they think fit, were successfully challenged when they sought, by virtue of that power, to introduce a scheme enabling old people to travel without charge. In fact the two modes of reasoning adopted in *Bromley* appear to be two facets of the same principle. This is illustrated most clearly by Lord Scarman who defines the fiduciary duty of the GLC to its ratepayers as "a duty which requires it to see that the services of its instrument, the LTE, are provided on business principles so as to ensure, so far as practicable, that no avoidable loss falls on the ratepayers." (p. 846).

Lord Diplock's speech is interesting because although concurring in the result he disagrees with the rest of the Lords on most of the issues concerning statutory construction. In particular, by examining legislative history, he convincingly demonstrates that the 1969 Act did not contemplate a duty on the L.T.E. to break even so far as practicable. He therefore clearly dissented from the mode of reasoning adopted by Lords Keith and Brandon. Diplock took the view that the only statutory constraint on revenue support was to be found in the GLC's general duty under section 1 to provide "integrated, efficient and economic transport facilities." The precise nature of that constraint could be ascertained only by taking a purposive construction of it in the context of the legal structure and status of the GLC as a local authority.

Diplock identified three groups to whom the GLC owed a duty in respect of public transport: (1) potential passengers, (2) Greater London residents who benefit from the general mobility of the transport system whether or not they use public transport, and (3) the ratepayers, to the extent that they are required to contribute to the cost of the system. Diplock considered that the people in the first two categories were almost identical but that there was no such coincidence between those categories and the ratepayers; the ratepayers "constitute only 40 per cent. of the residents and that 40 per cent. bears only 38 per cent. of the total burden borne by all ratepayers" (p. 829). Consequently, a conflict of interest lay between passengers and ratepayers. He was conscious of the fact that this relationship was recognised in law in the form of a fiduciary duty which the local authority owes to ratepayers "not to expend (the ratepayers') money thriftlessly but to deploy the full financial resources available to it to the best advantage" (p. 829). The key question was whether the GLC could be said to have breached this duty in the circumstances of this case. Diplock thought that it would be difficult so to hold if the issue was merely one of lowering fares by 25 per cent. and transferring the cost to its ratepayers. But here the loss of rate support grant meant that the GLC's decision was not simply about allocating a total financial burden but also "a decision to increase that burden so as nearly to double it and to place the whole of the increase on the ratepayers" (p. 830). For Diplock that was clearly "a thriftless use of moneys obtained by the GLC from the ratepayers and a deliberate failure to employ to the best advantage the full financial resources available to it by avoiding any action that would involve forfeiting grants from central government funds. It was thus a breach of the fiduciary duty owed by the GLC to the ratepayers" (*ibid.*).

While Diplock's analysis has certain similarities with the speeches of Lords Wilberforce and Scarman, their approach in fact has more in common with Lords Keith and Brandon, since all four apply principles in order to construe the nature of the statutory scheme under the 1969 Act. And Lord Diplock specifically disagrees with their construction. Furthermore, Diplock's analysis seems more coherent. Thus the majority position converts the GLC's duty under section 11(2)(*d*) to approve a fares *policy* into a mere accounting exercise; it transforms section 3 subsidies "for any purpose" into the marginal one of making up deficits only after the L.T.E. has striven, so far as practicable, to meet operating expenditure from fare income; it effectively destroys the stated policies behind the legislative changes in 1968 and 1969 which were identified in the White Papers (Ministry of Transport 1966; 1967); and it seems incoherent since there is no means of striving to break even "so far as practicable" without first deciding what quantity of service is required (Foster 1982, p. 107).

The difference between the Diplock and the Wilberforce/Scarman approach is that the latter invokes the concept of fiduciary duty in order to interpret the nature of the statutory scheme whereas in the former the fiduciary concept seems to assume the status of a quasi-constitutional principle. The latter approach has specific implications for transport policy whereas the former is potentially more far-reaching in its consequences. The significance of the fiduciary concept is examined in section 9.4.3. However, we must here evaluate Diplock's specific treatment of the fiduciary concept. In general, his approach is marked by extreme formalism and lack of rigour. His formalism is seen most clearly in his analysis of the antagonism between ratepayers and passengers/residents and his argument that only 40 per cent. of residents are ratepayers. Presumably this means that only 40 per cent. of residents are heads of households. If so this argument is extremely formalistic since in reality the rates constitute a tax on the household and the fact that formally it is levied on one person is irrelevant from the viewpoint of household burden. In reality there is little antagonism between residents and domestic ratepayers.

But, as Lord Diplock points out, 62 per cent. of the rate burden is borne by commercial and industrial ratepayers. What is not clear, however, is why the interests of non-domestic ratepayers are in conflict with the group of people who benefit from the general mobility of the transport system. In fact, non-domestic ratepayers potentially could benefit substantially from an increase in mobility: either in greater accessibility (of customers and clients to them or their products to various outlets) or in the alleviation of increased cost-inspired wage demands of employees. Consequently it is submitted that, within Lord Diplock's framework, there is no fundamental imbalance in using rates to finance fares reductions on the public transport system. Without this imbalance the invocation of the fiduciary concept seems illegitimate since it amounts to an unjustifiable judicial curb on the autonomy of local authorities to fix their budget levels and standards of service provision.

The lack of rigour in Diplock's analysis is seen most clearly in his argument that the decision to reduce fares constituted a thriftless use of ratepayer's money because of the rate support grant implications of this decision. This conclusion was reached without any examination of the nature of the block grant system (see sections 2.3.3., 2.3.5.). If the system had been examined Diplock would have realised that, as a result of the techniques used for equalisation purposes, the GLC received negative marginal rates of grant throughout the entire range of budgetary choice. If the strict logic of his analysis were adhered to the only safe budgetary position of the GLC would have been at a point approximately 50 per cent. below its G.R.E., at which its entire expenditure would be financed by R.S.G.! Furthermore, Diplock did not rigorously examine the nature of the grant loss. He noted that the £69 million cost of fares reduction resulted in R.S.G. loss of £50 million. But he did not mention the fact that almost one-third of that grant loss was attributable to holdback penalties. Yet at that time the holdback system lacked any statutory foundation and the penalties could not actually be levied until the Local Government Finance Act 1982 retroactively authorised their use.

Consequently it is submitted that none of the speeches in the House of Lords' decision in *Bromley London Borough Council* v. *GLC* reach an acceptable standard for decision-making in this complex and sensitive area of public law adjudication. The result of the decision was to create a great deal of uncertainty in both the field of transport and beyond. The GLC's response was to ask the Secretary of State for Transport to introduce legislation which would validate the "Fares Fair" scheme. This the Transport Secretary refused to do, but he was prepared to allow the GLC to fund concessionary fares for pensioners and to enable it to borrow money to cover the deficit arising as a result of the decision to quash the supplementary precept. The Travel Concessions (London) Act 1982 did permit the L.T.E. to operate a concessionary fares scheme for pensioners. But the GLC refused the loan sanction option because of the effective cost of borrowing and because the resulting break in the tradition of local authorities not borrowing for revenue purposes might detrimentally affect the general borrowing status of local authorities in the financial markets. Consequently, as a result of the *Bromley* decision the GLC submitted a revised budget for 1981/82 in which public transport fares were approximately double those under the "Fares Fair" scheme.

3.4.2 The Ramifications of the Bromley Decision. Although the *Bromley* decision concerned the interpretation of the Transport (London) Act 1969, the decision resulted in widespread concern over the power of Metropolitan County Councils to provide revenue subsidies under the Transport Act 1968. All six Metropolitan County Councils were under Labour control and all were providing revenue subsidies to public transport undertakings. Although South Yorkshire County Council, which had frozen the level of its fares since 1975, was an obvious target for challenge most attention focused initially on the two metropolitan authorities in which, along with the GLC, Labour had gained control at the May 1981 elections. In both the West Midlands and Merseyside County Councils the incoming Labour administrations were pledged in their manifestos to a cheap fares public transport policy. Furthermore, both authorities had issued supplementary precepts to finance these policies.

Following the *Bromley* decision the M.C.C.s sought counsel's opinion on its implications for their schemes. The opinions received were almost universally conservative and, as a result, caused a certain amount of disruption. For example, both the leader and the deputy leader of Merseyside County Council resigned after the controlling Labour group rejected their recommendation that fares should be raised in order to keep their fares policy within the law. In Greater Manchester, following counsel's advice, the County Council agreed to raise fares by 15 per cent. The decision of the West Midlands County Council to raise a supplementary precept of 14p in the £ to finance a 23 per cent. cut in fares, however, was the first to be challenged in the courts. In *R.* v. *West Midlands County Council., ex p. Solihull Borough Council* (1982) (unreported) Woolf J. quashed the supplementary precept on the grounds that the Council in seeking to implement the election pledge of a cheap fares policy had not, as a council, properly brought its mind to bear on the issue but had slavishly followed what it had conceived to be its electoral mandate. However, the day before the judgment was announced, as a result of counsel's advice, the Council had itself declared the supplementary precept null and void. Finally, South Yorkshire County Council, following the receipt of advice that their policies seemed unlawful and that members ran the risk of surcharge if they were not changed, were also under great pressure to increase fares.

It should be noted, however, that the provisions of the Transport Act 1968, although similar in several respects to the Transport (London) Act 1969, were not identical. The key provision was section 9(3) which imposed on the transport authority and the passenger transport executive a duty "to secure or promote the provision of a properly integrated and efficient system of public passenger transport to meet the needs of that area with due regard to the town planning and traffic and parking policies of the council's of constituent areas and to economy and safety of operation." In this section it is noteworthy that the term "economy" clearly seems to be qualified by the words "of operation." Furthermore, although section 11(1) of the 1968 Act required that at the end of any accounting period the consolidated revenue account must not be in deficit, section 13(3) implied that this duty to balance the account did not mean that only self-generated income could be included in the account since that provision authorised the transport authority to make grants to the executive in respect of revenue.

These issues were eventually tested in *R* v. *Merseyside County Council, ex p. Great Universal Stores Ltd.* (1982) 80 L.G.R. 639, in which the applicant, a ratepayer, sought an application for judicial review to quash the County Council's supplementary precept. Woolf J., in dismissing this application, noted that while there is a "very marked similarity" between the provisions of the 1968 and 1969 Acts "there is an important distinction as to emphasis" (p. 650). Thus, while under the 1968 Act the authority had to be mindful of expense, cost was only one among many factors to which the authority had to have regard. Consequently, particularly given the terms of section 9(3) of the 1968 Act and the fact that the general duty of the Executive under that provision was not made expressly subject to its financial duties, the difference in emphasis was significant. Woolf J. therefore held that "the Authority can require the Executive to run a service which the Executive consider cannot be justified on ordinary business principles if the Authority is prepared to undertake to meet the extra cost of running that service" (p. 648). The applicant's first argument, that the Authority had not power under the 1968 Act to provide revenue subsidies, thus failed.

The other major ground of challenge was whether the authority had exercised its discretion properly. Woolf J. considered that, given the broad range of issues to which the authority had to have regard and the fact that no issue arose in this case concerning the impact of the subsidies paid on the loss of rate support grant, it could not be said in this case that Merseyside County Council had not properly considered and balanced the financial burden on ratepayers arising from the policy. Furthermore, although the policy originated in the manifesto and was implemented quite speedily Woolf J. considered that there was no evidence that the Council after the May elections "did not consider the proposal contained in the manifesto afresh on its merits." (p. 657). As a result it was not possible to say that the authority had not exercised its discretion properly.

One immediate result of the *Merseyside* decision was to alleviate the pressure on South Yorkshire County Council to abandon its commitment to a fare freeze. Nevertheless, the *Bromley* and *Merseyside* decisions still left a degree of uncertainty over the limits of a local authority's power to provide revenue subsidies to public transport undertakings. This was highlighted by the GLC's proposal to provide revenue subsidies to reduce fares to L.T.E. services by 25 per cent. for 1983/84. In what was termed "the Balanced Plan," the objective of the GLC was to return to the fares levels which existed immediately prior to the introduction of the "Fares Fair" scheme. The L.T.E., however, were advised that, given their duties under the 1969 Act, they were not empowered to accept this subsidy. Since the GLC and the L.T.E. were unable to reach agreement on this matter the GLC applied to the High Court for judicial review, seeking declarations that its "Balanced Plan" constituted a lawful exercise of its powers under the 1969 Act and that it was accordingly entitled to maintain a direction which it had given to the L.T.E. to put those proposals into operation.

In *R.* v. *London Transport Executive, ex p. GLC.* [1983] 2 W.L.R. 702 a unanimous Divisional Court granted the declarations sought. Kerr L.J. stated that the decision of the House of Lords in *Bromley London Borough Council* v. *GLC* had been "widely misunderstood and indeed misrepresented" (p. 707). He accepted the position that the requirement that a transport undertaking be run on business principles was "primarily intended to exclude philanthropic considerations and to emphasise the need for the proper and cost-effective use of resources" and that it did not mean that "in the context of a public transport system, fare revenue was required to be maximised on ordinary business principles of profit and loss." (p. 714). Provided that the GLC had regard to its duty to promote "an integrated, efficient and economic" public transport system, the balance struck between farepayers and ratepayers was a matter of discretion for the GLC, subject only to the requirement that "if the balance was arbitrary or clearly unfair, then it would be invalid under the *Wednesbury* principle" (p. 717).

The Divisional Court's decision in this case is particularly interesting because, although the form of the judgments closely follow the majority position of the House of Lords in *Bromley*, there seems little doubt that the primary influence in interpreting the nature of the scheme under the 1969 Act, was Lord Diplock's speech in that case. Thus, although lipservice was paid to the L.T.E.'s "duty to break even, so far as practicable" it seemed clear that, for the Divisional Court, it was in section 1 of the Act and in the local authority's fiduciary duty that the primary legal constraints were to be found. It must therefore be emphasised that the issue of fiduciary duty was not of relevance in this case. Thus, while the Divisional Court's decision clarified the GLC's powers under the 1969 Act, the uncertainty of the nature of its fiduciary obligation to ratepayers remained.

3.4.3 The Transport Act 1983. Although the Government had refused to introduce legislation designed to legitimate the GLC's "Fares Fair" scheme, in July 1982 the Secretary of State did announce that a Bill would be introduced to establish a "clear and consistent legal framework" for the payment of urban public transport revenue subsidy. This framework was designed to provide the basis for "a reasonable, stable and lawful subsidy regime" in Greater London and the metropolitan areas. (DoT 1982, paras. 1, 5). This Bill became the Transport Act 1983.

The main reform introduced by the Transport Act 1983 was to require the preparation of an annual plan, covering a three-year period, which contains proposals relating to the provision of transport services and the general level and structure of fares to be charged for such services (s. 3). Responsibility for drawing up this plan lies with the Executive, although the plan must then be approved, with or without modifications, by the Authority (s. 4). Before the plan is adopted, however, the Authority must submit it to the Secretary of State and must take into account his guidance as to the maximum amount of revenue grants which would, in his opinion, be appropriate for the Authority to provide in that year

(s. 4(4), (5)). The aim of this revenue grant plan thus seems to be that of ensuring that the Authority has fully considered the question of the extent to which proposed public transport subsidies are justifiable in terms of demonstrable transport benefits.

The Act also imposed a common financial duty on the Executives. Sections 7(3) and 7(6) of the 1969 Act, which attracted so much judicial attention in the *Bromley* case, were repealed, along with the equivalent provision in section 11(1) of the 1968 Act. They were replaced by section 2 of the 1983 Act which provides a common and simplified version of the financial duty:

> "2(1) An Executive shall so perform their functions as to ensure so far as practicable that the combined revenues of the Executive and any subsidiaries of theirs for any accounting period are not less than sufficient to meet their combined charges properly chargeable to revenue account in that period."

Since the Act also recognises that the plan drawn up by the Executive may be formulated "on the assumption that the authority will in the relevant period make revenue grants of such amounts as the Executive may determine" (s. 3(3)), the Act makes it clear that revenue grants are included in "the combined revenues of the Executive." This provision therefore indicates that the financial duty of the Executives is essentially an accounting duty and does not incorporate any limitation on the power of Authorities to subsidise the transport undertaking. This is an important clarification and seems to suggest that the majority in the House of Lords misconstrued the 1969 Act in reaching their decision in *Bromley*. Section 2(1) of the 1983 Act thus re-establishes a logical structure to the Transport Acts of 1968 and 1969 by indicating that the statutory limitation on the power of the GLC and the metropolitan authorities to provide revenue subsidies is not to be found in the financial duty of the Executives, but rather in section 1 of the 1969 Act and section 9(3) of the 1968 Act respectively, which set the transport policy objectives for the Authorities.

However, the objective of the 1983 Act was not merely that of clarification. The aim was also to convert those transport policy objectives into justiciable constraints. This is to be achieved by requiring the Executives, in drawing up the plan, to undertake a cost-benefit exercise (s. 3(4)) so as to demonstrate the transport benefits which result from the revenue subsidies which they receive from the Authorities. This is not uncontroversial. First, although the

Authorities already prepare T.P.P.s which include a review of local transport problems and proposals to deal with them, responsibility for plan preparation under the 1983 Act is vested with the Executives. The relationship between this new plan and T.P.P.s thus seems unclear. Secondly, and more importantly, the Secretary of State has the power to give the Executives advice not only on appropriate revenue support levels but also on the methods to be used in calculating the costs and benefits of services (s. 3(5)). There is therefore the danger that this power could be used to make it very difficult to demonstrate that benefits outweigh costs at a given subsidy level.

Although the Authority may modify the plan before approving it, they must have regard to the costs and benefits of services, the guidance provided by the Secretary of State and "the need to achieve a proper balance between the interests of ratepayers in their area and the interests of transport users." (s. 4(3)). Furthermore, before approving the plan, the Authority must submit it to the Secretary of State and take into account his "guidance as to the maximum amount of revenue grants, if any, which would in his opinion be appropriate for the Authority to make." (s. 4(5)). Finally, section 5(2) empowers the Secretary of State to determine a protected expenditure level (P.E.L.) for each authority. If the Authority's revenue grant does not exceed the P.E.L. it shall "be regarded for all purposes as a proper exercise of that power." This is an unusual provision. The White Paper clarified the objectives of P.E.L.s by stating that it will give the Authorities protection from legal challenge, adding that if Authorities decide on a higher level of subsidies "councillors will know that they run the risk of surcharge should their action be challenged by the Auditor and found by the Courts to be unlawful." (DoT 1982a, para. 13).

Thus the manner in which this planning framework has been established suggests that the Government's objective was not to resolve legal uncertainties, but rather to exploit them in order to coerce Authorities into compliance with the Government's guidelines on acceptable levels of revenue support. The uncertainties in the statutory frameworks had been more or less resolved by the decisions of the Divisional Court in the *Merseyside* and *L.T.E.*, cases. The main legal uncertainty following the *Bromley* decision concerned the reactivation of the fiduciary concept. The Transport Act 1983 thus seemed designed to exploit the ambiguity inherent in the concept, in the context of the new system of targets and grant penalties (see section 2.3.5), in order to require compliance with the P.E.L. guidelines.

In practice this immediate objective was not achieved. The main reason was that the courts were unprepared to use the fiduciary concept as a powerful anti-public expenditure device (see section 9.4.3). Consequently, although six of the seven Authorities exceeded their P.E.L. in 1983/84 none were challenged in the courts. However, another reason concerned the planning process itself. The Department of Transport made it clear that they intended to use the techniques of cost-benefit analysis in order to assess the Authorities' proposals for revenue support (DoT 1983a, Annex A). For this purpose they developed a mathematical model to assist them in assessing value for money of subsidy in each conurbation (DoT 1982b; Glaister 1984). However, even on the Department's model all the metropolitan areas showed a positive net return for the levels of subsidy provided (Glaister 1984). Consequently the planning process actually became a mechanism through which local authorities could justify their revenue support policies.

Nevertheless, even if the process causes local authorities to provide a reasoned justification for their policies, cost-benefit analysis is not without its problems. It may demonstrate conclusively that the decision of the House of Lords in *Bromley* was indefensible (Morriss 1983) but there is a danger that it will distort both issues and values. As the main architect has admitted of the Department's model:

> "There are a number of other effects that many will consider to be important but that are not included explicitly. These include: any energy considerations that are not captured adequately in the various vehicle operating cost calculations; accident benefits ... ; the effects of increased subsidies on labour productivity and wage costs; the long-term effects of transport policies on urban form; and the wider, social aspects of the problem" (Glaister 1984, p. 197).

Finally, although the Transport Act 1983 was enacted to provide the basis for a "stable ... subsidy regime" (DoT 1982a, para. 5) this has not proved to be the case since it has been rapidly overtaken by proposals to reorganise public transport in London and to abolish the metropolitan county councils and the GLC.

3.5 The Reorganisation of London Transport

In 1980, before Labour gained control of the GLC, the House of

Commons Transport Committee decided to undertake a review of the organisation and financing of transport in London. It reported in 1982 and concluded that the existing system required reform. It proposed the establishment of a Metropolitan Transport Authority, composed of nominees of both the local authorities and the Transport Secretary, which would have responsibility for trunk and metropolitan road planning, strategic traffic management policies and public transport planning throughout the London region. The objective was to achieve an integrated and effective transport system for the London region (House of Commons 1982b).

The Government took the opportunity which this report presented to deal with the challenge to their preferred policies presented by the GLC's public transport revenue support schemes. It announced that the case for change in the organisation of transport in London was now compelling and proposed new legislation to transfer control of the L.T.E. from the GLC to the Secretary of State so that it could be reconstituted as a holding company, London Regional Transport, with its bus and underground operations established as separate subsidiaries (DoT 1983b). This was not the integrationist solution proposed by the Transport Committee but was essentially a measure to transfer control of the L.T.E. from local to central government so as to ensure that central government's public transport policies were implemented.

These proposals were enacted in the London Regional Transport Act 1984, which repealed Parts I and II of the Transport (London) Act 1969 and provided that the L.T.E. shall continue to exist, but shall be known as London Regional Transport (s. 1). L.R.T. is under a general duty "to provide or secure the provision of public passenger transport services for Greater London" (s. 2(1)) and in carrying out that duty must have due regard to "the transport needs for the time being of Greater London" and to "efficiency, economy and safety of operation" (s. 2(2)). It is given general powers to facilitate the achievement of its general duty (s. 3) and is required to co-operate with the Railways Board to secure the proper discharge of its duty (s. 2(3)). This general duty must be carried out "in accordance with principles from time to time approved by the Secretary of State" (s. 2(1)).

The corporate structure of L.R.T. indicates that the Government's objective is to break down L.T.E.'s organisation into smaller management and operating units with a view to the privatisation of certain units. Thus L.R.T. is under a duty, subject to the Secretary of State's approval, to form separate companies to provide bus and underground services (s. 4). L.R.T. will nevertheless retain sufficient control over any subsidiaries so as to enable them to control the general level and structure of fares to be charged and the general structure of service routes (s. 8). Subject to the Secretary of State's consent, L.R.T. may dispose of the whole or any part of the undertaking of any of their subsidiaries (s. 9). Furthermore, the Secretary of State is empowered to direct them to do so (s. 10). L.R.T. is also empowered to invite other persons to submit tenders to carry on any of their or their subsidiaries' undertakings and must accept that tender "if it appears to them that to do so would result in the relevant activities being carried on in a satisfactory manner and at less cost to them ... than if they ... were to carry on those activities" (s. 6).

Under the 1984 Act control of L.R.T. is effectively vested in the Secretary of State. In addition to the powers already mentioned, the Secretary of State has power to appoint the members of L.R.T. (Sched. 1), set financial objectives for L.R.T. (s. 16), receive and advise L.R.T. on their policy statements (s. 7), provide guidance on the form and content of L.R.T.'s business plan (s. 29), receive their annual report (s. 34), and has extensive powers to require information, give directions and establish guidelines for the general conduct of L.R.T.'s undertaking (s. 32). Furthermore, and perhaps of greatest importance, the Secretary of State controls the funding of public passenger transport services through his power to make grants to L.R.T. "for any purpose and on such terms and conditions as the Secretary of State thinks fit"(s. 12(1)). The Secretary of State may then recover a contribution from the ratepayers of Greater London towards his estimated expenditure on section 12 grants (s. 13(1)). This contribution may not exceed two-thirds of the estimated expenditure (s. 13(6)). The contribution is obtained by making a levy on the rating authorities in Greater London (s. 13).

Almost inevitably, the implementation of the 1984 Act led to conflicts between the Secretary of State and the GLC. First, the GLC appointees to the L.T.E. were dismissed by the Transport Secretary. Secondly, a dispute arose over the direction given to the GLC by the Transport Secretary under section 49 of the 1984 Act to pay £281.3 million in grants to L.R.T. for the initial year. This direction was challenged in the courts. In *R.* v. *Secretary of State for Transport, ex p. GLC* [1985] 3 W.L.R. 574 McNeill J. found in favour of the GLC on both procedural and substantive grounds. On the procedural issue it was held that natural justice required that the GLC first be given an opportunity to make representations concerning the appropriate financial contribution, and this had not been done. One result was that the GLC was required to pay more than section 49 permitted. Consequently, McNeill J. also found that the direction exceeded the powers of the Secretary of State under section 49 and therefore quashed the determination. The Government's response was not to appeal but instead to introduce a Bill retrospectively amending section 49 of the 1984 Act. The London Regional Transport (Amendment) Act 1985 was thus enacted on March 11. This Act substituted section 49(1)–(4) of the 1984 Act with a provision requiring the GLC to pay L.R.T. "by way of grant for the initial year...the sum of £258,179,588." It is clear, therefore, that the Government was not prepared to allow any obstacles to prevent the expeditious implementation of the reform of the arrangements for London Transport.

The Government have stated that L.R.T. will have four initial tasks: to improve services within the available resources; to reduce costs and the call on taxpayers' money by securing better value; to involve the private sector in the provision of services; and to promote better management through the establishment of smaller and more efficient operating units (DoT 1983, para. 18). These objectives are to be achieved within tight financial constraints. The Government has set financial targets requiring L.R.T. to make a 2.5 per cent. reduction in costs in each year for the next few years and a progressive reduction in subsidy from £190 million in 1984 to £95 million in 1987 (Wheen 1985, p. 47). This will require some reduction in manpower and probably also in service levels. Finally, in October 1984 L.R.T. invited private operators to submit tenders for 13 of its bus routes; this competitive franchising system could well be extended to cover a greater proportion of London's transport routes.

3.6 Abolition of the Metropolitan County Councils

In 1983 the Government announced that it was proposing to abolish the GLC and the Metropolitan County Councils; the Local Government Act 1985 provides that this takes effect on April 1, 1986. (For details see Chap. 8). Responsibility for public transport in the metropolitan counties becomes that of joint authorities (see section 8.4.3). These joint authorities will be subject to strict central control, since the Secretary of State for the first three years of their operation has powers to determine their expenditure levels, manpower levels and management structure.

3.7 Deregulation of Bus Services

3.7.1 Introduction. The road passenger transport system has been subject to a strict regulatory regime since 1930. Operators must possess not only a public service vehicle (P.S.V.) operator's licence in respect of the fitness of their vehicles and their employees, but also require a road service licence, which controls fares and stopping places, before they are permitted to run a service on a particular route. This regulatory regime is operated by traffic commissioners, who are appointed by the Secretary of State with a regional jurisdiction.

The vast majority of local (known as "stage carriage") bus services are provided by public operators: the L.T.E. (now L.R.T.) in London, the P.T.E.s in the metropolitan areas, 51 municipal operators and the various subsidiaries of the National Bus Company (N.B.C.). These together account for about 95 per cent. of bus miles, with the remainder being provided by a large number of small private operators. As a result of the pressures on the public transport system identified in section 3.3 above, the traffic commissioners have used their discretionary licensing powers to promote the standardisation of fares, to protect existing operators from competition and thereby to encourage cross-subsidisation between profitable and non-profitable routes provided by the operator.

Given the trends in public transport over the last 30 years and the Conservatives' policy of limiting or cutting subsidies to the public transport system, the Government have sought a deregulatory solution:

> "Without the dead hand of restrictive regulation fares could be reduced now on many bus routes and the operator would still make a profit ... [Operators] will be stimulated to provide a greater variety of services, using different types of vehicles running on different routes or frequencies, offering more choices to meet peoples' needs ... Competition also brings continuing pressure to keep costs down." (DoT 1984, paras. 1.5–1.7).

However, with the growing need for revenue subsidies to preserve the national bus network and with the increasing involvement of local authorities in the field of public transport, it could be argued that effective control of this regulatory system had passed from the traffic commissioners to the county councils. That is, the pattern of services may be determined not primarily through the licensing system but rather as a result of the policy and planning functions of county councils under the Transport Acts of 1968, 1969 and 1978. If so, it seems likely that a liberalisation of the Traffic Commissioners' licensing regime would not in itself significantly alter the system. Consequently, the decisions to remove the GLC's control over London Transport and to abolish that authority along with the Metropolitan County Councils, could also be related to the Government's public transport policy objectives.

3.7.2 The Transport Act 1980. The Conservative Government's first reform was nevertheless to seek to liberalise this licensing regime. This they did in the Transport Act 1980. Since the Public Passenger Vehicles Act 1981 consolidated the law in this area the statutory notations refer to the 1981 Act. Four main reforms were introduced.

First, express carriage services, which carry passengers 30 miles or more (s. 2), could be operated without a road service licence. This introduction of competition on express services did not affect stage carriage services directly, although it could if the operator was cross-subsidising from express to stage carriage services.

Secondly, although the requirement of a road service licence was retained in respect of stage carriage services, the presumption was altered. The traffic commissioners "shall grant the licence unless they are satisfied that to do so would be against the interests of the public" (s. 31(2)).

Thirdly, the traffic commissioners' control over fares was reduced. Conditions relating to fares could not be attached to a road service licence unless it was essential in order "to protect the public from unreasonable use by the holder of the licence of his position ... or ... to regulate the terms of competition between stage carriage services on any route or routes" (s. 33(3)).

Finally, provision was made to experiment with deregulation of stage carriage services in certain areas. These "trial areas" are designated by the Secretary of State by order on the application of the local authority (s. 38). Once designated, a road service licence is not required for the provision of a stage carriage service within a trial area (s. 39). An operator merely has to inform the local authority and the district council, and publish in a local newspaper notice of any new service, or any changes to or discontinuance of an existing service within the trial area (s. 40).

The effect of these measures on local public transport services has not been of great significance. Fare arrangements have generally not altered: most of the fare agreements between public and private sector operators reached before the 1980 Act have been maintained;

the commissioners have never intervened to prevent overcharging and have rarely done so to control the terms of competition; and while the rate of increase in bus fares has declined, this is attributable mainly to the combined effects of a falling rate of inflation, loss of patronage as a result of economic recession and the revenue support policies of the GLC and the M.C.C.s since 1981 (DoT 1984, Annex 3, para. 11).

While the criteria for the grant of road service licences has been eased, there have been few cases in which operators have obtained licences permitting them to compete with established operators. Of crucial significance has been the traffic commissioners' interpretation of "the public interest." The key issue was their attitude to the argument that permitting licences to operate competitive services would reduce the revenue of the existing operator and thereby reduce their ability to cross-subsidise unremunerative but socially desirable services. This argument came to a head in *R. v. Secretary of State for Transport, ex p. Cumbria County Council* [1983] R.T.R. 129. In this case a private operator was refused a licence to operate a service in Whitehaven in competition with the existing operator, a subsidiary of the N.B.C., on the ground that the resulting loss of profit to the existing operator would require it, in order to balance its books, to cut its unprofitable rural routes. The applicant for the licence appealed from the traffic commissioners' decision to the Secretary of State. The inspector appointed to inquire into the commissioners' decision recommended that the appeal be dismissed, but the Secretary of State granted the appeal on the grounds that the evidence of the existing operator and the county council had been accepted uncritically and that the objectors had not demonstrated satisfactorily that the service would be against the public interest. Cumbria County Council sought an application for judicial review of this decision on the ground that there was no evidence on which the Minister could properly conclude that he was not properly satisfied that the service would be against the public interest. This application was dismissed in the Divisional Court but was granted on appeal. Lord Lane C.J., giving the judgment of the Court of Appeal, was particularly critical of the form of the decision letter: "it would be very reprehensible for the Secretary of State to use the formula of not being satisfied to avoid the scrutiny of this court and to disguise the true reasons for his decision" (p. 135).

It has been suggested, however, that since that decision the commissioners have reappraised the question of "the public interest" and now require objectors to support their cases in a more analytical and a quantitative manner (DoT 1984, Annex 3, para. 7). Nevertheless, in the few cases in which operators have obtained licences to compete they have faced resistance in the form of pricing policies and increased service frequencies. These tactics by existing operators have generally been successful (Hibbs 1982, pp. 58–59; DoT 1984, Annex 3, para. 8).

The trial area scheme has similarly had limited success. Only three trial areas have been designated, covering mainly rural areas in parts of Norfolk, Hereford and Worcester and Devon (S.I. 1981, No. 373; S.I. 1981, No. 885; S.I. 1982, No. 1243). Little has changed in the Norfolk and Devon areas as a result of trial area designation but in the Hereford area there have been some important changes. This has arisen because at the same time the County Council introduced a new system of competitive tendering for revenue subsidy on unprofitable routes, and also because it is the only trial area which includes a sizeable town. As a result, the main N.B.C. subsidiary reduced services in the trial area by 170,000 vehicle miles per annum and 85 per cent. of the mileage withdrawn was replaced by private operators. In 1981 the County Council saved £62,000, or 38 per cent., in revenue support on bus services in the trial area as a result of competitive tendering. And in Hereford four private operators competed with the N.B.C. subsidiary; this has resulted in that company reducing fares and increasing services. However, the main concern has been over the safety standards of the private operators as one firm lost its operator's licence after inspection and another secured licence renewal only on a limited basis (DoT 1984, Annex 3, Pt. II).

3.7.3 The Transport Act 1985. Despite the limited impact of deregulation in the trial areas, the Government announced in 1984 that it was effectively to extend this deregulatory regime throughout Britain (DoT 1984). However, the Government also recognised that deregulation in itself might not significantly alter the public transport system; first, because the large public sector transport operators might use their dominant market position to thwart competition and, secondly, because the county councils might use their planning and grant powers to protect public sector operators. They therefore proposed fundamentally to reorganise the public transport system. These reforms were enacted in the Transport Act 1985.

Basic changes to the regulatory regime are enacted in Parts I and II of the 1985 Act. The main effect is to deregulate outside London by abolishing the system of road service licensing contained in Part

III of the Public Passenger Vehicles Act 1981 (s. 1). As a result, the regulatory framework is to be streamlined, with the body of traffic commissioners being replaced by a single traffic commissioner for each traffic area (s. 3, Sched. 2) and the licensing system replaced by a registration system (s. 6). The traffic commissioner may nevertheless regulate service routes, stopping places and the like by determining traffic regulation conditions (s. 7). This power may be exercised only at the request of any traffic authority (s. 7(1)) and only if the commissioner is satisfied that the conditions are required in order to prevent danger to road users or reduce severe traffic congestion (s. 7(4)). Furthermore, before determining traffic regulation conditions the commissioner must generally hold an inquiry (s. 7(9)–(11)). The commissioner may vary or revoke any conditions on being requested to do so by a traffic authority or the operator of a local service affected by the conditions (s. 7(14)). There is also a power of appeal to the Secretary of State, and subsequently to the High Court on a question of law, in relation to any determination, variation or revocation of traffic regulation conditions (s. 9).

The Act provides for a period of transition towards deregulation which will last until October 25, 1986 (s. 139(1); Sched. 6). During this period Part III of the 1981 Act will apply with certain modifications, the effect of which is essentially to require the traffic commissioners to grant applications for road service licences unless they are satisfied that to do so would "interfere with the transition to deregulation." (Sched. 6, paras. 2–4).

Deregulation of road service licensing is not extended to London. Part II of the 1985 Act therefore re-enacts Part II of the P.P.V.A. 1981 as it applies in London by virtue of sections 43–45 of the London Regional Transport Act 1984. The reason deregulation has not been extended to London is that the 1984 Act has given powers to the Secretary of State effectively to control L.R.T. and has established a framework which requires L.R.T. to engage in competitive tendering for bus services. The Government therefore proposes to defer deregulation in London until they see the results of the experiment of this system of competitive franchising within a regulatory framework. The Secretary of State is nevertheless empowered to repeal this London regime by an order subject to affirmative resolution (s. 46).

Finally, Part I modifies the licensing regime applicable to taxis (ss. 10–17), minibuses (ss. 18–23) and the P.S.V. operator's licence (ss. 24–31).

Associated with deregulation, the 1985 Act has fundamentally reorganised the structure within which public transport is provided. Part III makes provision for the privatisation of the N.B.C., but of greater significance for local government are Parts IV and V which make alterations to the structure and functions of local authorities and P.T.E.s with respect to public transport.

The structural reforms basically require P.T.E.s (s. 59) and district councils which operate bus undertakings (s. 66) to form companies limited by shares registered under the Companies Act 1985 and to transfer their undertaking to the company. (ss. 59; 67–70). The Secretary of State may direct the P.T.E. to transfer all shares in the company held by them to the P.T.A. for their area (s. 59(8)) and may make provision for the transfer of all the P.T.E.'s functions, property, rights and liabilities to the P.T.A. (s. 85). The Secretary of State may also require the Authority to divide the undertaking of the company into two or more companies (s. 61). Provision is made to enable the local authority to control the constitution and activities of these public transport companies (ss. 72–74). The local authority may make loans to the public transport company at the going rate (s. 79). Financial assistance by way of grants, loans or guarantees to any company which has incurred losses affecting the viability of its business, however, may only be provided with the consent of the Secretary of State and in accordance with an approved plan for improving the efficiency of the company's operations (s. 79(8)(9)). Finally, subject to the consent of the Secretary of State, the local authority has the power to provide for the disposal of any shares in, or other securities of, the company (s. 75(2)(3)).

The primary objective of these structural reforms, particularly since the main objective of the N.B.C. in preparing a privatisation programme will be "to promote sustained and fair competition" (s. 48(1)), is to ensure that the deregulatory scheme in Part I of the Act will lead to competition. This will be achieved by breaking up the larger public sector operators to ensure that they do not suppress competition through market dominance, and by requiring public transport companies to operate on ordinary business principles. Through this structure it is also presumably envisaged that there will be some incentive to privatise the public transport companies.

Finally, the 1985 Act made certain basic alterations to the functions of local authorities in respect of public transport. Section 57 replaces the general duty of P.T.A.s and P.T.E.s to secure an integrated public passenger transport system with a duty on P.T.A.s to formulate general policies as to the provision of services appropriate to the area's requirements and a duty on P.T.E.s to secure such provision. In formulating and carrying out such duties the Authority and Executive shall so conduct themselves "as not to inhibit competition between persons providing or seeking to provide public passenger transport services in their area" (s. 57(2) providing a new s. 9A(6) of the Transport Act 1968). Similar duties are imposed on county councils in non-metropolitan areas (s. 63). Furthermore, the Act imposes a duty on all authorities exercising public transport functions "to co-operate with one another so as to secure, in the interests of the ratepayers of their areas, the best value for money from their expenditure on public passenger transport, taken as a whole" (s. 88(2)).

Authorities retain the power to secure the provision for their area of public transport services which would not otherwise be available by entering into agreements providing for service subsidies, but only in accordance with a strict tendering system (ss. 88–92). Furthermore, the Secretary of State is empowered to make grants directly to persons operating or proposing to operate public transport services in rural areas (s.108). Finally, the Act empowers any local authority to establish travel concession schemes for old age pensioners, the blind, the disabled and children (ss. 93–102).

The reforms of the Transport Act 1985 thus constitute the most fundamental alterations to the regulatory system since regulation was introduced in 1930. The reforms are based on the view that the regulatory system based on the principle of cross-subsidisation which has emerged stifles innovation and encourages inefficiency. The objectives of the 1985 Act are therefore to deregulate in order to promote efficiency consequent on competition; to break the public sector monopoly and require public sector operators to function on market criteria; to make competition a reality; and to switch public support from general subsidies to large networks towards the support of specific routes which although unprofitable are socially desirable.

Undoubtedly the Act is a highly controversial measure. It is based on the idea that there is one network which the market can provide to which an additional network to meet social objectives could be attached. Most of the advances in integrated transport systems in the metropolitan areas in recent years, however, emphasise the fact that what passengers want to purchase is not an individual bus route but access to the entire network (Quarmby 1984). Also it is widely feared that any "savings" which can be achieved will be the result of lower wages and lower maintenance standards—neither of which are efficiency savings in the true sense. Indeed the House of Commons Transport Committee has criticised the Government's proposals on the grounds that they would cause wasteful and unsafe competition, destabilise bus networks and damage co-ordination of services (House of Commons 1985).

Nevertheless the signs seem to indicate that the Government intend the urban public transport network to be run more or less on a self-financing basis. The T.S.G. from 1986 will not be available for public transport revenue support (S.I. 1984, No. 1863) and it has been estimated that public expenditure projections indicate that public transport subsidies in the metropolitan areas will be reduced by 40 per cent. in the two years following abolition of the metropolitan county councils (Carvel 1985a).

3.8 Conclusions

Developments in the public transport field constitute a microcosm of developments affecting local government generally. The pace of change has been rapid and has resulted in major reforms to local government structures, functions and financial arrangements in respect of public transport. These reforms have been introduced against a backdrop of a crisis in public transport policy and a basic conflict between urban local authorities and central government about the most efficacious solution. The revenue-support solution favoured by urban local authorities was destabilised by judicial intervention in the *Bromley* case and the resulting legal uncertainty has been exploited by central government with the enactment of the Transport Act 1983. With the first signs that the 1983 Act was not producing the desired results, however, more radical initiatives followed: "nationalisation" of London transport, the replacement of metropolitan county councils with joint authorities subject to central control, the deregulation of local public transport, and the break up of the market dominance of public sector operators in an attempt to ensure "sustained and fair competition." In terms of central government action there are parallels between this experience and developments affecting the system of local government finance since the introduction of the block grant mechanism: *viz.,* hyperactivism, retroactivism and central government subjectivism.

Cumulatively these developments have had a significant impact on local government autonomy: from the restrictions arising from the invocation of the fiduciary concept, through the statutory procedural rules laid down in the 1983 Act, to the reconstruction of the local public transport system on essentially market-based lines. In particular these developments have curtailed the discretionary redistributive function of local authorities in the field of public transport.

Chapter 4

HOUSING MARKETS AND HOUSING POLICY

4.1 Developments in Housing Policy

The growth in council housing this century has been a major social achievement. At the turn of the century 90 per cent. of the housing stock was owned by private landlords. Since then the combination of more attractive investment opportunities and statutory restrictions on the landlord-tenant relationship have led to the fairly rapid demise of private landlordism. Today the private rented sector provides for only 12 per cent. of the market. In its place, alongside the growth in owner-occupation, there has emerged the public rented sector which accounts for around 30 per cent. of the housing stock.

The emergence of council housing has been merely one expression of growing state involvement in housing markets throughout this century. The concern over housing standards has also led to a major role for local authorities; nearly 2 million houses have been demolished since the 1930s through programmes of slum clearance, and since 1949 over 3 million houses have been renovated with the aid of improvement grants (Gibson and Langstaff 1982, p. 11). Furthermore, the growth in owner-occupation has been fuelled in part by various tax policies which subsidise the cost of home-ownership. As a result of these various policies housing conditions have significantly improved. The number of households living in unfit or substandard housing has fallen from 7,500,000 in 1951 to 1,650,000 in 1976 and the number of overcrowded households over the same period has fallen from 650,000 to 150,000. Also, there is no longer an absolute shortage of houses; whereas in 1951 there were about 750,000 more households than houses in England and Wales, by 1976 there were about 500,000 more houses than households (DoE 1977b, pp. 10–11).

The housing role of local authorities particularly increased in importance after the Second World War when local authorities became the primary instruments through which the housing policies of the Welfare State were carried out. Under the post-war Labour Government local authorities played the dominant role in house-building as part of a deliberate policy of directing resources to building for the needs of lower income groups. However, as Kirwan (1984, p. 134) has pointed out, although the principles of non-profit housing (embodied in the historic cost financing system) and housing as a social right (reflected primarily through the creation of the housing waiting list) were established, the welfare function of local authority housing remained ambivalent. This was mainly because housing lacked the dimension of universality which characterised education, health and social security programmes.

By the late 1970s, however, the ambivalence which had characterised much of the post-war development of housing policy seemed to have been replaced by a view that owner-occupation was the dominant, if not "natural," tenure form and that the function of council housing was to provide a minimal residual service. There were many reasons for this shift in emphasis.

First, housing policy was used as a tool of Keynesian macro-economic policy. Local authority growth rates, subsidy levels and building standards were manipulated as growth regulators. This had the effect of devaluing the importance of social needs in housing policy since economic rather than social variables seemed crucial. Furthermore, the consequences of this orientation during a period of economic recession and public expenditure restraint seem obvious.

Secondly, no post-war government had been prepared to construct a rational policy covering the entire area of housing finance. Consequently, even the benefits of the historic cost financing system seemed more the result of the failure to predict rates of inflation than an expression of a socialist approach to value (Kirwan 1984, p. 138). The failure to construct a rational policy thus made it difficult to defend historic cost financing, particularly since subsidies to council housing constituted an item of public expenditure while owner-occupiers' income tax relief on mortgage repayments did not.

Thirdly, while much of the council housing stock is of good quality, a high proportion of the inner city and overspill stock built primarily during the 1960s by industrialised methods has been extremely unpopular (Dunleavy 1981, pp. 353–355). The problems which have arisen in relation to these units have been used to create a climate of popular dissatisfaction with the entire tenure form.

Finally, while the declining private rented sector has been regulated by a large and complex body of law the local authority landlord-tenant relationship has been insulated from legal regulation. This autonomy in the management of their housing stock was based on the assumption that local authorities could be expected to act as model landlords. Unfortunately this assumption did not always prove to be justified (National Consumer Council 1976; Housing Research Group 1981).

For a combination of these reasons, council housing never fully achieved its potential as an alternative tenure form constructed on alternative principles. Consequently, when by the 1970s a crude housing surplus had been created the role of council housing seemed vulnerable. Public expenditure constraints added impetus to this vulnerable state. If housing problems could be characterised as residual then housing could be a prime target not only for public expenditure cuts but also for a re-examination of the local authority role.

The Labour Government's Housing Policy Review (DoE 1977b) seemed to accept this analysis. The review, which was "the high point of post-war complacency over housing provision" (Ball 1983, p. 3), took the view that the major problems had been dealt with and the minor problems were all that were needed to be solved. The Conservative Government in 1979 also accepted this analysis but placed much greater emphasis on the ideological strand of the analysis. They have propounded a clearer role for the State in housing provision, based on the view that housing ought to be seen as a private commodity which is best provided through the market. Their policies are therefore directed primarily towards supporting market processes, with the result that the role of the state is to cater for the needs of the residual population who cannot fend for themselves in the private market. This approach has profound implications for the local authority role:

> "The combination of changes suggests that the late 1970s and early 1980s are an important watershed in policy .... They imply a new era for council housing in which a concentration on special needs is accompanied by a reduction in the actual size of the council stock, a minimal rate of new building, a decline in the quality of new and existing council dwellings and a reduction in subsidy for council housing (but not owner occupation). ... It involves a ... rejection of ideas of optimal public service provision and a reassertion of the role of the market backed by a minimal poor law service." (Murie 1982, p. 34).

Some indication of nature of policy change is obtained from the fact that the Conservative Government planned to reduce public expenditure on housing by 48 per cent. between 1980/81 and 1983/84. This accounted for 75 per cent. of the planned reduction in total public expenditure over that period (H.M. Treasury 1980, Table 2.7). In addition to public expenditure cuts the Government proposed radically to alter the legal and administrative framework relating to council housing. This was achieved primarily through the Housing Act 1980 which introduced three major reforms to the council housing system: it gave tenants a right to purchase the freehold of their homes on favourable terms (Pt. I, Chap. I);[1] tenants were given security of tenure and certain rights in relation to housing management (Pt. I, Chap. II);[2] and it introduced a new housing subsidy system (Pt. VI).[3]

4.2 Council House Sales

The most controversial reform in the Housing Act 1980 was the statutory right of public sector tenants to purchase their homes. The power of local authorities to sell council houses is not a new phenomenon; the power was first contained in the Housing Act 1925 and, prior to the 1980 Act, was conferred on local authorities by section 104 of the Housing Act 1957. The power to sell, however, has been subject to Ministerial consent and post-war governments have modified the terms of such consents in accordance with their ideological views (see Murie 1975). This discretionary system was completely transformed by the provisions of Chapter I of Part I of the Housing Act 1980.

The 1980 Act conferred on a "secure tenant" of three years standing the right to acquire the freehold of their house or a long lease of their flat (s. 1).[4] The "secure tenant" is a key concept under the 1980 Act; the term is defined in detail in section 28[5] but generally the vast majority of tenancies are secure and the exempt categories are tightly drafted (Hoath 1982, pp. 8–19). Similarly, the categories of exempt properties are tightly defined (s. 2; Sched. 1; *Freeman* v. *Wansbeck District Council* [1984] 2 All E.R. 746).[6] Furthermore, the terms on which the tenant may exercise the right

---

[1] Housing Act 1985 Pt. V. (All the following references refer to the Housing Act 1985).
[2] Pt. IV.
[3] ss.421–427.
[4] ss.118, 119.
[5] s.79.
[6] s.120, Sched. 5.

to buy are extremely favourable. The purchase price is based on
market value (s. 6).[7] But the tenant was entitled to a discount on
market value of 33 per cent., plus 1 per cent. for each complete year
by which his or her period as a secure tenant exceeded three years
up to a maximum discount of 50 per cent. (s. 7).[8] Provision was
made for requiring repayment of the discount if the property was
subsequently resold within five years, reduced by 20 per cent. for
each full year of occupation between conveyance and disposal
(s. 8).[9] Also the tenant was given the right to a mortgage from the
council (ss. 1(1), 12).[10]

Given these incentives it seemed likely that the demand to
exercise the right to buy would be substantial. On the basis of
previous experience with discretionary sales it also seemed likely
that many local authorities would be reluctant to sell. The
Government, in laying down a fairly rigorous procedure, seemed
conscious of this difficulty. The 1980 Act imposed three main
procedural obligations on a local authority.

(1) To serve a written notice *within four weeks of receiving an
     application to buy* stating that the authority either admits or
     denies the right to buy (s. 5).[11]

(2) Thereafter, if the right to buy is admitted, *as soon as
     practicable* to serve on the tenant a notice stating the
     purchase price (s. 10).[12]

(3) To convey the property as soon as all matters relating to the
     transfer and mortgage have been determined (s. 16).[13]

These obligations are reinforced by very broad supervisory
powers which are vested in the Secretary of State and are designed
to avoid a repetition of the Clay Cross episode which arose in
relation to the Housing Finance Act 1972 (Skinner and Langdon
1974; Mitchell 1976). Section 23 enables him to intervene "where
it appears to the Secretary of State that tenants... have or may
have difficulty in exercising the right to buy effectively and

[7] s.127.
[8] s.129.
[9] s.155.
[10] ss.132, 133.
[11] s.124.
[12] s.125 (Since the 1984 Act, below, the duty arises after 8 or 12 weeks,
     depending on whether the property is a house or flat).
[13] s.138.

expeditiously."[14] Under this provision "the Secretary of State may do all such things as appear to him necessary or expedient to enable secure tenants... to exercise the right to buy" (s. 23(3))[15] and "the costs incurred by him in doing so... shall be a debt from the landlord to the Secretary of State payable on demand, together with interest at a rate determined by the Secretary of State from the date the sum was certified" (s. 23 (9)).[16]

Resistance of various kinds from local authorities did in fact occur (Ascher 1983). Central government's monitoring of the progress of local authorities in processing applications was unusually vigilant. The first formal approach to an authority about progress was made only five weeks after the Act came into force and 33 local authorities had already been approached by the time Norwich City Council were formally contacted by the DoE concerning their rate of progress (Forrest and Murie 1985, Table I). Nevertheless, it was Norwich City Council against which a formal notice under section 23 was eventually issued by the Secretary of State on December 3, 1981. This notice proposed that the Secretary of State's representatives would process sales on behalf of the City Council. The notice followed several meetings between the Council and the DoE. Norwich thereupon unsuccessfully sought judicial review of the Secretary of State's decision.

In *Norwich City Council* v. *Secretary of State for the Environment* [1982] 1 All E.R. 737 the Court of Appeal held that, although the Secretary of State must give the authority a fair opportunity of making representations before intervening and must act in good faith and without taking into account extraneous considerations or without misdirecting himself in fact or law, there was no evidence that he had not done so. The Court also rejected an argument that the local authority must be acting unreasonably before the Secretary of State may exercise his powers to intervene. The Court of Appeal nevertheless expressed some concern over the breadth of the Secretary of State's power under section 23. They referred to it as a "coercive" (p. 744) and "draconian" (p. 748) power which "may well be without precedent in legislation of this nature" (p. 749) and that "short of seeking to exclude altogether any power of review by the courts, the wording of section 23 has clearly been framed by Parliament in such a way as to maximise the power of the

---

[14] s.164.
[15] s.164 (5).
[16] s.166 (4).

Secretary of State and to minimise any power of review by the court" (p. 748).

After this decision Norwich City Council decided to co-operate fully with the Secretary of State (Forrest and Murie 1985, pp. 114–130). But the DoE has maintained its active role in monitoring generally the progress of local authorities in selling council houses. On January 26, 1984, for example, the Minister reported that the Department was in formal contact with 176 councils concerning their performance (House of Commons 1984e).

The impact of the right to buy was such that between 1980 and 1983 over half a million dwellings, representing 10 per cent. of the public sector stock, were sold under the scheme (House of Commons 1983a). This resulted in a decline not only in the relative but also the absolute number of public sector dwellings: see Figure 4.1. Nevertheless, sales peaked in 1982 as the pent-up demand was exhausted. In an attempt to maintain the impetus the Government therefore provided additional incentives in the Housing and Building Control Act 1984.

Under the 1984 Act, residential qualifications were reduced and the maximum discount increased. The three-year residential qualification for exercise of the right to buy was reduced to two years (s. 3(1) substituting new s. 1(3) of the 1980 Act)[17] and the determination of the residential qualification was harmonised with the discount qualification period and extended (s. 3(5), Sched. 2 inserting a new Sched. 1A into the 1980 Act).[18] The minimum discount was reduced from 33 to 32 per cent., reflecting a reduction in the residential qualification period, and the maximum discount increased from 50 to 60 per cent. (s. 3(2) substituting new s. 7(1) of the 1980 Act).[19] Also, children succeeding to their parent's tenancies were given the right to count the time spent in the property since the age of 16 for qualification and discount purposes (Sched. 1A, para. 4 of 1980 Act).[20]

The 1984 Act also provided certain new rights relating to purchase. First, the right to buy was extended to situations in which the landlord does not own the freehold; tenants are entitled to a lease expiring five days before the landlord's interest provided that interest is, in the case of a house, sufficient to grant a lease exceeding 21 years (50 years in the case of a flat) (s. 1, Sched. 1 of

[17] s.119.
[18] Sched. 4.
[19] s.129.
[20] Sched. 4, para 4.

Figure 4.1 Sales and Construction Rates in England and Wales 1970–1985.

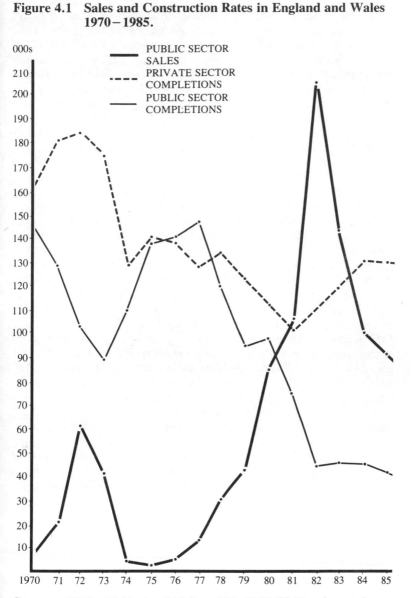

000s

PUBLIC SECTOR
SALES
PRIVATE SECTOR
COMPLETIONS
PUBLIC SECTOR
COMPLETIONS

Sources: 1970–82 Boyne (1984), p.181; 1983-85 Housing and Construction Statistics, HMSO (1985 estimates).

1984 Act).[21] Secondly, where a tenant's income is such that they are not entitled to a mortgage amounting to the purchase price of the property, there is a right to a "shared ownership lease." (ss. 12–17 and 37; Sched. 11).[22] Under this scheme the tenant purchases a minimum 50 per cent. slice of the equity, with the aid of a mortgage, and pays a reduced rent on the remainder (see Hughes 1981, pp. 83–85). The tenant may then purchase, again with the aid of a mortgage, further tranches until the whole is acquired. Thirdly, certain provisions ensuring that these rights could be beneficially exercised were enacted; in particular, the categories of dwellings exempt from the exercise of the right to buy were more restrictively defined (s. 2)[23] and a service charge protection scheme, similar to that which exists for flats (Sched. 19 of the 1980 Act), was introduced for houses (s. 18; Sched. 4).[24]

Finally, the 1984 Act makes amendments to the procedures relating to the right to buy which have the effect of rendering the tenant's right more efficacious. Thus the landlord's procedures are tightened up and those of the tenant liberalised (s. 6).[25] More importantly, however, the Secretary of State is given broader powers of intervention. These powers empower the Secretary of State to direct that certain covenants or conditions not be included in conveyances or grants (s. 9, inserting new s. 24A and B into the 1980 Act);[26] to require the landlord to provide information needed in connection with the exercise of his powers under sections 23, 24A and 24B of the 1980 Act (s. 10, inserting new s. 24C into the 1980 Act);[27] and to provide assistance (including the giving of advice and arranging for legal representation) to any person who has exercised or is seeking to exercise the right to buy and where the issue raised is one of principle or is otherwise complex or raises special considerations (s. 11, inserting new s. 24D into the 1980 Act).[28]

The most recent enactment relating to council house sales is the Housing Defects Act 1984.[29] In recent years it has become apparent that certain types of system-built public housing have inherent

[21] s.118, Sched. 5, para 4.
[22] ss.143–153.
[23] s.120, Sched. 5.
[24] ss.45–51.
[25] ss.140–142.
[26] ss.167, 168.
[27] s.169.
[28] s.170.
[29] Pt. XVI.

structural defects. Approximately 16,500 of these types of dwellings have been sold by local authorities. Since these defects may not have been discoverable by structural survey the Government felt that they owed a special duty to these purchasers. Consequently under the Act, owners of certain designated types of dwellings which are defective by reason of their design or construction (ss. 1, 2, 12;[30] DoE 1984) may apply to the local authority for assistance (s. 3(1)).[31] Assistance may take the form either of a reinstatement grant (ss. 3, 5),[32] if it is a house on which work can be carried out to provide satisfactory accommodation for 30 years, or repurchase by the authority of the defective dwelling (ss. 6, 7),[33] giving the applicant a right to a secure tenancy (s. 10).[34] The Government have estimated that the likely cost of these provisions will be £170–250 million, the financial and administrative burden of these provisions of which will be borne primarily by local authorities.

The Conservative Government have therefore shown unprecedented vigilance, and have sought and obtained unusual powers, in order to ensure that the right to buy became a material reality. There seem to be political, economic and ideological aspects to this policy. The political aspect focuses on the importance of this policy for the Conservatives' electoral strategy; the right to buy has proven electorally popular and has encouraged traditional Labour voters to vote Conservative. The economic aspect links into the general policy of reducing the size of the public sector and the burden of public expenditure. This is not insignificant since sales between 1979 and 1983 have generated around £2,000 million in cash receipts. The ideological aspect stresses the importance of owner-occupation in encouraging thrift, the work ethic and political stability in particular and anti-collectivist values in general.

The ideological aspect, with its focus on tenure-form, seems particularly significant. With the slump in the private sector— between 1970 and 1980 private construction rates fell by 35 per cent. and the size of the private rented sector decreased from 20 to 13 per cent. (Boyne 1983, p. 182)—council house sales seemed by far the most important means of maintaining growth in owner-occupation. Furthermore, the subsidies in the form of discounts appear unjustified on efficiency grounds (Whitehead 1984a). Indeed, the

[30] ss.527, 528, 559.
[31] s.534.
[32] ss.537–539, 541–2.
[33] s.547, Sched. 20.
[34] ss.553–558.

evidence suggests that, as expected (House of Commons 1981a), the impact of the policy is highly inequitable. The policy is leading to a regional polarisation of tenure—with sales highest in the outer metropolitan south east and lowest in the north—and also an inner/outer urban polarisation, since sales are low in inner urban areas. Three-bedroomed houses are most popular, whereas flats, although they constitute 30 per cent. of the public sector stock, account for under 3 per cent. of sales (Forrest and Murie 1984). The Government's concern over such statistics is reflected in the proposal, in clause 1 of the Housing and Planning Bill, to introduce a new discount rate of 42 per cent. rising to 70 per cent. for tenants of flats.

The effect seems likely to be a reduction in the range and probably the standard of the remaining public sector stock; an increase in the average costs of maintaining it, since economies of scale will be lost; and, to the extent that older dwellings are sold, to put pressure on the historic cost financing system. Furthermore, since the unemployed, single parents, the retired and others in need are significantly over-represented in council housing, there is a danger of creating ghettos of poor quality public housing and converting council housing into a residual welfare sector. Consequently, however the problems of the public rented sector are analysed, it seems unlikely that these will be alleviated by a policy enabling a minority of better-off tenants to convert their tenancy to ownership, while leaving the most disadvantaged tenants in council housing which, according to public expenditure projections, seems likely to be decreasing in quality. A key issue, therefore, is the policy for public investment in the public housing stock, especially the subsidy policy and reinvestment of cash receipts from sales. It is to these policies that we must now turn.

4.3 The New Housing Subsidy System

The growth of council housing in the twentieth century has been aided by the provision of Exchequer subsidies. Indeed, reform of the subsidy system has been a primary mechanism for enabling central government to encourage or discourage aggregate building rates for particular forms or types of council housing. It was hardly surprising, then, that the Conservative Government introduced a new housing subsidy system.

Local authority housebuilding is generally financed by borrowing. All local authority borrowing tends to be amalgamated in a Consolidated Loans Fund. As a result the costs of servicing this

Fund are averaged out and the Fund in turn lends to the Housing Revenue Account (H.R.A). Local authorities are required to keep a H.R.A. (Housing Finance Act 1972, s. 12)[35] into which is paid rent income, Exchequer subsidies and contributions from the general rate and from which the cost of debt charges, management, and repairs and maintenance is deducted. The general principle was that this account must balance (Housing Rents and Subsidies Act 1975, s. 1(3)). Through the operation of this system, therefore, rent levels are effectively determined.

Traditionally, local authorities have been given a great deal of discretion in determining rent levels, the exception being the period 1972–75 when, under the Housing Finance Act 1972, central government rent-fixing arrangements applied. The formal legal position is that an authority may "make such reasonable charges for the tenancy or occupation as they may determine" and "shall from time time review rents and make such changes, either of rents generally or of particular rents, as circumstances may require." (Housing Act 1957, ss. 111(1), 113 (1A)).[36] The courts have held that authorities, in determining the level and structure of their rents, may apply a social policy and charge differential rents: *Luby* v. *Newcastle-under-Lyme Corporation* [1965] 1 Q.B. 214; Hoath 1982, pp. 137–141; Hughes 1981, pp. 117–118. Nevertheless, the general level of rents is significantly influenced by subsidy policy.

In addition to levels of subsidy, the historic cost financing system has been very important in the development of council housing. This system arises because of the averaging out of the cost of debt charges. As a result, although the average cost of building a council house today may be in the region of £20,000, the average debt per council house which local authorities are servicing is around £3,000. Local authorities with higher proportions of older housing can thus balance their H.R.A.s at lower rent levels than those with lower proportions. These benefits are then redistributed through rent pooling arrangements. Thus the rents of council houses are determined not by the actual debt charges for individual houses nor by reference to its current market value (exchange value) but by reference to relative use values, so that the rent structure of a local authority is determined by the size and quality of dwellings. The result is that, in the aggregate, rents will be equal to total expenditure in the H.R.A. less the total amount of subsidies.

[35] ss.417–420.
[36] s.24.

The subsidy system, however, has probably been of greater significance to rental levels. The traditional method of providing subsidies was under a "unit cost" system through which a subsidy of £x per annum for the notional life of the dwelling was paid to a local authority for each dwelling built. This unit cost system came under great strain as a result of inflation and the resulting increases on the expenditure side of the H.R.A., and after 1967 it was replaced with a system which provided subsidies to local authorities as a percentage of their debt charges (Merrett 1979, pp. 177–191). Part VI of the Housing Act 1980 enacted a new housing subsidy system, although the system is essentially the same as that introduced in the previous Labour Government's Housing Bill which fell with the dissolution of Parliament in 1979.

The new subsidy system is based on a deficit-financing principle. This means that the amount of subsidy a local authority receives will be related not to dwelling costs or debt charges but to the state of its entire H.R.A. Thus the amount of subsidy received depends on an evaluation of its annual expenditure on servicing its debt and its management and maintenance costs (reckonable expenditure : s. 99(2))[37] on the one hand and the amount which the local authority can be expected to raise from rents and rate fund contributions (reckonable income: s. 100(2))[38] towards meeting these costs on the other. However, the Secretary of State is empowered to determine what expenditure is reckonable for subsidy purposes (s. 99(2))[39] and what income the authority is assumed to receive for that year as reckonable income (s. 100(2)).[40] In determining reckonable income the Secretary of State "shall state the assumptions on which it is based and the method of calculation used in it, and in making it ... shall have regard, among other things to past and expected movements in incomes, costs and prices" (s. 100(3)).[41] These determinations may be made for all local authorities, or different determinations may be made for authorities of different descriptions or for individual authorities (ss. 99(3), 100(4)),[42] but before making a determination for all local authorities the Secretary of State "shall consult with organisations appearing to him to be representative of local authorities" (ss. 99(4)), 100(5)).[43]

[37] s.424 (2).
[38] s.425 (2).
[39] s.424 (2).
[40] s.425 (2).
[41] s.425 (3).
[42] s.424 (3), 100 (4).
[43] s.424 (4), 100 (5).

The calculation of a local authority's housing subsidy is based on the amount of subsidy received in the previous year. This figure is known as the *base amount* (B.A.), although if the Secretary of State is of opinion that particular circumstances require it, he may increase or decrease the base amount, either generally or in relation to any description of authority or any particular authority (s. 98).[44] The amount of subsidy received in any particular year depends on the adjustments made to the B.A. by adding the difference between the increase in reckonable expenditure over the previous year, known as the *housing costs differential* (H.C.D.) (s. 99(1)),[45] and the increase in reckonable income over the previous year, known as the *local contribution differential* (L.C.D.) (s. 100(1)).[46] This yields the following formula for determining the amount of housing subsidy a local authority receives (s. 97):[47]

$$\text{Subsidy} = \text{B.A.} + \text{H.C.D.} - \text{L.C.D.}$$

This system clearly gives a great deal of discretionary power to the Secretary of State (for a detailed explanation see DoE 1982a). In particular, the assumption which the Secretary of State makes concerning rent increases for the purpose of determining reckonable income and the L.C.D. will impose a great deal of pressure on local authorities to comply with such guidance. Any authority which refuses to increase rents in accordance with such guidance would be obliged to increase its rate fund contribution to meet the shortfall. But, as seen in Chapter 2, the operation of the target and grant penalty system and also rate-capping has significantly restricted an authority's ability effectively to do so.

The Government in fact have used the new housing subsidy system to pressurise authorities into increasing rents by reducing the level of housing subsidies. Central government subsidy has declined from £1,423 million in 1980/81 to £305 million in 1984/85. As a consequence, council housing rents have increased dramatically; using a 1975 index base, council housing rents stood at 336.8 in 1983, compared with a retail price index of 257.6 and a mortgage interest repayment index of 264.3 (Bailey 1984). Indeed, as a result of the Government's use of the new subsidy system rent increases have been "considerably larger in real terms over a three year

[44] s.423.
[45] s.424 (1).
[46] s.425 (1).
[47] s.422.

period than those which caused all the uproar under the Housing
Finance Act 1972" (McCulloch 1982, pp. 98–9). Thus the financial
constraints, particularly when combined with the legal uncertainties
arising from the application of the fiduciary concept articulated in
the *Bromley* case to the area of council housing rents (although see:
R. v. GLC, ex p. Royal Borough of Kensington and Chelsea (1982)
The Times, April 7) caused most authorities to comply with central
government guidance.

   The Government's objective seems to be to destroy the historic
cost financing system by using the subsidy system to push up rents
to a level nearer to current market value rentals. As a result, there
was the likelihood that local authorities, particularly those with a
higher proportion of older stock, would make a profit on their
H.R.A. The 1980 Act therefore abolished the requirement that an
authority may not make provision for a surplus in its H.R.A. and
permitted an authority to carry to the credit of its general rate fund
the whole or part of any balance in its H.R.A. (s. 134.).[48] By 1983,
71 per cent. of local authorities were deemed to be breaking-even
or making a surplus on their H.R.A.s and were therefore not
receiving subsidies (Bailey 1984). In fact, 58 per cent. were doing
so and one authority had an annual H.R.A surplus of over £3.5
million (Audit Commission 1984a, pp. 34–35). With such steep
rent increases there has been speculation over whether a local
housing authority could be in breach of its legal duties to charge
"reasonable" rents (Housing Act 1957, s. 111(1))[49] or to maintain a
balance between tenants and ratepayers when fixing its rents
(*Belcher* v. *Reading Corporation* [1950] Ch. 380, 391). This seems
highly unlikely, given the market ideology which tends to per-
meate judicial thinking.

   That a primary objective of the new housing subsidy system was
to attack the historic costs financing system seems to be borne out
by the fact that what essentially is taking place is not a reduction in
subsidy but a restructuring in the nature of subsidies. Thus,
although housing subsidies have fallen by over £1,000 million
between 1980/81 to 1984/85, this reduction has been entirely offset
by the growth in the amount of income-related rent assistance
claimed by council tenants (Robinson 1984); as rents (and
unemployment rates) have increased, greater numbers of council
tenants have become entitled to assistance with rent payments. The

[48] s.418; Sched. 14, Pt. V.
[49] s.24 (1).

effect has therefore been to restructure the form of subsidy from a collective form through the historic costs financing system to an individual income-related allowance.

Income-related housing allowances were administered through a range of schemes dealing with rent and rate rebates, private sector rent allowances and supplementary benefit housing payments. In Part II of the Social Security and Housing Benefits Act 1982, however, these various schemes were amalgamated in the form of a housing benefit scheme administered by local authorities (for details see Arden and Partington 1983, Chap. 6). Many difficulties have arisen through the implementation of this scheme and many have argued that the housing benefit system cannot provide an adequate basis for subsidising housing costs without fundamental reform of the entire structure of housing finance and the establishment of a universal housing allowance, which incorporates subsidies to owner-occupiers (Raynsford 1984, Whitehead 1984b).

The new housing subsidy system has thus been utilised as part of an attack on collectivist forms of housing provision. As a result, the level of council housing rents has risen sharply and the nature of subsidy has switched primarily to individual income-related housing benefit. Even attempts by local authorities to utilise this framework in order to protect their collective organisation have been blocked. For example, Sheffield City Council in 1984 proposed to alter the terms of its tenancy conditions to enable tenants in receipt of housing benefit (and others) to opt into a scheme under which, in return for a higher rent, the council would assume responsibility for all repairs, but this proposal was blocked by amendments to the regulations (S.I. 1984 No. 1001). Their revised scheme, based on the principle of contracting out of a full repairing scheme and higher rent in return for a "do-it-yourself repairs grant," failed to achieve its objective: *R. v. Secretary of State for Health and Social Security, ex p. Sheffield City Council* (1985) *The Times*, August 2. One effect of these changes is that the level of rent arrears of council tenants has significantly increased (Audit Commission 1984b), a situation not made any easier by the problems arising from the implementation of the housing benefit system. An even more important effect, however, has been to provide a powerful incentive for higher income council tenants to exercise their right to buy and thus to reinforce the effects which the sale of council houses is having in transforming the public rented sector into a residual welfare sector. Furthermore, the manner in which this is being achieved is particularly controversial since no attempt has been made to devise a rational rents policy based on current market values; rather, rent increases have tended to be a response to centrally-determined finance-led targets.

4.4 Capital Expenditure

Controls over local authority capital expenditure were dealt with in section 2.5 above. Those controls form the framework for the control of housing capital expenditure, especially since housing accounts for over half of total local authority capital expenditure. In fact, it could be argued that the model for the framework of capital expenditure controls in the Local Government, Planning and Land Act 1980 is to be found in Housing Investment Programmes (H.I.P.s) which were introduced in 1977.

The H.I.P. system was based on the idea that local authorities, after undertaking a survey for assessing local housing need, would formulate comprehensive housing strategies linked to a five-year operational programme which would be submitted to central government on an annual rolling programme basis. These H.I.P. submissions are then used for determining capital expenditure allocations to authorities (DoE 1977c). This system, which emerged from the Labour Government's Housing Policy Review (DoE 1977b), seems in turn to be based on the T.P.P. experience. However, whatever their original rationale, the planning dimension to H.I.P.s has all but disappeared and H.I.P.s have in recent years been used as a tool through which central government can more rationally allocate a steadily diminishing aggregate housing capital allocation (Leather 1983). That is, in the context of retrenchment the expenditure control objective has dominated the H.I.P. system.

Since the H.I.P. system was introduced housing capital expenditure has been more than halved in real terms. This process commenced in the late 1970s but has been more marked during the 1980s. Consequently, as Figure 4.1 above shows, the level of local authority housing construction has dramatically reduced and is now at an all-time low. This is a direct result of the fundamental changes to the system of housing finance—sales, subsidy system and capital controls—introduced since 1980. The traditional housing finance system had been established on the assumption that there was a housing shortage and local authorities had an important role to play in dealing with it; the reforms since 1980 have established a series of incentives based on the opposite set of assumptions.

However, in addition to housing capital expenditure levels being reduced, basic changes in the composition of capital expenditure have occurred. Housing capital expenditure not only funds the provision of new council housing but also such items as the modernisation of the existing council housing stock and private sector renovation grant programmes. As Table 4.1 shows, there has been a switch in the balance of capital expenditure away from new building towards the rehabilitation of the existing public and private sector housing stock. The basic changes to the system of housing finance are largely responsible for this reallocation of expenditure, although this is formally sanctioned in the system of Housing Project Control introduced in 1981 (see DoE 1982b).

Table 4.1   Components of Local Authority Housing Capital Expenditure 1978/79 – 1983/84 (£,000m., 1982 prices).

	1978/79	79/80	80/81	81/82	82/83	83/84
Capital expenditure on new dwellings	1.8	1.5	1.1	0.8	0.7	0.6
Capital expenditure on improvement	0.8	1.0	0.8	0.7	0.9	0.9
Improvement grants	0.2	0.2	0.2	0.2	0.5	0.7

Source: Robinson (1984), p.6.

Project control forms part of a move from detailed to strategic central government administrative controls over capital projects. From 1981/82 local authorities were no longer required to conform to detailed controls such as Parker Morris space and heating standards and housing cost yardsticks (see Merrett 1979, p. 105). However, although local authorities are given borrowing approval *en bloc* for expenditure up to the level approved in their H.I.P. allocation, the project control system requires that for certain categories of expenditure the specific consent of the Secretary of State is required. The main categories are the acquisition of land for new housebuilding and certain municipalisation schemes. These administrative controls over new council house-building thus reinforce the incentive effects of the new financial framework.

The emphasis is therefore placed on renovation rather than new building and so expenditure on renovation of both the public and private sector stock has increased in real terms in recent years. In particular central government has encouraged local authorities to provide grants for the renovation of private housing (see generally Hughes 1981, Chap. 10). Thus between 1982 and 1984 the improvement grant level was raised from 75 to 90 per cent.; in 1983 an incentive scheme was introduced whereby any local authority which spent over a certain threshold of its capital allocation on improvement grants qualified for additional subsidy; and local authorities were encouraged to undertake enveloping schemes in which the external fabric of entire terraces or blocks of private housing which have deteriorated beyond the scope of routine maintenance are renovated with the aid of local authority grants (DoE 1982c).

There are several reasons for this strategy. First, it enables central government to maintain tight control of capital expenditure since expenditure on grants can more easily be controlled than large capital projects. Secondly, the private sector are more likely to be involved in the building work on renovation. And thirdly, this strategy closely fits the dominant ideology of promoting owner-occupation. The English House Condition Survey 1981 showed that the number of unfit houses had not decreased over 15 years and that since 1976 the number in disrepair had increased by 44 per cent. More than half of these houses were owner-occupied. Consequently, if the Conservative Government's goal of a property-owning democracy is to be achieved it is essential that they deal with the difficulties of low income owner-occupation; the provision of improvement grants is one attempt to do so.

The major challenge faced by this strategy of reducing housing capital expenditure and directing public expenditure primarily towards private rehabilitation is how it might meet the real housing needs of the 1980s. How can the Government ensure that limited improvement grants are made available to those in the greatest need? How can the Government find the estimated £19,000 million needed to repair defects in the English council housing stock (A.M.A.1985)? Consideration of the first issue has led the Government to propose subjecting improvement grant entitlement to means-testing or changing grants into loans redeemable as an equity stake in the property (DoE 1985a). In attempting to deal with the second issue the Secretary of State has suggested that local authorities should "make strenuous efforts to find private sector partners" for involvement in public sector rehabilitation schemes (Matthews 1985). This has led to various schemes in which blocks of council houses (*e.g.* in North Tyneside Metropolitan District Council) and even entire council housing estates (*e.g.* in Knowsley Metropolitan District Council) have been sold to the private sector for improvement for sale; proposals have been made (*e.g.* by

Glasgow D.C.) for the transfer of blocks of council houses to ownership co-operatives run by former tenants which would enable them, for example, to obtain grants to rehabilitate their property (Stubbs and Mundy 1985). Provisions to encourage such schemes, which are said to constitute the first phase of the Government's plans to privatise most of the remaining council housing stock, are included in Part I of the Housing and Planning Bill which was introduced in the 1985/86 Parliamentary session.

Finally, in relation to housing capital expenditure there is the issue of capital receipts. Basic H.I.P. allocations to local authorities have been very low indeed, because the Government have expected this allocation to be supplemented by a prescribed proportion of capital receipts generated through sales (section 2.5). This is advantageous to the Government both because it encourages authorities to co-operate with council house sales and also because it reduces borrowing requirements. Capital receipts have thus become a significant element in capital expenditure; since 1982/83 they have financed over one-quarter of local authority capital expenditure. The problem is that capital receipts are not necessarily accrued by authorities with the greatest housing needs. One solution to this problem would be to incorporate a higher proportion of anticipated receipts in the authority's basic H.I.P. allocation by reducing the prescribed proportion of capital receipts (Leather 1984). The reductions in the prescribed proportion of capital receipts (section 2.5) might be seen as a step in this direction. However, since it has been accompanied by reductions in the overall totals of housing capital expenditure, the move will do little to resolve this problem. Given these general developments, perhaps the most intractable problem facing the Government in the longer term is the range of policy choices facing it when the level of capital receipts significantly diminish.

4.5 Management of Council Housing

Traditionally, local authorities have had a great deal of discretion in the management of their housing stock. They are vested with general powers of management, regulation and control over their housing (s. 111, Housing Act 1957).[50] The procedures for housing allocation have been largely beyond legal regulation; they must merely ensure that they give reasonable preference to persons

[50] s.21.

occupying insanitary or overcrowded houses, having large families
or living in unsatisfactory housing conditions, and to homeless
persons to whom they owe duties (Housing Act 1957, s. 113(2)).[51]
Central government's role traditionally has been *advisory* rather
than *supervisory*. But by the late 1970s there was a broad-based
consensus that legal rules should structure the landlord-tenant
relationship in the council housing context. These rules were
enacted in Chapter II of Part I of the Housing Act 1980, as
amended by the Housing and Building Control Act 1984.[52] The
effect is to provide secure tenants with a status and a bundle of
legal rights.

Secure tenants are given security of tenure which is similar in
spirit to that provided to private sector tenants by virtue of the Rent
Act 1977. Thus a secure tenancy cannot be brought to an end
without the landlord authority obtaining an order for possession
from the court (s. 32);[53] the grounds for possession are set out in the
Act (s. 34; Sched. 4).[54] A secure tenancy is not generally assignable
(s. 37)[55] since that would severely circumscribe an authority's
powers of management. But a secure tenant has the right to take in
lodgers (s. 35);[56] the right to sublet with the consent of the authority
(such consent not to be unreasonably withheld) (s. 35,36);[57] and the
right to exchange the tenancy with any other secure tenant with the
consent of the authority (such consent not to be withheld except on
certain specified grounds) (s. 37A; Sched. 4A).[58] The Act also makes
provision for rights of succession (ss. 30, 31);[59] the right to make
improvements with the consent of the authority (such consent not to
be unreasonably withheld) (ss. 81–83, 38, 39);[60] and the right, in
accordance with a scheme made by the Secretary of State, to carry
out repairs which form part of the landlord's obligation and to
recover certain sums from the landlord for so doing (s. 41A).[61] (And
see DoE 1984, para. 117.)

These rights provide the secure tenant with a legal status. In

[51] s.22.
[52] Pt. IV.
[53] s.82.
[54] s.84, Sched. 2.
[55] s.91.
[56] s.93.
[57] ss.93, 94.
[58] s.92, Sched. 3.
[59] ss.87–90.
[60] ss.97–101.
[61] s.96.

addition, the 1980 Act contained provisions which relate more directly to the policy formation aspect of the authority's housing management role. Thus, the authority must publish each of the following: information concerning the terms on which secure tenancies are held (it must also make available to each secure tenant a copy of such document) (s. 41);[62] a summary of its rules relating to housing allocation and exchanges (s. 44);[63] and the procedures which have been established for consultation with its secure tenants on housing management matters (s. 43(3)).[64] The final requirement is the result of a basic substantive rule. Every landlord authority is required to make and maintain "such arrangements as it considers appropriate to enable those of its secure tenants who are likely to be substantially affected by a matter of housing management" both to be informed of the authority's proposals and to make their views known to the authority (s. 43(1)).[65] The authority must then consider any representations made, in accordance with these arrangements, before making its decision (s. 42(2)).[66] A matter is one of housing management if "in the opinion of the landlord authority" it:

"(a) relates to management, maintenance, improvement or demolition of dwelling-houses let by the authority under secure tenancies, or to the provision of services or amenities in connection with such dwelling-houses; and

(b) represents a new programme ... or a change in the practice or policy of the authority; and

(c) is likely substantially to affect its secure tenants as a whole or a group of them." (s. 42(2)).[67]

Thus, in addition to being provided with a protected legal status or sphere of autonomy, secure tenants are given rights to be informed and consulted about certain housing management matters.

What is noticeable about these reforms concerning housing management is that rights of an individualistic nature are well-

---

[62] s.104.
[63] s.106.
[64] s.105 (5).
[65] s.105 (1).
[66] s.105 (1).
[67] s.105 (2) (3).

defined, but rights which could assume a collective character are much less strictly drafted. This is seen most clearly in relation to the tenants' consultative scheme. During the 1970s many local authorities experimented with a variety of tenant participation arrangements (Richardson 1977) and the Labour Government's 1979 Housing Bill went much further in reflecting that experience (Hoath 1982, p. 210). Furthermore, that experience has been carried through into the 1980s by local authorities which have initiated schemes to decentralise housing services to neighbourhood offices in an attempt to make services responsive to tenants' needs (Fudge 1984; Wright 1984). By comparison, the arrangements in the Housing Act 1980 are greatly diluted; the precise nature of the arrangements are within the control of local authorities since no detailed consultation mechanism is prescribed and the crucial issue of rents and other charges are excluded from the consultation process.

This raises a more general issue concerning developments in public sector housing law in the 1980s. The language of housing policy is increasingly the language of rights—the right to buy, the right to a mortgage, the right to a shared ownership lease, the right to security of tenure, the right to exchange, rights of succession, the right to carry out repairs, the right to make improvements, right to a reinstatement grant, and the like. These are formal rights vested in existing council tenants. But they provide little which will guarantee a right to a good quality living environment to council tenants, let alone to the increasing numbers of households living in substandard accommodation for whom access to council housing has been their best opportunity of obtaining a decent home. Indeed, these formal rights are provided as part of a package of fundamental reforms in financial arrangements which will make the likelihood of local authorities being able to do so even more remote.

4.6 Housing Markets and Housing Policy

The Conservative Government's housing policies seem to be founded on the view that the housing problem has been basically solved and that the main issue concerns the balance of households in the public and private sectors. Consequently, the "politics of construction rates" has been replaced by the "politics of tenure form" (Boyne 1984, p. 180). The Government's view is that the proportion of households in the private sector is too small and therefore housing policies have concentrated on privatising public housing, providing assistance for increasing the level of owner-occupation and attempting to regenerate the private rented sector.

In addition to the right to buy, various measures have been promoted to increase levels of owner-occupation: various forms of shared ownership schemes exist (Forrest, Lansley and Murie 1984); a special loan scheme was introduced to assist first-time purchasers in the Home Purchase Assistance and Housing Corporation Guarantee Act 1978[68]; a local authority mortgage guarantee scheme to help overcome the risk-adverse attitude of mortgagees was introduced under section 111 of the Housing Act 1980[69]; local authorities have been encouraged to undertake voluntary sales and building and improvement schemes for sale (Housing Act 1980, Pt. V);[70] and measures have been taken to increase competition in mortgage and savings markets.

The Government have also taken measures to regenerate the private rented sector. They have introduced the new concepts of shorthold tenancy (fair rent but limited security of tenure: Housing Act 1980, ss. 51–55) and assured tenancy (security of tenure but market rent: Housing Act 1980, ss. 56–58) and have generally liberalised the regulatory regime to the benefit of landlords (Housing Act 1980, Pt. II; Hoath 1981). There has even been some discussion of the removal of controls over the private rental sector, although the Government has now deferred action on this issue (Minister without Portfolio 1985, para. 3.15).

Other than for the right to buy, these various measures to stimulate the private sector have not been particularly successful. Low-cost home ownership initiatives were estimated by 1983 to have added only 23,000 units to the owner-occupied stock (House of Commons 1983b, Chap. 3) and the measures for increasing owner-occupation generally have given a wider choice and greater flexibility to those who can afford to buy rather than extending the opportunity to buy to new sections of the population. Also, only about 5,000 shorthold or assured tenancies had been created by 1982 and in all probability these were mainly the result of conversion of former regulated tenancies to shorthold (House of Commons 1982c).

The impact of these policies, however, has dramatically affected the role of local authorities in the field of housing. There has been an absolute reduction in the size of the council housing stock, rates of local authority completions are at an all-time low and there has

[68] ss.445–450.
[69] s.442.
[70] ss.32–44, 429.

been an overall decline in the quality of the stock. In so far as there is a need for a public rented sector the Government seem more concerned to promote the housing association movement than protect and promote the local authority role. Alan Murie (1985, p. 199) has summed up the present position well:

> "Those who are unemployed or in the least well-organised and well-paid sections of the labour force are now more concentrated in council housing. This is now less a matter for congratulation about channelling good housing to poor people but more a matter of concern over multiple and reinforcing disadvantage. The potential role envisaged for council housing has not been realised."

Consequently, the effect of the Government's policies has not been to remove paternalism but to change its nature (Whitehead 1984, p. 131). It has reduced the social valuation of housing as a consumer good and increased the social valuation of housing as an investment good (*ibid.*). Relative subsidies to owner-occupiers have significantly increased; in 1983 owner-occupiers received an average subsidy of £170 *per annum* while the average council tenant did not receive any housing subsidy (Ermisch 1984, pp. 45,50). Since owner-occupiers are on average wealthier than council tenants this has increased the regressive impact of housing subsidies, has polarised housing tenure forms and reinforced a role of council housing as a residual welfare sector. And this has been achieved through imposition of a structure of rules on local authorities which, while giving certain rights to existing council tenants, has significantly reduced their ability to meet the growing number of claims on their limited housing resources.

Chapter 5

EDUCATION

5.1. Relationships in the Education System

The Education Act 1944, which provided the legal framework for the reconstruction of educational provision in the post-war period, remains the principal statute governing education today. This Act establishes the roles, responsibilities and legal relationships between the central department, local authorities, school governing bodies, parents and teachers in the provision of primary, secondary and further education. Nevertheless, during this period these relationships have changed in response to social and political change and changes in educational philosophy. The Act retained its authority essentially because it established a flexible framework within which the demands of the various interests could be mediated. In recent years, however, this flexible framework has been placed under considerable strain. Since the education service accounts for about one-half of aggregate local authority expenditure, public expenditure constraints are likely to have a significant impact on the system. But relationships have also been affected both by demographic changes, which have resulted in a fall in the numbers of schoolchildren, and various ideological factors.

Under the 1944 Act the primary duty is that of the parent of every child of compulsory school age "to cause him to receive efficient full-time education suitable to his age, ability and aptitude and to any special educational needs he may have" (s. 36). The local education authority (L.E.A.) is under a duty to secure that there shall be available for their area sufficient schools, so that no parent is unable to discharge the duty imposed on them by section 36 (s. 8). In order to fulfil their duty the authority are empowered to establish and maintain schools and to assist any school not maintained by them (s. 9). The schools available for an area shall not be deemed to be sufficient unless they are "sufficient in number, character, and equipment to afford for all pupils opportunities for education offering such variety of instruction and training as may be desirable in view of their different ages, abilities, and aptitudes" (s. 8(1)). Finally, the duty of the Secretary of State is to "secure the effective execution by local authorities under his control and direction of the

119

national policy for providing a varied and comprehensive educational service in every area" (s. 1(1)).

The 1944 Act thus implies that the primary agents in the education system are parents and the Secretary of State; the duty of the Secretary of State under section 1 is a uniquely strong expression of the principle of central control and direction and both the Secretary of State and L.E.A.s are required to "have regard to the general principle that . . . pupils are to be educated in accordance with the wishes of their parents" (s. 76). However, this would not be an accurate characterisation of the system. On the one hand, there is a mismatch between the duty of the Secretary of State and the powers available to secure it. While the Secretary of State has powers to intervene where L.E.A.s "have failed to discharge any duty imposed on them" (s. 99) or where they "have acted or are proposing to act unreasonably with respect to the exercise of any power conferred or the performance of any duty imposed" on them (s. 68), it is not obvious that this is sufficient to "control" and "direct" local authorities. Also, other parts of the Act suggest that the relationship is more complex; section 23, for example, states that "secular instruction to be given to the pupils shall . . . be under the control of the local education authority." On the other hand, the courts have been very reluctant to interpret the 1944 Act in such a way as to give parents enforceable rights against the L.E.A.: *Watt* v. *Kesteven County Council* [1955] 1 QB. 408; *Cumings* v. *Birkenhead Corporation* [1972] Ch. 12; *Wood* v. *Ealing London Borough Council* [1967] Ch. 364; *Winward* v. *Cheshire County Council* (1978) 77 L.G.R. 172.

Consequently, the nature of the relationships between the principal parties in the education system seems inherently uncertain. In the post-war period the relative powers and duties of the parties have been tested primarily in relation to the issue of the organisation of secondary schools. The 1944 Act did not lay down any particular form of secondary school structure but most L.E.A.s, in accordance with Government advice, adopted a tripartite division of secondary schools into grammar, technical and modern. Although not designed to provide a hierarchy of achievement—the Government's view was that they were of equal status but serving different ends—the experience of the 1950s and 1960s suggested a sharp segregation and fuelled a demand for the abolition of selection and the establishment of comprehensive secondary schools.

When Labour were returned to office in 1964 they issued a circular announcing their intention of eliminating selection and separatism in secondary education and requested L.E.A.s to submit plans for reorganisation of their schools along comprehensive lines (D.E.S. 1965, 1966). Although this acted as a catalyst for change, there were several disputes over the next decade which highlighted ambiguities in the legal relationships between the parties. The most important were those in Enfield and Tameside. The *Enfield* case in particular raised issues concerning the status of parents in the system: *Bradbury* v. *Enfield London Borough Council* [1967] 1 W.L.R. 1311, *Lee* v. *Enfield London Borough Council* (1967) 66 L.G.R. 195, *Lee* v. *D.E.S.* (1967) 66 L.G.R. 211, Education Act 1968. (See Buxton 1970, pp. 206–215). On the other hand, the *Tameside* case focused on the relationship between the Secretary of State and the L.E.A: *Secretary of State for Education and Science* v. *Tameside Metropolitan Borough Council* (1977) A.C. 1014 (see Loughlin 1983, pp. 74–82). Both affairs demonstrated not only the ambiguous nature of the relationships but also the difficulties faced by the courts in providing an adequate interpretation of the statutory scheme. And since in *Enfield* the courts could be viewed as blocking a hastily prepared reorganisation scheme whereas in *Tameside* they prevented the Minister from blocking a hastily prepared unravelling of a proposed reorganisation scheme, the courts inevitably could be seen as engaging in matters of political controversy.

Since 1965 central government policy on comprehensive schools has altered with each change in government (Regan 1977, pp. 46–53). This process culminated with the enactment by Labour of the Education Act 1976, empowering the Secretary of State to require L.E.A.s to submit proposals for giving effect to the comprehensive principle, and the subsequent repeal of those provisions by the Conservatives in the Education Act 1979. Nevertheless, despite this latest Act, the principle of comprehensive schooling is now entrenched; between 1965 and 1979 the proportion of secondary school pupils educated in comprehensive schools increased from 8 to 85 per cent. (Dennison 1984, p. 3).

Nevertheless, concern over the nature of relationships in the education system has increased in recent years and some believe that a new basic statutory settlement is needed (Aldrich and Leighton 1985). This is highlighted by the fact that certain fundamental changes have been made by the Conservative Government which have had the effect of increasing consumer choice and strengthening the power of central government. These changes have been brought about as a result of a series of reforms and initiatives which have also had an effect on the nature and goals of the education service. These developments are examined in this chapter.

5.2 Further Education

The legal foundation for the provision of further education by local authorities is unclear. Under section 41 of the 1944 Act L.E.A.s are required to secure the provision for their area of adequate facilities for further education. However, this responsibility exists only in accordance with schemes drawn up by the L.E.A. and approved by the Secretary of State (s. 42) and few schemes have been submitted and approved. Nevertheless, L.E.A.s in fact maintain a range of institutions including polytechnics, colleges of education and tertiary colleges (although universities, which are self-governing institutions, are excluded) and this has never been subject to challenge.

Recent developments, however, have had a profound effect on this sector. The changes have been caused by the impact of the economic recession on employment opportunities for school-leavers, resulting in the majority of school-leavers at the age of 16 having no prospect of finding a full-time job. One response may have been to expand traditional further education opportunities for all school-leavers. However, the Government, taking the view that both the D.E.S. and L.E.A.s had generally neglected to provide non-advanced further education (N.A.F.E.), instead extended the range of training opportunities provided under the aegis of the Department of Employment. The agency used was the Manpower Services Commission (M.S.C.), established under the Employment and Training Act 1973.

The most important initiative of the M.S.C. has been the Youth Training Scheme (Y.T.S) which aimed from 1983 to offer every 16 year-old school-leaver an opportunity to receive a year's training (extended in 1986 to two years: DES 1985a) as a bridge between school and work. Y.T.S. was designed as providing training with private sector employees, with the L.E.A. providing certain support services such as off-the-job training and careers advice. This is known as "mode A." However, in order to deal with the mismatch between supply and demand "mode B" was established to accommodate those people not able to obtain a place on a "mode A" scheme. Under "mode B" the L.E.A. provides the basic training (Mason 1984). As a result, L.E.A. provision of N.A.F.E. has been increased, although essentially its function is as a support service for the Y.T.S.; it is reimbursed for the cost of such provision from the M.S.C. (DES 1982a).

The M.S.C. has thus taken over as the lead agency in the

provision of N.A.F.E. Nevertheless, L.E.A. provision of N.A.F.E. has also increased as it has been called on to provide support services. However, it would appear that the Government intend to privatise a certain amount of the L.E.A.s' work in this sector; in 1984 the Government announced that by 1986/87 it was proposed to divert R.S.G. covering a high proportion of the cost of further education colleges away from local authorities and directly to the M.S.C which will purchase courses from providers as it sees fit (Department of Employment 1984). The objective seems to be to promote the growing industry of private training agencies which establish themselves as managing agents to run Y.T.S. for profit (B.T.U.R.C. 1983). Consequently, local authorities are being displaced in the N.A.F.E. sector both by the Government's decision to give the lead-agency role in training policy to the M.S.C. and by ancillary provisions requiring the L.E.A. to compete with the private sector for the provision of supportive training courses.

As a result, as Ranson (1985, p. 63) has observed, the institutions of tripartite education, which have been largely removed from the secondary sector through the establishment of comprehensive schools, are reappearing and being reinforced in the tertiary sector; "A" Level courses parallel the grammar stream, advanced technical and business courses (T.E.C. and B.E.C.) the technical stream, and Y.T.S. the modern stream. Although the D.E.S. believe that these streams should achieve "parity of esteem" (Macfarlane Report 1980, p. 18) this seems even more unlikely than the attempt at the secondary education level. Y.T.S. does not, of itself, produce greater employment opportunities, but it does mark an attempt more directly to educate people in accordance with their employment opportunities in a contracting labour market. Inevitably, these central government initiatives have led to central-local conflict which has manifested itself in court action: see *R.* v. *Secretary of State for Education, ex p. I.L.E.A.* (1985) (unreported).

5.3. The School System

5.3.1 Stratification and Vocationalism in Secondary Schools. The experience of policy developments in further education, a response to the problem of youth unemployment, has recently been evaluated with a view to assessing its suitability for adaptation to the secondary sector. The first product of this assessment was the M.S.C.'s Technical and Vocational Educational Initiative (T.V.E.I.) which was established on an experimental basis in 14 local authorities in 1983/84. The objective is to provide additional

funding for schools operating new technical and vocational courses for certain groups of students aged between 14 and 18 (Moon and Richardson 1984). The scheme was expanded in 1984/85 with more than half of L.E.A.s being involved. T.V.E.I. may well be dovetailed with the new Certificate of Pre-Vocational Education (C.P.V.E.), which is a "17 plus" qualification of technical orientation and is being introduced in colleges of further education and some sixth form colleges from September 1985 (D.E.S. 1985a).

Another initiative is a D.E.S. special project generally known as the "Joseph scheme" and aimed at what Sir Keith calls "the bottom 40 per cent." of the school population, who are branded as failures by the examination system. This scheme aims to instil greater student motivation by giving more "relevant" education and training from the age of 14. In order to encourage L.E.A.s to undertake these vocational preparation schemes central government is providing financial incentives through education support grants. Provision for the payment of education support grants was made in the Education (Grants and Awards) Act 1984, which empowers the Secretary of State to pay grants not exceeding 0.5 per cent. of the aggregate amount of expenditure which the Secretary of State believes it would be appropriate for L.E.A.s to incur. In effect the 1984 Act embodies the principle of the D.E.S. using specific grants for encouraging particular innovations. The significance of this trend is highlighted by the fact that, in December 1985, the Government introduced a Bill to increase to 1 per cent. the proportion of aggregate L.E.A. expenditure which may be allocated as education support grants (Education (Amendment) Bill; 1985–86; H.C. 39).

At the other end of the academic spectrum "for the purpose of enabling pupils who might otherwise not be able to do so to benefit from education at independent schools," the Secretary of State was required by section 17 of the Education Act 1980 to establish and operate an assisted places scheme. Under this scheme participating independent schools remit the whole or part of the fees of pupils holding assisted places and are reimbursed by the Secretary of State. The amount of assistance depends on the pupil's parents income (ss. 17, 18, Sched. 4; for regulations see Liell and Saunders 1984, D214–248). In effect the assisted places scheme is designed to reverse section 5 of the Education Act 1976 which revoked the approvals given to L.E.A.s which met the expenses of children attending direct grant schools.

These initiatives highlight the extent to which stratification and vocationalism within secondary schooling is being reinforced. The tripartite system, which was largely eliminated with the establishment of comprehensive schools, is now being re-asserted *within* comprehensive schools; the standard examination system exists for the brighter pupils, while T.V.E.I. is promoted as a technically based initiative and the Joseph scheme exists to give more vocational preparation for less able pupils. Finally the assisted places scheme exists to attract the brightest students from moderate income families into the private sector.

5.3.2 Standards in Schools. In 1980 the Government projected that public expenditure on education would fall by 6.5 per cent. in real terms between 1978/79 and 1983/84 (H.M. Treasury 1980). This was a significant reduction, although not as great as the rate of decline in the school-age population. Nevertheless these trends indicated that considerable changes would be taking place in the education system; more of the same was not an option from the Government's viewpoint, less of the same did not seem attractive, and innovation therefore became the name of the game. In particular, raising standards through increased effectiveness of the system became the priority of the D.E.S.

This priority has led to a range of initiatives including much greater involvement by the D.E.S. in the school curriculum (D.E.S. 1981a), proposals to reform the examination system, proposals to enact legislation to enable the Secretary of State to require L.E.A.s regularly to appraise the performance of their teachers (D.E.S. 1985b), grants for in-service training courses on management responsibilities and special initiatives (D.E.S. 1983), and a proposal that new headteachers should undergo a two-year probationary period (D.E.S. 1984a) (see now Education Bill 1985–86. H.L. 87). Also, in order to promote public awareness of performance, there have been a number of reforms (see section 5.3.4 below) including publication since 1983 of the reports of H.M. Inspectors of Education (H.M.I.). The overall objective appears to be to attempt to set performance objectives for measuring effectiveness in education.

However, the publication of H.M.I. reports has also highlighted deficiencies in educational provision. Of particular interest have been the annual reports of H.M.I. to the Expenditure Steering Group (Education) of the Consultative Council on Local Government Finance (see Figure 2.7) which have been published since 1980. In the report published in 1984, for example, only 14 of the 97 English L.E.A.s were judged to have at least satisfactory levels across all main aspects of provision (D.E.S. 1984b). Such deficiencies have led various groups to call upon the Secretary of State to use his powers under sections 68 and 99 of the 1944 Act to intervene or, under section 93, to hold a local inquiry (Meredith 1982). These complaints have so far been rejected without inquiry, which may not seem surprising since they result, at least in part, from the Government's expenditure policies. However, the D.E.S. have also relied on the restrictive interpretation provided by the House of Lords in the *Tameside* case of their powers under section 68 in order to stress their limited supervisory responsibilities (D.E.S. 1982b, p. 11). This contrasts both with the results of a major study of central-local government relations in the mid-1960s which concluded that the D.E.S. "are the clearest example of a Department with a positive, promotional attitude to local authorities" (Griffith 1966, p. 522) and with the Department's role in establishing educational performance objectives. Furthermore this view has been roundly criticised by the House of Commons Environment Committee:

"... it appears to be the Department's view that sections 68 and 99 are dangerously primitive measures, difficult to enforce in the courts, and that they are measures of absolute last resort. We do not take that view. We see, rather, these sections of the 1944 Act as being part of the means by which the Secretary of State may discharge his duty 'to promote the education of the people' in the words of section 1 of the Act. We also believe that these provisions in the Act were designed precisely to avoid the *necessity* of parents taking their problems to the courts. This is both because litigation is inherently vexatious and expensive, and also because many of the issues that might arise could be of a specialist and technical character, and it would be better if the first source of redress were to be someone who might be expected to have specialist advice readily available." (House of Commons 1981b, para. 9.16).

This view has recently been supported by Woolf J. in *R.* v. *Secretary of State for Education, ex p. Chance* (1982) unreported (Liell and Saunders 1984, F 132). However, the D.E.S. view appears to be that, unless an L.E.A. is in breach of its statutory responsibilities, the Department is unable to act. Consequently it seems likely that aggrieved persons will seek individual application for judicial review rather than by way of complaint to the Secretary of State. This raises the question of the nature of the minimum legally enforceable standards of educational provision. That is, when would it be possible to hold that L.E.A.s are failing to provide and maintain schools sufficient in "number, character and equipment to afford for all pupils opportunities for education" (s. 8 of 1944 Act)?

The D.E.S. view appears to be that it would not be until a comprehensive school was failing to provide any science or any modern languages for any of its pupils that there would be a breach of duty (House of Commons 1981b, para. 9.11–9.13). So far the courts have not been asked to adjudicate directly on this issue. The closest case was *R. v. Hereford and Worcester Local Education Authority, ex p. Jones* [1981] 1 W.L.R. 768 in which the applicant challenged the decision of the L.E.A., faced with diminishing resources, to charge for the provision of music tuition in schools. Forbes J. had no hesitation in granting a declaration; music tuition was capable of forming part of the school curriculum and section 61(1) of the 1944 Act states that "no fees shall be charged ... in respect of the education provided." However, he also was of the view that the question of whether such tuition is to be included in the curriculum is a matter for the authority to decide and that if the L.E.A. had decided they could no longer afford to deploy resources on individual music tuition "I could not say that ... that would be something which this court could interfere with." Given the way in which the basic statutory obligation of L.E.A.s is formulated the courts seem ill-equipped adequately to deal with the issue. Nevertheless, if expenditure constraints continue and the D.E.S. maintains its non-interventionist stance, it seems likely that the courts will be asked to adjudicate on the issue.

5.3.3 Rationalisation. The number of secondary school pupils has been forecast to fall by almost 30 per cent. between 1979 and 1992. Consequently, the issue of public expenditure cutbacks is complicated by the effects of changing demographic structures. Since projected expenditure cutbacks are not as great as the projected rate of decline in school population the Government has urged L.E.A.s to use the opportunity to redeploy resources in order to make improvements in educational provision. However, the urban local authorities in particular have argued that the Government's calculations do not fully take into account adjustment costs and the diseconomies associated with the rapid decline in school numbers (Jackson *et al.* 1982; Bailey 1982; Bramley 1984). Both Labour and Conservative governments responded to the issue of falling rolls and surplus school places by exhorting L.E.A.s to rationalise school provision (DES 1977, 1981b). The Conservative Government has also modernised the statutory regime governing school reorganisation procedures.

These procedures are contained in sections 12–16 of the Education Act 1980 and they replace section 13 of the 1944 Act which lay at the centre of the legal disputes over comprehensive organisation proposals highlighted by the *Enfield* cases (see section 5.1). Where an L.E.A. intend to establish, maintain, cease to maintain or "make any significant change in the character or significant enlargement of the premises" of a county school (s. 12(1)), or to reduce the number of pupils below a certain level (s. 15), they must comply with the procedures laid down in section 12. This requires that the L.E.A. publish their proposals in accordance with regulations (see S.I. 1980 No. 658) and they must submit a copy of the proposals to the Secretary of State (s. 12(1)).

Any 10 or more local government electors may, within a period of two months after first publication of the proposals, submit an objection to the proposals to the L.E.A. (s. 12(3)). These objections, together with the L.E.A.'s observations on them, must be submitted to the Secretary of State within one month of the end of the two-month period (s. 12(3)). Certain types of proposals require the approval of the Secretary of State (s. 12(4)); others require approval only if all the objections have not been withdrawn, although even then the Secretary of State is empowered to notify the L.E.A. that the proposals require approval (s. 12(5)). If the proposals require approval, the Secretary of State may "reject them, approve them without modification or, after consultation with the L.E.A., approve them with such modifications as he thinks desirable" (s. 12(6)). (On the nature of modifications see *Legg* v. *ILEA* [1972] 1 W.L.R 1245.) The L.E.A. are under a duty to implement approved proposals but the Secretary of State may, at the request of the L.E.A., modify any proposals which they are required to implement (s. 12(8)).

These statutory procedures govern major reorganisation proposals which arise as a result of falling rolls. They apply not only when L.E.A.s propose to open and close schools but also when they intend to make significant changes in the character of schools. L.E.A.s are given a degree of freedom to engage in planned contraction but if they intend to reduce the number of pupils in any relevant age group below a certain level then the statutory procedures will be triggered (s. 15). This level is generally 20 per cent. or more below the "standard number" (s. 15(1)), this being the number of pupils admitted to that school in that age group in September 1979 (s. 15(5)). The Secretary of State is empowered to vary the standard number by order (s. 15(8)).

The Government in 1981 urged L.E.A.s to make much faster progress on removing surplus places (D.E.S. 1981b), a view which has been supported by the Audit Commission (1984c). This objective has been pursued by the D.E.S. in a highly interventionist manner. The Department has also used the same policy instruments which were used to encourage comprehensive reorganisation; circular advice rather than law, financial pressures, and its powers of approval in such a way as to promote its own education policies. The first two factors are illustrated in Circular 2/81 which used exhortation, a requirement of detailed monitoring and the promise of financial incentives to L.E.A.s which rationalised their stock (DES 1981b, paras. 20–29). The last factor is highlighted most clearly by the Secretary of State's decision in 1981 to reject Manchester City Council's proposals to reorganise its school system by eliminating sixth forms from secondary schools and establishing a city-wide system of sixth form colleges (Meredith 1984, pp. 215–217). The aim of the Manchester scheme was to avoid the polarisation and classification of schools between those, generally in higher-class areas, which could sustain a sixth form, and those which could not. Both the Secretary of State's decision to reject the proposal and the terms of a subsequent circular stressed "the need to retain what is best and has proved its worth within the existing system" (DES 1982c, para. 3).

Finally, the statutory procedures governing school reorganisation proposals under the 1980 Act still provide for a largely closed administrative system. The Manchester episode demonstrates that parents' groups can succeed in frustrating the L.E.A.s intentions provided they obtain the support of the Secretary of State but interested parties have few legal rights. D.E.S. circular advice indicates that the L.E.A. should engage in consultation prior to the publication of proposals (D.E.S. 1980, para. 5.1), but, provided the procedures are complied with, it will be extremely difficult successfully to challenge the Secretary of State's decision to confirm the L.E.A.'s reorganisation proposals: *R.* v. *Secretary of State for Wales, ex p. Hawkins* (May 28, 1982) (C.A.) (unreported); *R.* v. *Secretary of State for Wales, ex p. Russell* (June 28, 1983) (Q.B.D.) (unreported); *R.* v. *Secretary of State for Education and Science, ex p. Collins* (June 20, 1983) (Q.B.D.). Nevertheless, recently the courts have held that parents have a right to be consulted by the L.E.A.

before it decides to adopt a reorganisation proposal: *R.* v. *Brent London Borough Council ex p. Gunning* (1985) *The Times*, April 30. Furthermore, although in *Coney* v. *Choyce* [1975] 1. W.L.R. 422 it was held that publicity requirements are generally to be treated as directory rather than mandatory and are primarily enforceable by the Secretary of State rather than the courts, in the *Gunning* case it was held that the consultation process was wholly inadequate as to content and timing, that these deficiencies were not curable by subsequent procedures for hearing objections after the proposals were made, and that therefore the decision would be squashed (see also *R.* v. *Secretary of State for Education and Science, ex p. Birmingham City Council* (1985) 83 L.G.R. 79). The courts thus seem increasingly prepared to engage in supervision of the procedures governing the formulation and implementation of reorganisation proposals.

5.3.4 Consumer Choice. A central theme in the Conservative Government's social policies has been the encouragement of competition and the stimulation of consumer choice. This theme has also been important in the field of education. Consequently there has been much discussion of the possibility of establishing a market-based education system by introducing an education voucher scheme (*e.g.* Kent County Council 1978; Blaug 1984). The Conservative Government were initially very interested in establishing such a scheme but the proposal no longer seems to be on the Government's agenda. Nevertheless, they have introduced certain reforms which are designed to establish some form of surrogate market system by increasing the power of parents in the education system.

Although section 76 of the 1944 Act requires the Secretary of State and L.E.A.s to have regard to the general principle that pupils are to be educated in accordance with their parents' wishes, as we have seen (section 5.1), the courts have not generally interpreted this provision in such a manner as to give parents enforceable rights. Sections 6–9 of the Education Act 1980 seek partially to remedy this by institutionalising a system of parental preferences.

Thus, every L.E.A. is required to make arrangements for enabling parents "to express a preference as to the school at which he wishes education to be provided for his child ... and to give reasons for his preference" (s. 6(1)). The L.E.A. is under a duty to comply with this preference unless compliance would prejudice the provision of efficient education or the efficient use of resources, or if the preferred school is a voluntary maintained, special agreement or selective school and admission would not be in accordance with or compatible with the school's admission arrangements (s. 6(2) (3)). Arrangements must be made for appeals against admission decisions to an appeal committee, whose decision shall be binding (s. 7.; Sched. 2). Appeal committees come under the direct supervision of the Council on Tribunals and within the jurisdiction of the Local Commission for Administration (s. 7(6) (7)). The L.E.A., or governors in the case of every aided or special agreement school, are also required each year to publish particulars of the arrangements for the admission of pupils to schools, including arrangements for transport, meals and school clothing, examination-entrance policies, provision for special educational needs and the particulars of individual schools (s. 8; S.I. 1981, No. 630).

This system has significantly affected school admission procedures. Before the system came into force in 1982, the Secretary of State received around 1,000 complaints per year on allocation; in about one-third of these the Secretary of State used his powers of direction under section 68 of the 1944 Act. Between 1982 and 1984 around 10,000 cases went before the appeal committees, of which about one-third were successful (Rogers 1984). One result of this statutory appeals system is that the Secretary of State seems generally unprepared to consider complaints from unsuccessful parents. Their primary means of redress now appears to be through the Local Commission for Administration, with the Council on Tribunals being responsible for supervising the general operation of the appeal committees. These agencies have in fact issued reports critical of the manner in which some appeal committees have operated (*e.g.* Council on Tribunals 1983, paras. 3.4–3.5). The ultimate form of redress, however, is action in the courts. In *R.* v. *South Glamorgan Appeals Committee, ex p. Evans* (May 10, 1984) (unreported) Forbes J. laid down a two-stage test which appeal committees should apply to determine whether the L.E.A.'s duty to comply with parental preference may be overridden: (1) will efficient education or efficient use of resources be prejudiced if the child is given the desired place?; and (2) does the degree of prejudice outweigh the parents' right to choose?

Parental influence over schools has also been a theme which has influenced the reform of school governing bodies. School governing bodies derive their authority from sections 17–22 of the 1944 Act. All maintained schools must have an Instrument of Government, providing for the constitution of a governing body, and Articles of

Government, providing for the conduct of the school (s. 17). In so far as school government is effectively shared between the L.E.A. and the school governing body the general principle tends to be that the L.E.A. settles "the general educational character of the school and its place in the local system" while the governors have "general direction of the conduct and curriculum of the school" (Board of Education 1944, para. 18; see *R.* v. *Manchester City Council, ex p. Fulford. The Times*, October 26, 1982, *Honeyford* v. *Bradford City Council. The Times*, November 14, 1985).

These provisions of the 1944 Act have been amended and supplemented by sections 1–5 of the Education Act 1980. In particular, this provides for the first time that each governing body should include parent governors (s. 2(5)). These reforms to school government embody, in a significantly modified form, the recommendations of the Taylor Report of 1977 (Taylor Report 1977; Rogers 1980, Chap. 14). These moderate reforms to school government, however, have recently been overtaken by more radical proposals. A Green Paper published in 1984 proposed two fundamental legal changes; first that the functions of school governing bodies be clearly defined in legislation and secondly that parent governors be given the right to form a majority on school governing bodies (D.E.S. 1984c). These proposals seem to constitute an alternative means of establishing consumer control to that of the education voucher system, particularly since governors would have the power to determine curriculum objectives and to control the school budget. The proposals generated a great deal of controversy and, as a result, the Government decided to introduce legislation to establish a modified reform of school governing bodies (D.E.S. 1985b, paras. 216–229). In the November 1985 Queen's Speech the Government promised a Bill to strengthen the role of school governing bodies and to provide for an equal number of local authority representatives and parents on these bodies (see now Education Bill 1985–86. H.L. 87).

The strengthening of the influence of consumers in the education system has thus been a central theme in the 1980s. In addition to the provisions of the Education Act 1980 the rights of parents were given a great deal of emphasis in the drafting of the Education Act 1981, which establishes a statutory code for the assessment and the provision of facilities for children with special educational needs (Liell and Saunders 1984, A33). Furthermore, the Education (Corporal Punishment) Bill introduced by the Government in 1984/85 Parliamentary session reflected this ethos since it did not propose to abolish the use of corporal punishment in schools but rather to give parents the right to exempt their children from the use of corporal punishment. After being amended in the House of Lords, however, it was decided not to proceed with the Bill during that session (House of Commons 1985b).

5.4 Ancillary Services

Ancillary educational services have also been a target for expenditure savings. Under the 1944 Act L.E.A.s have certain duties to provide school meals and school transport. By altering the nature of these obligations the Government hoped to encourage L.E.A.s to make substantial savings. In the 1980 Public Expenditure White Paper, for example, it was assumed that L.E.A.s would halve their net expenditure on school meals and school milk in 1980/81 in order to yield savings of £200 million (HM Treasury 1980, pp. 95–96). Savings of this order clearly would require changes in the L.E.A.'s legal obligations.

Under section 49 of the 1944 Act and section 1 of the Education (Milk) Act 1971, L.E.A.s were under a duty to provide meals "suitable in all respects as the main meal of the day" for pupils and to provide milk for certain categories of pupils. These provisions were replaced by section 22 of the Education Act 1980. This imposes a duty on the L.E.A.s merely to "provide such facilities as the authority consider appropriate for the consumption of any meals or other refreshment brought to the school" by pupils, and thereafter the L.E.A. is *empowered* to provide pupils with milk, meals, or other refreshment and make such charges as they think fit for anything provided by them (22(1) (3)). The L.E.A., however, must ensure that a mid-day meal is made available for pupils whose parents are in receipt of supplementary benefit or family income supplement and that the provision is such "as appears to the authority to be requisite" (s. 22(2)). Finally they are empowered to remit the whole or part of any charges "if, having regard to the particular circumstances of any pupil or class or description of pupils, they consider it appropriate to do so" (s. 22(3)(b)). This enables them to remit charges in, for example, family financial circumstances not provided for under section 22(2).

The result of these changes, given financial constraints, has been predictable. Between 1979 and 1982 charges for school meals increased significantly, nutritional quality standards have gone down and the take-up of school meals decreased by 22 per cent. (House of Commons 1982e). Several L.E.A.s have also been reported as considering ceasing to provide any general school meals service at all (*e.g.* House of Commons 1984g).

The Conservative Government also proposed a similar scheme for school transport. Section 55 of the 1944 Act requires L.E.A.s to make such provision of transport as they consider necessary or as the Secretary of State may direct for the purpose of facilitating the attendance of pupils at schools. Such transport must be provided free of charge. The L.E.A.'s discretion in the provision of public transport is curtailed by section 39 of the 1944 Act which effectively requires the L.E.A. to make suitable arrangements for the transport to and from school of pupils who do not live within "walking distance" of the school: see *Surrey County Council* v. *Ministry of Education* [1953] 1 W.L.R. 516. Walking distance means three miles, two in the case of children under the age of eight, measured by the nearest available route (s. 39(5); see *Rogers* v. *Essex County Council* [1985] 2 All E.R. 39).

In the Education (No. 2) Bill the Government proposed that these duties would be replaced by a power to provide transport charging such fares as they thought fit, subject only to the requirement that pupils living beyond the walking distance would be entitled to free transport provided their parents were in receipt of supplementary benefit or family income supplement. This proposal however, was defeated by a combination of the rural and religious lobbies in the House of Lords, and the Government decided to withdraw the clause (House of Lords 1980).

Nevertheless, expenditure constraints have caused some L.E.A.s to seek school transport savings. Suffolk County Council, for example, in 1981 abandoned their practice of providing free transport to all pupils travelling to and from school, and required those pupils living within the statutory walking distance to pay for school transport. This decision was unsuccessfully challenged in the courts: *R.* v. *Suffolk County Council ex p. Jones* (March 11, 1981) (Q.B.) (unreported).

Consequently, with regard to ancillary educational services the Conservative Government's policy has been to seek to eliminate the redistributive element of the general service, to target subsidy by means-testing and to provide the general service on ordinary commercial lines.

5.5 Conclusions

The functions of the D.E.S. are to ensure that adequate public resources are allocated for education and to promote and improve standards of education. But the D.E.S. lacks an executant capacity and is dependent on local government to implement education policies. The tension between the roles of these two institutions has been highlighted in a period of fiscal retrenchment. In particular the D.E.S. has sought to ensure that the resources which it has won in public expenditure negotiations are actually spent by local authorities on education. As a result, the Department has attempted to take control over key aspects of education policy and expenditure. Thus in the early 1980s the D.E.S. proposed a separate block grant for education as a solution to control over local government expenditure (DoE 1981a, Annex B) and more recently, with the Education (Grants and Awards) Act 1984, it has begun to use specific grants to target expenditure to particular schemes. This assertion of a hierarchical relationship between the centre and the localities may also be seen in the context of such key aspects of education policy as examinations and curriculum.

Central government's policy, however, should not be seen merely as a defensive strategy in the context of scarce resources. Central government has, in the process of centralising power, also promoted a certain vision of education policy and desired organisational arrangements. Education policy has been based on the principles of *rationalisation* of education resources, *stratification* by differentiation of educational provision in accordance with students' abilities and aptitudes, and *vocationalism* by targeting education more directly to the roles students might be expected to play in the labour market (Ranson, 1985). Furthermore, administrative and governmental arrangements have sought to promote consumer sovereignty by strengthening the mechanisms of parental influence over education. This may also serve to strengthen stratification and vocationalism. The effect of both trends, however, has been significantly to restrict local authority autonomy in educational provision.

Chapter 6

LOCAL GOVERNMENT AND PRODUCTION

6.1 Introduction

The local government functions examined thus far have been essentially consumption-orientated redistributive services. As we saw in Chapter 1 this type of service has increased in significance this century. Indeed some have argued that the production-consumption cleavage provides the key to understanding recent conflicts between central and local government (Saunders 1982; Sharpe 1984). While there certainly have been tendencies towards functional specialisation between central and local government this century, particularly with the loss of many trading services, local authorities still have various responsibilities which are of great importance to the efficient functioning of production processes.

Many of these local government activities revolve around land as an element in the production process. We have seen (Chap. 1) that the growth in local government functions in the nineteenth century was largely the result of the social, economic and locational changes brought about by the forces of industrialisation and urbanisation. It was as a result of such changes that state intervention was required to deal with the land question. Local authorities have thus been heavily involved in the provision of various types of infrastructure which underwrite production; in regulating land use change to minimise externality effects and achieve efficiency in the operation of land markets; and generally in undertaking urban renewal and servicing land for private development.

The growth of these responsibilities during the twentieth century has resulted in some tension concerning the scope and nature of these powers, since they provide the state with the potential for significantly modifying the operation of land markets and the property development process. This is perhaps seen most clearly in the policies of post-war governments towards land value recapture mechanisms (Leung 1979). But it may also be seen reflected through other aspects of planning policy such as the attitude of government towards direct development undertaken by local authorities. In this chapter we shall therefore examine recent changes in local government functions which are more directly related to production processes.

136

6.2 Land Development

6.2.1 Introduction The Town and Country Planning Act 1947 introduced a highly sophisticated and comprehensive system of planning control. Under this, planning permission from the local planning authority (or, on appeal, from the Minister) was required before development could be undertaken. Development plans, drawn up by the local authority and approved by the Minister, were to provide the basic guide for decisions on planning applications. Development rights in land were nationalised and the regulation/compensation link, which had undermined the inter-war system, was finally broken. Except for the issue of land value recapture policies, this basic legal framework has remained intact ever since, the only major reform being the bifurcation of the development plan into structure and local plans in 1968. This is hardly surprising since the primary function of law in this area has been to provide an institutional and procedural framework through which conflicting interests can be mediated.

Nevertheless, major changes have occurred as the nature and importance of various interests have changed. The post-war planning system was founded on the need to contain urban growth, to reconstruct urban centres and to establish a new towns programme. Trends over the last 40 years have transformed the significance of these principles which underpinned this post-war planning consensus. First, there has been a growing realisation that planning policies cannot be devised without fully considering the broader social and economic issues which have an impact on land use; the establishment of structure planning, for example, stemmed in part from this realisation. Secondly, this realisation, combined both with the growth of the corporate approach in local government and the growth of the property development industry, has led to the emergence of an interdependent relationship between the public and private sector. This is reflected most clearly in the use of formal local authority/private enterprise joint venture schemes. Thirdly, the growing use of intensive farming methods has challenged the idea that agricultural and environmental interests are broadly compatible.

Of perhaps greatest significance, however, have been the locational effects of certain fundamental changes in the economic structure of the country. The significance of these changes (which arise from such factors as Britain's position in the world economy, the changing capital-labour ratio in industry and the growth in the service sector of the economy) were in part masked by the post-war period of economic growth. But since the 1970s the results have been stark and have most clearly manifested themselves in the phenomena of *deindustrialisation* and *deurbanisation* (Massey and Meegan 1978; Fothergill and Gudgin 1982; Scott 1982b; Young and Mills 1982). Deindustrialisation, deurbanisation and the restructuring of the space economy have profound implications for local government functions; after all, as we have seen, the growth of local government in the nineteenth century was largely a response to the forces of industrialisation and urbanisation. More particularly these changes directly challenge the post-war planning consensus since these economic forces militate against urban containment policies and the impetus to redevelop older urban areas.

In this section the general changes introduced in the planning system since 1979 in the context of these broader socio-economic developments are discussed. We shall also examine the policies and mechanisms introduced by the Conservative Government to encourage redevelopment of older urban areas.

6.2.2 The Regulatory Planning System. The primary objectives of the Conservative Government have been to establish a simpler framework for regulating development, to promote speed and efficiency within the planning system, and to ensure that, so far as possible, development should be facilitated. Because law provides a fairly flexible framework, very little in the way of new legislation has been needed in pursuing these objectives and the most significant reforms have come about through administrative changes.

Nevertheless, significant structural reforms have been made. The system of structure and local plans introduced in 1968 was designed to deal with such problems as delay, lack of responsiveness and narrowness in the old type of development plans drawn up under the 1947 Act. Through the establishment of structure plans, dealing with strategic issues, and local plans, examining detailed land use issues concerning smaller areas, it was envisaged that development plans could become more responsive, relevant and (selectively) rigorous. In the event the structure plan system has not been an unqualified success. The system was designed with the idea of unitary authorities in mind; as a result the two-tier reorganisation of 1974 significantly contributed to the complexities and delays which have been experienced. Furthermore, there has also been a widespread feeling that the reformed system was the product of an era of growth and was somewhat inappropriate in a period of retrenchment.

Reforms to the structure and local plan system have reflected these concerns. The Local Government, Planning and Land Act 1980 streamlined the procedures for the preparation and consideration of plans and simplified the form of structure plans by downgrading the reasons for policies and proposals to an explanatory memorandum which accompanies the plan (see s. 88; Sched. 14). This was followed by the Town and Country Planning (Structure and Local Plans) Regulations 1982 (S.I. 1982 No. 555) which simplified the content of the plans. The objective of these reforms, according to the Government, was to streamline the plans "and keep down the cost and manpower that goes into the plan-making end of the planning system" by concentrating "on essentials in the performance of these tasks and a determined elimination of the unnecessary" (DoE 1981b, para. I). The 1980 Act also reflected the sense of the inappropriateness of structure plans in a period of retrenchment by subtly diminishing the status of the structure plan relative to local plans (s. 88; para. 10(*d*) of Sched. 14).

The aim of establishing a simpler planning framework has also been reflected in changes to development control procedures. Thus the 1980 Act reformed the rather complicated county/district relationship concerning applications for planning permission, essentially by increasing the power of district councils and replacing the county council's power to issue directions to the district with a requirement that the district consult with the county on a range of matters (s. 86). As a result, the district council will be the local planning authority in respect of the vast majority of planning applications. As a sop to the county council, section 86(3) requires the local planning authority when determining planning applications "to seek the achievement of the general objectives of the structure plan." Consequently, one objective of the Government has been to establish clear and straightforward administrative and policy frameworks within which development decisions will be made.

A related concern has been to ensure that this administrative framework operates speedily and efficiently. This concern was one of the two main aims of DoE Circular 22/80, which replaced over 60 Circulars and provided a clear statement of the Government's attitude to development control. This circular emphasised the fact that "promptness, relevance and efficiency are characteristics of good planning" and asked authorities to examine their "office and committee arrangements closely to see what changes might be made to speed up matters" (DoE 1980c, paras. 3, 5). This emphasis on speed has been reflected in advice designed to simplify appeal procedures (DoE 1981c). Also the Department has experimented with novel methods of determining appeals such as *informal hearings* for cases which otherwise would go to more formal public local inquiry (Barker and Couper 1984, pp. 397–398), and *advance notice decisions* where, if all parties agree, preliminary indication of the result of the public local inquiry may be given within days of its conclusion (*ibid.* pp. 435–436).

Thus the Government's objective has been to establish a clear, concise, simple and efficient administrative and policy framework. These aims complement the final aim of facilitating development. This aim is also the second aim of Circular 22/80 which stated:

> "The planning system should play a helpful part in rebuilding the economy. Development control must avoid placing unjusti-fied obstacles in the way of any development especially if it is for industry, commerce, housing or any other purpose relevant to the economic regeneration of the country.... Local plan-ning authorities are asked therefore to pay greater regard to time and efficiency; to adopt a more positive attitude to planning applications; to facilitate development; and always to grant planning permission, having regard to all material considerations, unless there are sound and clear-cut reasons for refusal.... The Government want to make sure that the planning system is as positive and as helpful as it can be to investment in industry and commerce and to the development industry." (DoE 1980c, paras. 3,11).

Certain adjustments were signalled as a result of this attempt fundamentally to reorientate the planning system. Thus the Government have issued advice that "the fact that an activity is a non-conforming use is not a sufficient reason in itself for refusing planning permission" (*ibid.* para. 13); that enforcement of planning control is a "permissive power" and should be used "only where planning reasons clearly warrant such action" (*ibid.* para. 15); that aesthetics is "an extremely subjective matter," that authorities "should not therefore impose their tastes on developers simply because they believe them to be superior" and that "control of external appearance should only be exercised where there is a fully justified reason for doing so" (*ibid.* paras. 19, 21); that the "absence of a local plan, or the fact that one is in the offing, is not in itself sufficient reason for refusing a planning application" (DoE 1981b, para. 11); and have reiterated the policy that the use of conditions in planning permission should be kept to an absolute minimum (DoE 1985b). Also, in 1981 the General Development Order was amended to enable householders to extend their dwellings by 15 per cent. of cubic capacity (from 10 per cent.) and industrialists their buildings by 20 per cent. (from 10 per cent.), without the need for planning permission: S.I. 1981 No. 245. Greater deregulation was achieved as a result of further amendments in December 1985: S.I. 1985 No. 1981.

Essentially the Government's objective has been to establish a market-led planning system with the role of local authorities as that of aiding private developers and facilitating private development. This objective can be seen behind other modifications to the system, such as the abolition of office development permits (S.I. 1979 No. 908), the suspension of industrial development certificates (S.I. 1981 No. 1826) and the winding up of the new towns programme (Cullingworth 1985, Chap. 9 and pp. 407–408). Furthermore, it was hardly surprising that the Community Land Act 1975, in which it was envisaged that local authorities would play the dominant role in the assembling and marketing of development land, was repealed in 1980 (L.G.P.L.A. 1980 s. 101)—although for a combination of economic, political and administrative reasons, that scheme was already a dead letter (Grant 1979). Nevertheless, the Land Authority for Wales, which performed land assembly functions for Wales, was retained, albeit working within market norms (L.G.P.L.A. 1980, Pt. XII). As a result of these changes the importance of ensuring an adequate land supply for the development requirements of the private sector was emphasised.

These resulting arrangements are seen most clearly in relation to the availability of land for private housebuilding. Since the Government's housing policies relied heavily on the ability of the private sector to meet housing needs (see Chap. 4), ensuring that housebuilders had sufficient land to meet these needs became paramount (Rydin 1984). In order to achieve this the Government required local authorities to undertake studies in co-operation with the housebuilding industry to ensure that sufficient land was allocated to meet the needs of the industry for the following five years (DoE 1980d). The importance of such land availability studies was underlined by section 116 of the Local Government Planning and Land Act 1980 which empowered the Secretary of State to direct a local authority to undertake such assessments.

The critical issue, then, was the impact which such an explicit market orientation might have on the urban containment and conservation policies on which the post-war planning consensus was founded, particularly since today the most profitable areas for development are on the fringes of urban centres and in the smaller market towns. The Government announced, however, that their planning policies do "not mean that their commitment to conservation is in any way weakened" (DoE 1980c, para. 4). This seemed to be borne out by the fact that the Town and Country Planning (National Parks, Areas of Outstanding Natural Beauty and Conservation Areas) Special Development Order 1981 (S.I. 1981 No. 246), which came into force at the same time as the G.D.O. amendments, exempted those designated areas from the new relaxations on permitted development. But, although the designated areas seemed protected, concern was expressed at the Secretary of State's consistent policy in the 1980s of increasing housing land allocations when approving structure plans (C.P.R.E. 1981, p. 11). In particular it was felt that the green belt principle was threatened.

These issues came to a head with the publication in August 1983 of draft circulars on green belts and land for housing. These suggested that local authorities should review the inner boundaries of green belts around the peripheries of built-up areas and that they should consider withdrawing green belt status from pockets of open land surrounded by existing development. However, after intensive lobbying by local authorities and conservation interests and broad-based expressions of concern (House of Commons 1984f), the circulars were eventually published in a revised form which reiterated the importance of the green belts policy (DoE 1984b and c).

Nevertheless, central government policies have resulted in the imposition on local authorities of a more limited policy and administrative framework. Public expenditure constraints and the repeal of the Community Land Act have severely circumscribed the ability of local authorities to engage in positive planning. And central government has positively encouraged local authorities to promote and support private sector development initiatives. Consultation, negotiation and partnership between public and private sector has also been encouraged—but only so long as the private sector retains the upper hand (see DoE 1983b). All of these developments are part of a basic policy of reasserting the dominance of market mechanism, a policy which reaches its apogee with the abolition in 1985 of Development Land Tax (Finance Act

1985, s. 93). Planning activity in the 1980s consequently has been marked by a tension between the values of the market and the traditional planning policies of urban containment and conservation.

6.2.3 Urban Renewal Policies. One major issue for the Government has been its attitude towards urban renewal policies. Since development pressures are experienced primarily on the peripheries of large urban areas and in small towns and villages, the use of regulatory planning powers to support the market seems likely to hinder attempts to redevelop older urban areas. In these areas concern has been expressed about social, economic and physical conditions. Much of the physical and economic infrastructure is old and in need of renewal, and demographic trends, reinforced by overspill and new towns policies, have resulted in those groups which are more likely to be dependent on local authority services being over-represented in these areas.

Since the late 1960s central government has devised a number of programmes to tackle these problems. Primarily these have taken the form of area-based initiatives such as educational priority areas, general improvement areas, housing action areas and community development projects (McKay and Cox 1979, Chap. 7). These initiatives initially seemed to be inspired by the "culture of poverty" thesis (*e.g.* Banfield 1968, Chap. 3) since the implicit assumption was that the poverty of people in these pockets of deprivation could be eradicated by positive action, area-based action and the more effective delivery of local authority services. However, these views were challenged by the teams set up under the community development project, arguing that explanations of poverty were to be found in the distribution of power and in basic changes in the economies of inner areas (C.D.P. 1977a and b). Such analyses embarrassed the Government and the C.D.P. experiment was wound up in the late 1970s.

By the late 1970s, however, the Government appeared to have rejected many of the assumptions of the culture of poverty thesis and recognised that the key issue was economic rather than social. This policy realignment was reflected most clearly in the White Paper *Policy for the Inner Cities* (DoE 1977d) which emphasised the need directly to strengthen the economies of inner urban areas, and proposed to achieve this by readjusting the main policies and programmes of government and by introducing special central-local government partnership arrangements for certain inner areas. The

Conservative Government, after a review of inner city policy (House of Commons 1981c), accepted the need for special arrangements, albeit with an increasingly economic and private sector orientation.

These Urban Programme policy developments have largely been introduced without the need for new legislation. The reason for this is the breadth of the Secretary of State's power, under section 1 of the Local Government Grants (Social Needs) Act 1969, to pay grants to any authorities "who in his opinion are required in the exercise of any of their functions to incur expenditure by reason of the existence in any urban area of special social need." These grants, which are specific grants financing 75 per cent. of the cost of approved projects, can thus be switched from social to economic and revenue to capital projects in accordance with the prevailing policy. In 1978, however, inner city policy realignment was reflected in new legislation in the form of the Inner Urban Areas Act 1978. This Act provided a legal underpinning for inner city programme and partnership initiatives through which new central-local government planning arrangements were established (Hambleton 1981, Stewart 1983, Leach 1985). The Act also empowered local authorities in designated districts to declare industrial improvement areas and to make grants and loans for promoting development in these districts (ss. 1–11).

The Conservative Government have worked largely within this legal framework although new legislation has also been enacted. The orientation of inner city policy, however, has significantly changed. This change has had a serious impact on local government. The 1977 review, for example, placed great emphasis on mutual interdependence between the tiers of government in tackling urban problems, and recognised the predominant role of local government:

> "Local authorities are the natural agencies to tackle inner area problems. They are democratically accountable bodies; they have long experience of running local services, most of which no other body provides as effectively or as sensitively to local needs; and they have working links with other bodies concerned.... Local authorities will need the support and encouragement of all the central government departments and agencies concerned." (DoE 1977d, paras. 31, 33)

The Government's restructuring of inner city policy, however, has challenged this view of local government. This has been done by focusing on the amount of urban wasteland which is held by local (and other public) authorities (Nabarro 1984). The non-use of this land has been attributed to mismanagement by local authorities, who have thus been characterised as part of the problem rather than the lead agency in any solution. Their role has therefore been supplanted by central government, which in turn has directly involved the private sector both in the policy planning process and as an agent for renewal. This analysis may be illustrated by examining policy and legal developments.

The increased attention being paid to publicly owned urban wasteland led the Government to conclude that little was known about the land-holdings of public bodies. The result was the enactment of new legislation in the form of Part X of the Local Government Planning and Land Act 1980. Part X empowers the Secretary of State to compile and maintain a register containing the land-holdings of public bodies (s. 93; Sched. 16) in certain areas (s. 94) which, in his opinion, are "not being used or not being sufficiently used for the purposes of the performance of the body's functions" (s. 95). A copy of the register for designated areas must be sent to the local council and be available for inspection by members of the public (s. 96). Finally, the Secretary of State is empowered to compel a body to take steps to dispose of any land owned by it which is entered on the register (ss. 97–99).

After introducing the provisions of Part X in a limited number of areas on an experimental basis, the provisions were applied throughout England and Wales (S.I. 1981 No. 1618; S.I. 1984 No. 1493). According to the DoE nearly half of the land on the registers appears to possess medium to high potential for development (House of Commons 1984f, para. 59). In 1983, however, of the 63,304 acres of underutilised land recorded in the registers as owned by local authorities, only 3,222 had been disposed of and 2,743 of that brought into use (Cullingworth 1985, p. 399). Nevertheless it was not until late 1985 that the Secretary of State began to issue disposal directions.

Public land registers may *identify* underutilised land but, as the figures show, they will not ensure that land is brought into productive use. Nevertheless, the objective of the registers must be to encourage sales to the private sector, since otherwise the register would have been based on underutilised land rather than public land. The main problem, therefore, is the fact that profitability is the key criterion for determining whether the private sector will develop land. Consequently, if the Government wish to involve the private sector more directly in the redevelopment of inner urban areas they may be required to underwrite the profitability of redevelopment projects. In fact, this has been done through a range of measures, the most important of which are enterprise zones, derelict land grants (D.L.G.s) and urban development grants (U.D.G.s).

The enterprise zone idea began with a proposal to open up selected areas of inner cities to market inititatives with only the most minimal of state controls (Hall 1977). This radical proposal, which aimed to recreate the Hong Kong of the 1950s and 1960s in British inner cities in the 1980s, clearly appealed to the *laissez-faire* ideology of the Conservative Government. The proposal actually enacted in schedule 32 to the Local Government, Planning and Land Act 1980, however, although it aimed to minimise regulatory controls and provide financial inducements to undertake development, was very different from that original idea (Taylor 1981).

On the invitation of the Secretary of State an authority may draw up a scheme for an enterprise zone (para. 1). Provided the authority has given "adequate publicity" to the scheme and considered representations, it may adopt the scheme (para. 2); the Secretary of State may then designate it as an enterprise zone authority, and the area to which the zone relates as an enterprise zone (para. 5). The importance of the scheme is that it operates automatically to grant planning permission for any classes of development provided for within the scheme, subject only to the conditions or restrictions laid out in the scheme (para. 17). In effect the scheme introduces an arrangement analogous to the American zoning system in these areas. Although there are other regulatory concessions of a minor nature there is no relaxation to pollution and health and safety standards, and building regulations still apply. Furthermore, in order to protect amenity or sensitive uses, restrictions may be imposed in the scheme concerning the location of certain classes of development within a specified area (para. 17). Of probably greater importance in attracting private investment, however, are the financial advantages of locating within an enterprise zone; namely, exemption from development land tax (Finance Act 1980 s. 110) and on industrial and commercial buildings 100 per cent. capital allowances (Finance Act 1980 s. 74) and exemption from rates (para. 27). Local authorities are reimbursed by central government for any loss in rate revenue (para. 29).

In 1981 11 enterprise zones, each of about 500 acres were designated for a ten-year period; this was followed by a second round of a further 14 in 1983. But have these controversial schemes succeeded? The basic criticisms of enterprise zones are: that the idea is strong in rhetoric and weak in concept; that the benefits of the scheme will accrue mainly to landowners or developers rather than strengthen the local economy; and that it seems a spatially redistributive policy which is likely to shift rather than create employment (Massey 1982). The results of the monitoring research on the first round of designations have borne out many of these criticisms. Thus, despite the deregulatory rhetoric it is clear that the relaxed planning regime has done little to stimulate development. In fact, development activity has relied not only on enterprise zones subsidies but also on public sector intervention and expenditure. The level of subsidy provided to the private sector has been very high; £132.9 million in the period 1981–83, which in terms of employment generation represents a cost of about £16,500 per job created. Furthermore, the evidence suggests that most of the jobs might have been created locally anyhow (Roger Tym and Partners 1984; Hall 1984). Consequently, while the objective of stimulating property development has been achieved, that of generating new employment has not.

The Conservative Government has also extended and consolidated powers to provide grants for "derelict, neglected or unsightly land requiring reclamation or improvement" (L.G.P.L.A. 1980, s. 117; Derelict Land Act 1982). D.L.G. can thus be used in aid of redevelopment in inner urban areas. In fact the amount allocated on D.L.G.s has risen in real terms in the 1980s and in 1984/85 £74 million was allocated. Most of the approved projects are joint local authority/private sector schemes which lead to the immediate disposal of the site to private developers. 65 per cent. of the schemes are for private housing and in 1984/85 the total amount invested by the private sector in D.L.G. aided schemes was £440 million (House of Commons 1984f, para. 78).

The final initiative for underwriting private sector redevelopment schemes in inner urban areas is the U.D.G. scheme. The U.D.G. scheme was introduced in September 1982 following a recommendation of the Financial Institutions Group (F.I.G.), a group of managers from the financial institutions seconded to the DoE to explore investment in the inner cities following the urban riots in the summer of 1981. U.D.G. is designed to render private development projects viable by covering the gap between the project cost, including an allowance for the developer's profit, and the expected return. Suitable projects are nominated by local authorities and evaluated by the DoE's U.D.G. Appraisal Team, which consists mainly of private sector secondees. There are no restrictions on the type or size of projects although particular attention is paid to the "leverage ratio," the ratio between private investment and public subsidy, and the contribution the projects make to meeting the special needs of the area or generating private investment confidence in the area. U.D.G.s are a separately administered element of the Urban Programme and so the statutory basis of the scheme remains the 1969 Act. Any authority based on designated districts under the 1978 Act and those with enterprise zones may apply (DoE 1983c).

Between September 1982 and April 1984 446 bids had been submitted, of which 141 (32 per cent.) were given approval. If all projects materialise this will represent private investment of £260 million at a public expenditure cost of £65 million, a leverage ratio of 4:1. Approved projects include industrial (40 per cent.) and commercial (35 per cent.) schemes, and new and rehabilitated housing projects (23 per cent.) (Jacobs 1985). Prominent amongst the latter category are schemes for the privatisation and refurbishment of systems-built council housing (Munday and Mallinson 1983, see section 4.4).

Given that U.D.G. is explicitly a scheme for underwriting the profitability of private sector development, the key issues are whether the resources of the scheme are directed at the right targets and whether the scheme successfully promotes development which would not otherwise occur, or whether it is merely a hand-out to private developers. It is too early to assess the British experience but the evidence from the American Urban Development Action Grant (U.D.A.G.) scheme, which influenced the design of U.D.G.s, is useful. This suggests that U.D.A.G.s were most successful with market-led schemes. Also in one exercise it was found that 36 per cent. of U.D.A.G. supported projects involved some degree of substitution of public for private sector funds (Boyle 1985, pp. 207-208). Under the U.D.G. scheme there is the possibility of dealing with this by negotiating a clawback agreement, but costs and profits are extremely difficult to monitor (Mallinson and Gilbert 1983). Nevertheless, the DoE seem satisfied with the progress of the scheme so far (Jacobs 1985, p. 197).

Thus, by focusing on the underutilisation of publicly-owned urban land, central government has emphasised the contribution of local authorities to the creation of urban problems. This in turn has led to the promotion of the private sector as a primary agency in urban renewal and, as a result, schemes such as enterprise zones,

D.L.G.s and U.D.G.s have been established to underwrite the profitability of private sector redevelopment initiatives. However, the success of such schemes is still dependent on public sector intervention to facilitate such initiatives. In this vital role as facilitator of development the Government has also promoted a number of agencies in order to displace the local authority role.

The most important of these agencies is the Urban Development Corporation (U.D.C.) which the Secretary of State is empowered to establish under Part XVI of the Local Government, Planning and Land Act 1980. Under the 1980 Act the Secretary of State may designate any land in a metropolitan district or London borough as an urban development area (s. 134) and establish a U.D.C. for that area for the purpose of regenerating the area (s. 135). In pursuit of this objective U.D.C.s are empowered to acquire land owned by public authorities in the area (s. 141), to buy and sell land (ss. 142, 146) and may provide the finance needed to facilitate the development of land by any person (ss. 160–162). If the U.D.C. itself wishes to develop land it may submit a planning application directly to the Secretary of State (s. 148). The Secretary of State, however, also has the power to make the U.D.C. the local planning authority (s. 149) and the housing authority (s. 153) for the area and vest it with duties relating to building control (s. 151) and public health (s. 159).

The Government has used these powers to establish U.D.C.s for the dockland areas of London and Merseyside, where the decline, modernisation and relocation of port facilities have left huge areas of industrial obsolescence and dereliction. The development corporations have been vested with publicly owned land in their areas and have taken over development control functions (S.I. 1981 No. 561, S.I. 1981 No. 1082). Essentially the Government have used the development corporation model in place of the partnership arrangements which operated in the 1970s in order to try to attract private capital to the inner cities.

The apparent advantages of the development corporation model are that it is a single purpose agency which does not have to balance the demands of different claimants on its resources and is not swayed by democratic processes, and that, because it has no executive capacity, it is not a bureaucratic organisation which is hampered by a traditional departmental professional line management structure. (House of Commons 1984f, paras. 72–77). Undoubtedly much has been achieved by the U.D.C.s within a relatively short period (Adcock 1984). However, the crucial factor appears to be the financial resources allocated to the U.D.C.s. The London Docklands Development Corporation, for example, was allocated around £50 million for its activities in 1984/85; this compares with £74 million allocated *nationally* for D.L.G.s and £48 million for U.D.G.s. Clearly, when using U.D.C.s the Government have been more prepared to match resources against the scale of the problem.

Another agency established recently which undermines the local authority role is the Merseyside Task Force, set up following the Toxteth riots in 1981. The Task Force, which comprises 30 civil servants from various central government departments and 8 persons seconded from private firms acting under the direction of the Secretary of State for the Environment, aimed to generate new initiatives for reducing unemployment and improving the economic and social life of the conurbation. This initiative undermined the local authority role by seeking to bypass the established inner city partnership planning arrangements established under the 1978 Act, chaired by the Secretary of State. However, the Secretary of State, instead of trying to revive and develop partnership arrangements, used the Task Force initiative to bypass them (House of Commons 1983c).

In 1985 it was proposed that the Task Force model be extended to other urban areas through the formation of City Action Teams (Carvel 1985b). Impetus was added by the riots in Handsworth and Tottenham in 1985. The riots caused the Government to set up a Cabinet committee with priority status to undertake a review of inner city policies. The Government's primary concern was to ensure that central government grants were actually spent on projects of which they approved. Consequently the possibility of by-passing the local authority became a key theme. It was thus proposed first that "urban renewal agencies," private sector consortia which would spearhead regeneration, should be established and, secondly, that the Secretary of State should have power to provide grant aid direct to private sector bodies. Legislative sanction for the latter proposal is being sought in Part III of the Housing and Planning Bill. The former proposal builds on attempts by the Government to use the private sector more directly as a facilitator of development. Thus, in 1983, on the advice of F.I.G., Inner City Enterprises Ltd. (I.C.E.) was formed as a service company with institutional shareholders. Its function is to seek out development opportunities in inner areas, ensure that they are properly marketed and brought to the attention of funding institutions. It is too early to assess this company's success. However, this initiative provides a good illustration of the Government's attempts to involve the private sector in the search for development opportunities in the inner city (Hambleton 1980).

The pattern in the Conservative Government's urban renewal policy thus seems clear. *Policy for the Inner Cities* (DoE 1977d) aimed to explore the economic as well as the social dimensions to urban problems and in order to tackle these problems sought to redirect the main programmes of government by establishing novel central-local planning arrangements. There have been significant shifts in this strategy. The Government seems to have lost faith in planning processes and has turned to the private sector to play a major role in urban renewal. As a result, the key governmental roles have become those of *facilitator* of private development schemes and *underwriter* of their profitability. This implies a limited role for local government, especially since the concern with social deprivation has been replaced with the search for initiatives to stem urban economic decline. Finally, the financial arrangements reinforce this limited role. Rather than redirect main governmental programmes the Government has significantly reduced the resources available to urban authorities; at the same time the resources allocated to the Urban Programme have been increased (Boyle 1985, p. 206), presumably on the grounds that central government can more directly control expenditure through the allocation of specific grant aid.

6.3 Economic Development

6.3.1. Introduction. Local authorities are not vested with a general economic function although they have certain specific economic powers and are able to use other general powers for economic purposes. In recent years, however, they have once again become more directly involved in the operation of the local economy. The broadening of the conception of planning with the introduction of structure planning, for example, required them to assess the relationship between land use policies and economic policies. This was reinforced by the establishment in the 1970s of corporate approaches in local government. These led authorities to reflect on the aggregate impact of their activities on the economic and social well-being of their communities. And the economic crisis and rising levels of unemployment have caused authorities to examine closely both their own role in the local economy and methods of aiding and promoting local economic activity.

An examination of their own role in the local economy was required because of the scale of local government activities; in fact, in many places local authorities are the major employers and investors in their areas. With unemployment levels rising and social need increasing it is hardly surprising that many have been resisting the pressures by central government to reduce the size of their workforces. Furthermore, several authorities are beginning to examine more positively their functions as owners, employers and contractors, for example, by using their power of procurement to achieve socio-economic objectives (Blunkett and Green 1983, pp. 11 and 16; GLC Economic Policy Group 1983; and see *Wheeler* v *Leicester City Council* (1985) 3 W.L.R. 335). These initiatives, however, are being blocked by the Government (see section 7.3).

In this section we shall examine the legal restrictions imposed on the operation of the local authority's own productive workforce and the responses of central government to local economic initiatives.

6.3.2 Direct Labour Organisations. Local authorities undertake a great deal of construction, building and maintenance work, such as road construction and repairs to their housing stock. Much of this work is carried out by their own workforce, or direct labour organisation (D.L.O.). The annual value of D.L.O. work is in the region of £1,500 million. However, there has been no standard organisational structure or accounting method applied to local authorities' D.L.O.s; for example, the maintenance workforces of many authorities were integrated into the relevant departmental management structure whereas others had established a separate organisation. In Part III of the Local Government, Planning and Land Act 1980 the Conservative Government required D.L.O.s to operate as formal trading services by subjecting them to trading accountability.

Under the Act all authorities having D.L.O.s employing more than 30 people (s. 21) are required to keep separate revenue accounts for four basic categories of work undertaken: (a) general highway works; (b) major new construction works; (c) minor new construction works; and (d) maintenance work (s. 10). Authorities must then estimate the value of each item of work (s. 9(2)) and the actual costs incurred, and these must be credited and debited in the annual accounts (ss. 12, 13).

However, in addition to requiring authorities to maintain accounts on a commercial basis, the Secretary of State is vested with powers to ensure that the D.L.O. makes a profitable return on capital employed and to require a D.L.O. to compete directly with private contractors. Thus, D.L.O.s are required to earn a rate of return on capital employed which is specified by the Secretary of State (s. 16). Furthermore, the Secretary of State may direct that an authority produce a special report on the previous three years operations of the D.L.O. and, after so doing, may direct that it cease to undertake such work, or limit its activities to certain types of work (s. 17). Finally, the Secretary of State is empowered to draw up regulations requiring that, in respect of work worth more than a specified amount, the work may not be undertaken by the D.L.O. unless it has submitted a tender in competition with at least three outside contractors (s. 9).

As a result of this legislation about half of the local authorities had to reorganise their D.L.O.s to some degree. The Secretary of State fixed the rate of return on capital employed at 5 per cent. (DoE 1981d). The 1981/82 annual reports showed that this target was met by the majority of D.L.O.s (Flynn and Walsh 1982). However, a great deal of doubt has been cast on the appropriateness of this performance target since D.L.O.s are not very capital intensive. Consequently a fairly large number of authorities recorded high rates of return, the highest being 1,494 per cent. As Norman Flynn has commented, if rates of return on capital employed are a true measure of efficiency then that authority was operating 299 times more efficiently than those which merely met the Secretary of State's target (Flynn 1985)!

Of potentially greater significance were the regulations concerning competitive tendering. These regulations were first made in 1981 (S.I. 1981 No. 339, 340) but were then amended and replaced in 1982 (S.I. 1982 No. 1036) and 1983 (S.I. 1983 No. 685). The general effect of these amendments has been progressively to increase the volume of local authority work that must be put out to competitive tender. One reason for doing so was that the provisions had not stimulated much competition.

Although the impact of this legislation is at this stage uncertain, one clear effect has been the uncertainty caused in D.L.O.s by the new legislation. This arises in part from the problems of interpreting the legislation: *Wilkinson* v. *Doncaster Metropolitan Borough Council* (1983) (unreported), (see Cross 1984); *Inner London Education Authority* v. *Department of the Environment* (1985) 83 L.G.R. 24. But primarily it results from the fact that regulations have been constantly changed. As Flynn (1985) suggests, this stems from the fact that while central government knew the effect they wanted to achieve, they did not know precisely which rules and procedures would create these effects; they therefore devised legislation which enabled the rules to be changed as the results became apparent. This objective has been to privatise, or at least significantly to curtail, one form of municipal enterprise which survived the loss of most of local government's trading functions.

6.3.3 Local Economic and Employment Initiatives. Local authorities have in recent years become more concerned with economic and employment initiatives. This may reflect either their concern at economic decline in their areas as a result of changes in the industrial structure or more generally the economic recession. Although local authorities have no general economic function they have powers to aid economic development, mainly in relation to their land ownership and development functions; Local Authorities (Land) Act 1963; Local Government Act 1972 ss. 119, 120; Inner Urban Areas Act 1978. Additionally, they have general powers which could be used for economic development purposes. The most important is section 137 of the Local Government Act 1972 which empowers authorities to expend the produce of a 2p rate on activity "which in their opinion is in the interests of the inhabitants of their area or any part of it or all or some of its inhabitants." This very broad power is subject to the restriction that it may be used only where the authority has no other powers in relation to that purpose. Furthermore, during the 1960s and 1970s many authorities acquired further economic development powers through private Acts of Parliament (Minns and Thornley 1978, pp. 30–34; Rogers and Smith 1977).

The local authority role in economic development was formally recognised by central government in 1977 when they were encouraged to contribute to central government's industrial strategy by themselves formulating policies to promote economic development (DoE 1977e). The main thrust of local authority initiatives has been to provide serviced sites for industrial development with the emphasis being on the encouragement of small firms (Boddy 1982). Any employment policy was therefore indirect; it was assumed that the benefits of a property development approach would filter through to the job market and that small firms would eventually grow and provide further employment opportunities.

By the 1980s some local authorities felt that the traditional approach was not very productive as it led to wasteful competition between authorities over a declining amount of potentially mobile industry and because unemployment policy was secondary rather than primary. These authorities began to pursue alternative approaches which sought to make direct strategic interventions in the local economy by targeting mainly on medium-sized firms in order to protect existing levels of employment or create new employment. Assistance is provided in the form of loans, guarantees and equity investment, and planning agreements, specifying investment, employment and production targets, union recognition and wages levels, are negotiated. This approach is based on the model of the National Enterprise Board established under the Labour Government's Industry Act 1975. Alongside this approach was a concern about workplace organisation and this resulted with these authorities promoting worker involvement in management and producer co-operatives.

In 1981/82 the total amount of industrial assistance by local authorities in England and Wales was £218 million. In the same year the expenditure of local authorities in Britain on industrial assistance under section 137 of the local Government Act 1972 has been estimated at £14.38 million (Crawford and Moore 1983, p. 169). This suggests that the great bulk of industrial assistance by local authorities was of the traditional type because most of the finance for the alternative approach was provided under the authority of section 137. Nevertheless it was also clear that expenditure on alternative approaches was increasing. In 1982, for example, both the GLC and the West Midlands County Council established enterprise boards as independent companies to execute their economic and employment policies. These boards were given budgets for 1982/83 of £25 million and £3.5 million respectively, allocated under section 137 (Boddy 1984).

With the growing importance of local authority industrial assistance, certain legal uncertainties about the use of the section 137 power (Crawford and Moore 1983, pp. 173–183), and the need to review local Act powers because of section 262 of the Local Government Act 1972, the Government established the Burns Committee to review local authority assistance to industry and commerce (Burns 1980). The Report outlined possible amendments to existing powers and recommended that while local authorities should be able to plan for employment their activities should be complementary to, rather than competitive with, those of the private sector. The Government responded to the Burns Report by proposing that authorities designated under the Inner Urban Areas Act 1978 would continue to have access to the use of section 137 for providing industrial assistance but other authorities would be able to use only the product of a half penny rate on industrial assistance, and then only to assist independent firms employing up to 25 people (House of Commons 1982d).

After lobbying from the local authority associations, however, the Government did not proceed with these proposals. The result was that section 137 was amended in order to remove doubts about the use of that power for industrial assistance purposes: section 44 of the Local Government (Miscellaneous Provisions) Act 1982, inserting new sub-sections (2A), (2B), (4A), (4B) of section 137 of the Local Government Act 1972. In the following year, as a result of further doubts about the relationship between section 137 and other industrial assistance powers, the Local Authorities (Expenditure Powers) Act 1983 was enacted.

The Government therefore decided not to proceed with a proposal to curtail local authority powers to provide industrial assistance. Nevertheless the role of local authorities in this field remains a matter of concern to central government. Local authority involvement has been increasing, particularly as a result of changes in the Government's regional policy (Mawson 1981). The Government seems particularly concerned about the more interventist forms of economic policies adopted by some urban authorities. Steps have been taken to deal with these concerns through the abolition of the metropolitan county councils and the GLC. (see Chap. 8) and the establishment of the Widdicombe Committee in 1985 to examine, *inter alia*, discretionary expenditure by local authorities under section 137.

6.4 Conclusions

The post-war planning system provided for comprehensive control over development and vested local authorities with sufficient powers to enable them to play a positive and directive role in guiding development. It also aimed to sever the link between regulation and finance to enable authorities to devise planning policies free from financial pressures. The financial objective has never been realised and as a result the planning system has been required generally to follow the dictates of the market. In recent years, the combination of public expenditure constraints, which have limited the ability of local authorities to engage in positive planning policies, and economic trends, which impose pressures on urban containment policies, has seriously challenged what re- mained of the post-war planning consensus. The Government's industry and because employment policy was secondary rather than response has been to encourage partnership between the public and private sectors.

The result has been the establishment of an essentially market-led planning system. This means the establishment of a simpler system which is more speedily administered and in which the local authority role is not promotional but responsive. The most recent manifestations of these changes are the Government's proposals, in Part II of the Housing and Planning Bill to introduce the concept of Simplified Planning Zones, which are basically enterprise zones shorn of the financial inducements; to introduce further forms of deregulation through the General Development Order (see S.I. 1985 No. 1981); and to review the operation of the Use Classes Order (Minister without Portfolio 1985, para. 3.6). One critical test of this market-led planning system has been in relation to the redevelopment of older urban areas. Here central government have encouraged local authorities to play the roles of facilitator and underwriter of the profitability of private development proposals. To the extent that this has required a positive governmental role a great deal of initiative has been taken by central government and away from local authorities.

Finally, some local authorities, frustrated by indirect, property development-led economic development initiatives, have undertaken more positive and interventionist strategies for seeking to maintain or promote employment. Central government policies have not been supportive; the Government has taken indirect action to curtail these activities through the abolition of the GLC and the Metropolitan county councils and may yet take more direct action.

Chapter 7

FINANCIAL DISCIPLINE

7.1 Introduction

In Chapter 1 we postulated a view that the Conservative Government was seeking to impose a particular type of financial discipline on local government and that this underlay not only reforms to the system of local government finance but also the form of the restructuring of local government functions. This question must now be more directly examined. Essentially the Government's characterisation of the problems of local government appears to be drawn from an economic theory of politics called "public choice" (I.E.A. 1978). This theory challenges the assumption of orthodox welfare economics that the existence of market failure is sufficient reason for governmental intervention. The theory does so by applying the economic assumptions about the utility maximising behaviour of individuals to the arena of governmental decision-making and, as a result, challenges the assumption that government will act efficiently and in the public interest.

Public choice theory provides analyses both of administrative and political developments. The theory of bureaucracy starts with individual behaviour within bureaucracies and assumes that individuals will seek to increase the size of their departments, since salaries and other perquisites tend to be proportionate to the size of their budgets. Consequently, it is argued that bureaucracies have a built-in expansionary motive which results in operational inefficiencies (Tullock 1965; Niskanen 1973). The theory of politics is based on an analysis of the effects of electoral competition within the political market place. On the supply side, it is argued that political parties bid for support, with the result that they end up by promising more than they can deliver. This leads to inflated expectations on the demand side since the electorate have incentives to vote for increased services because they do not pay for them directly and because there may be little correlation between tax payments and benefits (Downs 1957; Breton 1974). These views of bureaucracy and politics in combination produce the argument that there is a "ratchet effect" in government of ever-increasing expenditure as a result of meeting new demands while being unable to cut back on entrenched programmes.

This type of analysis seems to have been applied to local government. Such analysis focuses in particular on post-war changes in functions and financial and administrative structures. Functional changes have led to a preponderance of redistributive services in local government; this has weakened the correlation between the amount of rates paid and benefits received. Changes in the financing system include diminishing the regressive nature of the rating system through the introduction of rate rebates and increasing the proportion of local government expenditure met by grants from central government. These changes contribute to service-demand inflation both by subsidising the local cost generally and in particular the cost to those who, although receiving substantial benefits, might otherwise exert a restraining influence because of the demands placed on their disposable income. In terms of administrative structure the analysis highlights the dominance of "managerial professionalism" in local government (see section 9.2) alongside the fact that around 85 per cent. of the local government workforce is unionised. Both aspects seem likely to strengthen the bargaining power of local government employees.

By utilising this form of analysis the Government have sought to argue that local government is a bureaucratic, self-serving institution which is especially susceptible to the phenomenon of political demand inflation and is subject to few mechanisms of restraint; in short, that the political market mechanism in local government is not functioning properly. Their objectives have therefore been to attempt to establish some form of equilibrium in this political market mechanism and to introduce a variety of mechanisms to counter the phenomenon of political demand inflation. Thus, reforms to the grant system (see section 2.3) can be examined as attempts significantly to transfer the cost of marginal expenditure decisions (which, after all, is the sharp edge of political decision-making) onto local ratepayers. Of potentially greater significance have been statutory reforms which seek, to varying degrees, to reconstitute a broad range of local government policy decisions in the form of monetary exchange relations. Examples include measures requiring privatisation of assets and contracting out of services, or competition with the private sector for the provision of services and the promotion of market-based pricing policies for local authority provided services. Finally, it should also be noted that at a crucial stage in policy development the courts played a catalytic role through their restatement of the concept of fiduciary duty in the *Bromley* case (see sections 3.4 and 9.4.3).

In this chapter we shall examine the main legal developments in this attempt to establish new forms of financial discipline on local authorities. These developments will be examined under the heads of financial discipline and market discipline.

7.2 Financial Discipline

7.2.1 Financial Administration. Every organisation must ensure that its financial transactions are honestly and assiduously conducted and that an effective system of accounting is established. The general legal framework governing the administration of the finances of local authorities is to be found in Part VIII of the Local Government Act 1972. These provisions require that all receipts and liabilities of a local authority be carried to and discharged out of their general rate fund ("county fund" for county councils) and that accounts be kept of these receipts and liabilities. And every local authority "shall make arrangements for the proper administration of their financial affairs and shall secure that one of their officers has responsibility for the administration of those affairs" (s. 151).

The financial security of local authorities is ensured through a range of provisions. First, local authorities are expected, on a year-by-year basis, to meet all of their expenses out of revenue. As a result, there is no general power to borrow for revenue purposes; a local authority may borrow for revenue purposes only "for the purpose of defraying expenses ... pending the receipt of revenues receivable by them in respect of the period of account in which those expenses are chargeable" (Local Government Act 1972, Sched. 13, paras. 5 and 10). A general power to borrow for any purpose exists but this requires the Secretary of State's sanction and is rarely used to permit borrowing for revenue purposes (Local Government Act, Sched. 13, para. 1.)

Secondly, central government controls a local authority's level of investment and amount of indebtedness through controls over borrowing (see section 2.5 above). Thirdly, all securities created by a local authority rank without priority and all money borrowed is charged indifferently on all the revenues of the authority (Local Government Act 1972, Sched. 13 para. 11). Finally, the charge on revenues is safeguarded by the power of an authority to make a rate or issue a precept; thus an authority is required to "make such rates as will be sufficient to provide for such part of the total estimated expenditure to be incurred by the authority during this period in respect of which the rate is made as is not to be met by other means"(General Rate Act 1967, ss. 2 and 11).

These measures ensure the financial security and creditworthiness of local authorities. The only recent developments affecting this position concern the power to make rates. The effect of these changes is examined in section 7.2.3 below, but first we must examine audit arrangements.

7.2.2 Audit. That the accounts of local authorities should be subject to external audit has long been established. The primary function of the auditor is as "a watchdog to see that the accounts are properly kept and that no one is making off with the funds": *Asher* v. *Secretary of State for the Environment* [1974] 2 W.L.R. 446, 472. This aspect of the auditor's role has never been controversial. However, controversy has surrounded certain incidental powers of the auditor to hold councillors personally liable for loss caused by unlawful acts or misconduct. This is because these powers have occasionally been used in the context of contentious policy decision-making and as a result the existence of the powers has been criticised on the ground that they stifle initiative and unduly inhibit councillors. In 1967 the Maud Committee recommended that these incidental powers of surcharge be abolished (Maud 1967, para. 290) but they were retained in the Local Government Act 1972, albeit in a modified form. The basic law on audit is now contained in Part III of the Local Government Finance Act 1982.

The basic powers and duties of auditors remains substantially unaltered by the 1982 Act and the major reforms introduced are of an organisational nature. These organisational reforms are a response to pressures for the audit service to be independent of both central and local government (Layfield 1976, Chap. 6) and for greater use to be made of management audit techniques and of private-sector auditors. The result was the establishment of an Audit Commission (s. 11; Sched. 3) whose primary responsibilities are to appoint auditors to audit the accounts of local authorities (s. 13), to prepare and keep under review a code to audit practice prescribing the way in which auditors are to carry out their functions (s. 14) and to "undertake or promote comparative and other studies designed to enable it to make recommendations for improving economy, efficiency and effectiveness in the provision of local authority services" (s. 26).

These changes are in part motivated by a desire of the Government to privatise a greater amount of audit work. The 1972 Act had provided local authorities with the right to choose between using the services of the district auditor and those of an approved private auditor; in practice, however, 95 per cent. of work was undertaken by the district auditor (Jones 1985, p. 16). The 1982 Act in effect takes away freedom of audit choice from local authorities and places it in the hands of a Commission appointed by the Secretary of State. The Commission's independence is limited by the Secretary of State's power to issue directions to the Commission (Sched. 3, para. 3(1)). Nevertheless the Commission have sought to establish a role independent of the central government (see, for example, their critical reports on the financial arrangements: Audit Commission 1984a; 1985). The final responsibility of the Commission, the promotion of management audit, is an attempt to adapt to governmental organisation an audit technique developed for commercial undertakings. Management audit goes far beyond an examination of records and implies a critical assessment of managerial efficiency within the organisation. Since the key to management audit is "productivity" it is not an easy concept to apply to local government as there is a danger that productivity will be examined purely in commercial terms (Marshall 1974, pp. 193–195).

The auditor appointed by the Commission must be satisfied that the authority's accounts are in order, that proper practices have been observed and that the authority has made "proper arrangements for securing economy, efficiency and effectiveness in the use of resources" (s. 15(1)). For this purpose the auditor shall have a right of access at all reasonable times to all documents of the authority as appear necessary for the purpose of the audit (s. 16). At the conclusion of the audit the auditor provides a certificate stating that the audit has been completed in accordance with the Act (s. 18(1)) although the auditor may produce an immediate report on any matter coming to his notice in the course of the audit if he considers that this is in the public interest (ss. 15(3), 18(2)–(5)). Any local government elector may inspect and make copies of the statement of accounts and auditor's reports (s. 24) and has the right to question the auditor about the accounts (s. 17).

The controversial powers of surcharge and disqualification arise under two heads. Under section 19 if it appears to the auditor that any item of account is contrary to law he may apply to the court for a declaration unless that item is sanctioned by the Secretary of State (s. 19(1)). If the court makes that declaration and is not satisfied that the person responsible for incurring or authorising the unlawful expenditure acted reasonably or in the belief that the expenditure was authorised by law, it may order that person to repay the whole or part or the amount (and where two or more persons are responsible they shall be jointly and severally liable). Furthermore, if the person is a councillor and the unlawful expenditure exceeds £2,000 the court may disqualify the person from being a member of a local authority for a specified period (s. 19(2) (3)).

The other head falls under section 20 which provides that if any person has failed to bring into account any sum which should have been so included or that a loss has been incurred or deficiency caused by the wilful misconduct of any person the auditor shall certify that the sum or the amount of the loss or deficiency is due from that person. The auditor or the authority may then recover that sum or amount for the benefit of that body. Persons certified under this section are jointly and severally liable for the sum or amount and may appeal to the court which may confirm, vary or quash the decision (s. 20(3)). If the certificate related to a loss or deficiency caused by wilful misconduct of a person who is a member of the authority and the amount due exceeds £2,000 that person shall be disqualified for being a member of a local authority for five years (s. 20(4)). Action for the recovery of such debts may be taken in the courts and orders for repayment are enforceable in accordance with the general rules applicable to judgments or orders of the court for payment of money (Jones 1985, pp. 230–4).

Whenever these powers are invoked against local authorities there is a tendency for the resulting disputes to attain the status of *causes celebres*; see for example the disputes over wage policies in Poplar (*Roberts v. Hopwood* [1925] A.C. 578; Keith-Lucas 1962; Branson 1979), and council house rents policies in St. Pancras (*Taylor v. Munrow* [1960] 1 W.L.R. 578) and Clay Cross (*Asher v. Lacey* [1973] 1 W.L.R. 412, *Asher v. Secretary of State for the Environment* [1974] 2 W.L.R. 446; Mitchell 1974; Skinner and Langdon 1974). After 1972 the district auditor's function in respect of unlawful expenditure (but not loss owing to wilful misconduct) changed from that of an adjudicator to quasi-prosecutor. However this did not deter the district auditor recently pursuing a surcharge action as a result of the decision of the London Borough of Camden to settle locally a national strike of manual workers employed by local authorities. The strike was settled on terms favourable to the local workforce and the district auditor applied for a declaration that an element of the wages paid to manual workers was contrary to law. In *Pickwell v. London Borough of Camden* [1983] 2 W.L.R. 583 the Divisional Court refused to make the declaration on the ground that the district auditor had demonstrably failed to make out the case that the wage rates were unlawful on the basis of *Wednesbury* principles of unreasonableness.

The *Pickwell* decision thus seems to indicate that the legal framework of the 1982 Act will not cause a new wave of auditor activism. Nevertheless, as we shall see (section 7.2.3), other legal and political developments suggest that the auditor's powers and functions will remain controversial.

7.2.3 Default. The financial security systems of local authorities are underpinned primarily by the authority's power to raise rates. So long as this power exists the creditworthiness of local authorities seems guaranteed. The restrictions imposed on the power in recent years, however, could potentially affect this system. Sections 1 and 2 of the Local Government Finance Act 1982 placed certain curbs on this power by prohibiting the making of supplementary rates and precepts, but of greater potential significance have been the powers in the Rates Act 1984 to limit the freedom of designated authorities to make a rate (see section 2.4). This raises the possibility of an unbridgeable revenue-expenditure gap emerging and requires a re-examination of local authority financial security systems. Furthermore, given the recent history of central-local conflicts, the possibility of local authority default is not entirely remote. Local authorities seeking to challenge central government expenditure policies have threatened two courses of action which could possibly lead to default; refusing to raise a rate and adopting a policy of deficit financing.

The tactic of refusing to raise a rate on the financial terms set by central government has been quite popular among confrontation-minded rate-capped local authorities for two main reasons. First, rating authorities were under no statutory obligation to make a rate by any particular date (*cf.* precepting authorities: General Rate Act 1967, s. 12(6)). Secondly, this tactic was used with some degree of success by Liverpool City Council in 1984. Labour took control of Liverpool in the 1983 elections and found their reflationary budget plans constrained by their historically determined expenditure target. The council therefore found itself unable to agree a budget and rate before the start of the 1984/85 financial year. Eventually, after negotiations with central government leading to concessions on Urban Programme allocation and modifications of housing subsidy arrangements (the latter affecting all authorities), the council agreed a budget and rate on July 11, 1984 (Midwinter 1985).

Inspired by the Liverpool approach, nine of the sixteen Labour-controlled rate-capped authorities commenced the 1985/86 financial year without having set a rate. They were joined by Liverpool who, although not rate-capped, still considered the available expenditure choices unacceptable. By the end of June, however, all but one authority, the London Borough of Lambeth, had made a rate. Pressure on these authorities arose from an action for judicial review against Hackney London Borough Council. In *R.* v. *London Borough of Hackney, ex p. Fleming* (Q.B.D.) April 16, 1985 (unreported) Woolf J. granted an order of mandamus requiring the council to make its rate but giving it until the end of May to do so. Woolf J. stated that, although there is no express provision stating by what date the authority should make a rate, in accordance with general principles and section 151 of the 1972 Act (see section 7.2.1 above), the authority is under a duty to exercise its discretion reasonably and in the interest of its ratepayers. Although the precise period depended on the facts of each case Woolf J. felt that, "in the absence of a reasonable explanation, not to make a rate by the beginning of a financial year or within a reasonable time thereafter—I have in mind weeks rather than months—would prima facie be unreasonable and, therefore, in breach of duty."

However, the main pressure on these authorities came from the threat of surcharge action. Indeed, the Audit Commission directed that an extraordinary audit, under section 22 of the Local Government Finance Act 1982, of the accounts of both Lambeth and Liverpool be held. Losses stemming from the failure of these authorities to make a rate (at this stage only the loss of interest on the withholding by the Government of the rate rebate element of housing benefit and certain Treasury grants) were calculated and notices under section 20 were issued to the responsible councillors certifying that these losses were caused by their wilful misconduct. The councillors appealed unsuccessfully against certification; *Smith* v. *Skinner* (1986) *The Times,* March 6. Since the auditors seemed to be seeking to determine in principle the issue of wilful misconduct the possibility of their bringing similar actions against councillors in other authorities which deferred rate-making remains a possibility. Finally, the Government have acted to prevent the future use of this tactic by introducing legislation to impose a duty on rating authorities to make a rate on or before April 1 of that financial year (Local Government Act 1986, s. 1).

The other confrontationist tactic is the threat of deficit financing. Several of the rate-capped authorities which reluctantly made a rate for 1985/86 had been reported in the press as threatening to engage on an expenditure programme which would not match available revenues. Such action would be unlawful since local authorities are not empowered to carry over expenditure deficits for subsequent years: *Smith* v. *Southampton Corporation* [1902] 2 K.B. 244. Nevertheless, it could prove difficult to avert this course of action at an early stage by applying for judicial review since under the Rates Act only the rate limitation and not the maximum expenditure level has statutory force. Consequently a court would need to be convinced that the expenditure programme of any authority was not being and could not be tailed to its revenue resources.

The use of this tactic also raises the prospect of local authority default. However, central government possesses no general power of intervention in the event of default (*cf.* Housing Finance Act 1972, ss. 95 and 96; the Boards of Guardians (Default) Act 1926; and for a catalogue of existing default powers see House of Commons 1984h). Consequently, although the Government presumably would seek default powers if the situation arose, at present the main remedies would lie with creditors. Precepting authorities can require the authority to hand over the precept by seeking an order of mandamus: *R.* v. *Poplar Borough Council (No. 1)* [1922] 1 K.B. 72. Section 15 of the General Rate Act 1967 provides an alternative remedy by enabling the precepting authority to obtain a certificate from the Minister enabling it to apply for a receiver. On appointment the receiver would have the same power as if the precepting authority were a secure creditor.

As seen in section 7.2.1 above, local authority borrowing is secured against revenues and there is no preferential security. Further, as a statutory corporation a local authority cannot be made the subject of a bankruptcy petition nor can proceedings for liquidation be commenced against it (Grant 1984a, p. 21). The remedy provided in the regulations governing borrowing for creditors is that an application to the High Court can be made for a receiver to be appointed once any money due on any mortgage, stocks or bonds remains unpaid for 2 months (S.I. 1974 No. 518, reg. 9; S.I. 1974 No. 519, reg. 22). This hardly seems an efficacious remedy given the potential impact of local authority default on the credit rating of local authorities in capital markets. In this respect the role of the Public Works Loans Board as lender of last resort seems significant (Grant 1984b, pp. 61–63). Thus, while precepting authorities and lenders rank as secured creditors others, such as suppliers, contractors and employees, would be unsecured creditors dependent on private law action for debt.

It thus seems clear that financial security systems of local authorities established in the era of consensus and partnership have not been adjusted to deal with the issues which seem to be emerging in the era of conflict in the 1980s. This was highlighted by the insolvency crisis facing Liverpool City Council in October–November 1985 as a result of its decision to pursue the deficit budgetting tactic. In the end the crisis was averted by a financial package which involved capitalising some items of revenue expenditure, selling some of their interests as mortgages of land and extending borrowing facilities. One response of the Government has been to include a provision in the Local Government Act 1986 requiring local authorities to obtain the consent of mortgagors before disposing of their interest as mortgagee (Pt. III).

7.3. Market Disciplines

The most important development in terms of financial discipline in local government has been the incorporation of market rationality into local services and local authority management structures. This development stems in part from the acceptance of analyses drawn from the school of public choice since market rationality is used as a criterion of restraint, accountability and effectiveness. We have already seen from the studies of functional developments that this trend may take various forms. In fact, 9 distinct though related forms of incorporating market rationality into local government may be discerned.

First, there are *asset sales*. These are a key part of the Government's economic policy. The main programme has been the transference of public corporations to the private sector (Brittan 1984). The main form of asset sales in local government has been the sale of land and buildings. Although the privatisation of public corporations has captured greater public attention, the amount raised by local government asset sales, mainly council house sales (section 4.2), has in fact realised more income than that received from the sale of public corporations.

Secondly, there is the requirement of *direct competition* with the private sector for service provision. This may clearly be seen in relation to the objectives of the Transport Act 1985 which deregulates road service licensing, thereby opening up the field of public transport to competition, and requires public transport operators so to conduct themselves as not to inhibit competition between persons providing or seeking to provide public passenger transport services (section 3.7). Another example is provided by the statutory requirement that certain categories of local authority construction and maintenance work be undertaken by the D.L.O. only if it has submitted a tender in competition with private contractors (section 6.3.2). Furthermore, the Government have also proposed introducing new legislation extending compulsory competition provisions to such service activities as refuse collection, street cleansing, cleaning of buildings, vehicle maintenance, ground maintenance and catering services. It is also proposed that this legislation would contain powers enabling the Secretary of State to direct the authority to reissue tendering invitations if it had been done in a way which unreasonably limited competition (DoE 1985). It was expected that this legislation would be included in the 1985/86 Parliamentary timetable but the Government decided that since there was not sufficient time for all proposed measures this Bill would be deferred.

The requirement of competition is itself a powerful mechanism of discipline but it is closely related to a third form of market discipline, that of requiring the *contracting out* of services. One example which has been dealt with is the assisted places scheme under the Education Act 1980 (section 5.3.1), a form of contracting out of education responsibility to the private sector. However the Government have tended to encourage rather than require contracting out of services. Consequently, since local authority powers and duties are generally formulated in terms of "securing" or "making arrangements" for the provision of services, there is no need for new legislation to enable local authorities to do so. Several Conservative-controlled authorities have done so, mainly in relation to labour-intensive services such as refuse collection, cleaning, maintenance and catering services (*e.g.* Scott and Benbow 1983, Minogue and O'Grady 1985). The only power in effect to require contracting out is section 17 of the Local Government, Planning and Land Act 1980 which empowers the Secretary of State to direct a local authority to cease to have the power to use its D.L.O in respect of certain types of work. Similar powers were contemplated for the proposed legislation relating to competition. This legislation was to include a power to enable any term or condition included in an invitation to tender or a contract to be declared void if it is not directly related to the performance of the contract. The aim was therefore to restrict the local authority's control over a contractor's employment arrangements and act as an aid to contracting out of services.

The fourth form of incorporating market rationality into local government is the promotion of *economic pricing* policies. The Layfield Report in 1976 expressed concern about inconsistencies in local authority charging policies, felt that charges could play a greater role in financing local services and recommended further study in this area (Layfield 1976, p. 140). This was accepted by the Labour Government (DoE 1977a, para. 6.25–6.26) and work has been undertaken (*e.g.* Coopers and Lybrand Assocs. 1981). This has been given a greater impetus by the Conservative Government. In some areas the aim has been to cover the administrative costs of the service; see, for example, the Local Government Planning and Land Act 1980, s. 87 which introduces a scale of fees payable for processing applications for planning permission. In others the objective has been to give local authorities greater freedom to charge and to encourage them to increase charges: examples of this may be seen in the Health and Social Services and Social Security Adjudications Act 1983, Pt. VII enabling authorities to charge such fees as they consider reasonable for a range of social services; the Education Act 1980, ss. 22 and 23 giving similar freedom in relation to school meals charges; and the Housing Act 1980, Pt. VI introducing a new subsidy system which has been operated in a manner designed to encourage authorities to increase housing rents (see section 4.3 above). Some of these policies are influenced by the aim of eliminating the redistributive element in collectively provided services on the ground that redistribution via income transfers is more efficient.

Fifthly, through a variety of mechanisms the Government has sought to advance *efficiency* in local government. This may be seen most clearly in the Audit Commission's remit to go beyond issues of financial probity and to undertake "'value for money" audits (section 7.2.2). While no objection may be made to the principle of having regard to economy, efficiency and effectiveness in any organisation, in the context of pressures for expenditure reductions the emphasis tends to be placed on undertaking cost-cutting exercises rather than improving the effectiveness of public services in meeting social need. Since the 1982 Act is geared primarily to the auditor's responsibilities the Government proposed to include a provision in the competition legislation making local authorities subject to an explicit statutory duty to have regard to value for money in relation to all their functions (DoE 1985, para. 8). A further example of the establishment of mechanisms to promote efficiency is Part II of the Local Government, Planning and Land

Act 1980 which requires local authorities to publish information on unit costs, performance indicators, manpower statistics and other financial information and to publish an annual report on financial affairs. The objective, it appears, is to promote comparison between authorities, although inter-authority comparison seems exceedingly difficult. Again, the emphasis in these "openness" provisions is on encouraging efficiency in the narrowest sense of that term,.

Sixthly, the Government is seeking to restructure local authority responsibilities in such a way that local authorities constitute *market support mechanisms* rather than being able to undertake their functions in a manner that challenges market rationality. The restructuring of public transport and housing responsibilities aims to establish public transport and public housing as residual activities which support private market provision rather than providing alternatives to the logic of the market. But this restructuring is probably seen most clearly in relation to planning and land development where local authority functions have been reorientated towards aiding, promoting and underwriting private sector initiatives (see Chap. 6).

The last three forms of injecting market rationality into local government structures are closely related. The seventh is the reorganisation of local authority services in accordance with *individualistic principles of action*. This primarily involves the elimination of systems based on the socialisation of costs or cross-subsidisation. Again it is most clearly to be seen in developments in public transport and housing; in housing, for example, it involves a weakening of the historic costs financing system, the increase of rents to economic levels and the targeting of subsidy on individuals through means-tested housing benefit.

The eighth and ninth forms are designed to provide external checks on local authority action through the promotion of *ratepayer influence* and *consumer influence*. The attempt to increase ratepayer influence can be seen in grant reforms which have transferred a greater proportion of the marginal cost of expenditure to local ratepayers (section 2.3). This strategy was given a tremendous boost by the reiteration in the *Bromley* decision of a fiduciary duty owed to ratepayers. Since then certain decision-making processes have been restructured in order to increase ratepayer influence; see, for example, section 13 of the Rates Act 1984 which imposes a duty on local authorities to "consult persons or bodies appearing to it to be representatives of industrial or commercial ratepayers in its area about its proposals for expenditure and the financing of expenditure in the next financial year." Consumer influence provides an alternative check on local authorities. The traditional discretionary powers of local authorities in the areas of education and housing, the main areas of collective service provision, have been restricted by imposing on local authorities a legal framework which gives greater parental choice in education (section 5.3.4) and provides for tenant consultation in housing (section 4.5). Even the extension of the rights of public access to local authority meetings, minutes of meetings and documents in the Local Government (Access to Information) Act 1985 can be viewed as another method of strengthening both ratepayer and consumer influence.

These various forms of injecting market rationality into local government structures potentially could have a profound cumulative influence on the status of local authorities. Public bodies can be involved in areas of social and economic activity in any of three ways; provision, subsidy and regulation (Le Grand and Robinson 1984, pp. 3–6). Local authorities traditionally have performed a governmental role as executant bodies organised around the principles of collective provision and collective financing of services. The introduction of market rationality into local government, however, implies a rejection of the efficacy of collective provision and financing of services. In effect, the Government's aim has been to require local authorities to withdraw from *public provision* of services, to *reduce subsidies* and to *deregulate*. These objectives directly cut across the traditional organisation of local government.

7.4 Evaluation

The sustained attempt by the Conservative Government to incorporate various forms of market rationality into local government structures is essentially ideological. The justifactory theory, public choice analysis, is long on theory and short on empirical study. In fact there is very little evidence to indicate that private sector organisations are more efficient than public bodies (Millward 1982), let alone that effectiveness can be equated with efficiency. Furthermore, the solutions which emerge depend on the analytical framework adopted for assessing the nature of the problem. Thus, cross-subsidisation is condemned as inefficient and inequitable, but is examined only within council housing or a public transport operator's network. If the framework of analysis were extended to include public subsidies to owner-occupiers through income tax relief on mortgage interest payments or tax relief on company cars (alongside other subsidies to private car users) the nature, efficiency and equity of cross-subsidisation within the local service would assume an altogether different tenor. Furthermore, cross-subsidisation seems to be an equally significant phenomenon in private organisations.

This is not to say that there are not problems within local government. It would be surprising indeed if organisations the size of local authorities were without their problems; a medium sized county council, for example, will employ around 20,000 people and have a property portfolio worth over £500 million on the open market (Banham, 1984 p. 274). Local authorities undoubtedly experience such problems as poor management, lack of co-ordination of their services, poor quality of service, insufficient sensitivity to local needs and lack of accountability to consumers or taxpayers (Donnison 1984). There are, however, a broad range of possible solutions which do not require withdrawal and the replacement of governmental initiatives with the processes and outcomes of the market.

There are thus many criticisms which may be made of the types of market-based disciplines which the Government is attempting to impose on local authorities. *Asset sales*, particularly council house sales, have generally been sold below market value and, given the nature and scale of social need, such sales are difficult to justify on equitable or efficiency grounds. *Competition provisions* are potentially unfair since local authorities are expected to act as model employers and, with the scale of surplus capacity currently in the private sector, it is highly likely that private bodies will be able to undercut local authority tenders. *Contracting out* can result in new problems of regulation by contract and may blur lines of accountability. *Economic pricing policies* may undermine the original redistributional objectives of service provision; these objectives may not adequately be dealt with through income transfers because of the problems of take-up and the poverty trap. The *promotion of efficiency* causes problems because there is a great deal of pressure to reduce costs by changing the nature of the service; this may in fact result in inefficiencies when seen from a broader viewpoint. *Market support policies* place a great deal of faith in the ability of market processes, even with subsidies, to solve problems which often the market originally created. And the promotion of *individualism, ratepayer and consumer influence* asserts an individualistic and atomistic explanation of the operation of social processes that is contradicted by many analyses of the functioning of structures of social action.

Thus it is hard to avoid the conclusion that the objective of imposing market-based disciplines on local authorities is an ideologically-motivated policy which is designed to lower the standards of local services and thereby to encourage people to turn to the private sector for the satisfaction of their needs, to reduce the wages and working conditions of local authority employees and diminish the strength of public sector unions, and to create new markets for private firms suffering the loss of markets and profitability as a result of economic recession.

Chapter 8

THE REORGANISATION OF METROPOLITAN GOVERNMENT

8.1 Introduction

The history of local government structure during the last 150 years has been closely tied to the phenomenon of urbanisation. Institutional reforms in the nineteenth century may be viewed as a response to the problems of urban growth which required public action. But these reforms created a local government system which was divided along urban-rural lines. As a result, further reforms required by continuing urban growth in the twentieth century did not materialise because authorities were locked into a conflict over territory, status and tax base which was imposed by the nineteenth century structure (Alexander 1985, p. 52). When the local government system was eventually comprehensively reorganised, the nature of reforms which materialised was significantly influenced by the problem of metropolitan areas, those large urban areas which formed a single integrated economic unit, but were composed of socially and politically distinct and diverse communities.

The London Government Act 1963 reduced the number of local authorities in the London area from around 100 to 34; the Greater London Council (GLC), 32 London borough councils and the City of London Corporation. The GLC was "essentially an embodiment of the idea of metropolitan unity"; the old London County Council (L.C.C.) had reached its peak population in 1901 and thereafter urban growth was accommodated outside its boundaries so that by 1939 the population of the outer built up area equalled that contained in the L.C.C. area (Young 1984, p. 70). Thus, although the boroughs were considered to be the primary units of local government, the GLC was intended to perform an important all-London strategic role.

London government reform demonstrated the possibility of achieving comprehensive structural reorganisation. Furthermore, when it was followed by the reorganisation of local government in England and Wales under the Local Government Act 1972, the form of this reorganisation also embodied the principle of metropolitan government. However, while the principle was readily accepted, there was a considerable amount of disagreement over number, boundaries and functions. The result was that, while metropolitan county councils (M.C.C.s) were established in the six major conurbations in England, their boundaries were drawn tightly around the built-up areas and their functions were limited, with the district councils exercising most powers (Leach 1985, pp. 18–23).

The contexts in which these metropolitan authorities had to operate were significantly different. The M.C.C.s were completely new authorities with no previous history and had to struggle to justify their existence in the face of district councils, many of which, as county boroughs, had been unitary authorities and resented the loss of functions to M.C.C.s. The GLC, having the traditional authority of the L.C.C. to build on, did not have this problem in inner London, where there had been no tradition of strong borough government, although they did have a somewhat analogous problem in their relations with outer London boroughs.

Nevertheless there are certain similarities, in particular because both sets of reforms were the responsibility of Conservative Governments which tend to be ambivalent about creating strong metropolitan authorities. Many believe, as a result, that the metropolitan authorities created were inherently unstable institutions; as Ken Young (1984, p. 171) has put it, they have too little power to be effective but too much to be acceptable. Thus, while they have promoted imaginative policies in public transport, waste disposal, the arts and, against a background of urban decline, economic development, they have been unable to develop a powerful strategic role (Flynn *et al.* 1985, Chaps. 2, 3; Forrester. *et al.* 1985, Chaps. 6, 8). In the M.C.C.s this has been highlighted in their planning role, where the tightness of their boundaries has resulted in clashes between the M.C.C. and surrounding shire counties (*e.g.* Bridges and Vielba 1976). With the GLC the crucial battle has been with the outer London boroughs over its attempt to develop strategic housing policies (Young and Kramer 1978).

The boundary issue has been a further source of tension and instability; by drawing the boundaries tightly to protect the Conservative power bases in the shire counties the Government made it more likely that the metropolitan authorities would be Labour-controlled. Thus, although political control of the metropolitan authorities has changed regularly (Flynn *et al.* 1985, pp. 56, 76), since May 1981 all have been under Labour control. After 1981 the metropolitan authorities were all to varying degrees pursuing policies, such as public transport fares policies (section 3.4) or economic development and employment policies (section 6.3.3), which were opposed by the Conservative Government. All were overspending against the Government's expenditure targets (section 2.3.5); indeed the GLC and ILEA together accounted for around 40 per cent. of national overspend and those authorities, together with Merseyside County Council and South Yorkshire County Council, were on the Government's 1984/85 list of 18 rate-capped authorities (section 2.4). These developments essentially sealed the fate of the metropolitan authorities.

The catalyst was the impending election in 1983 and the Government's need for a major initiative in local government for their election manifesto. For a decade the Conservatives had been pledged to abolish rates but their 1981 Green Paper (DoE 1981a) had indicated that there were no viable and acceptable alternatives. At the last moment, therefore, they proposed two major reforms: rate control and the abolition of the GLC and the M.C.C.s (Forrester *et al.* 1985, pp. 60–66).

8.2 Streamlining the Cities?

When the Thatcher government was returned to power for a second term consideration had to be given to the abolition manifesto commitment, which had been included without detailed work on its implications having been done. The product of this exercise was the White Paper, *Streamlining the Cities* (DoE 1983d), published in October 1983. In this 32-page document the case for change was presented in 10 paragraphs. Three main reasons were given for abolishing the GLC and M.C.C.s: that the authorities have limited operational responsibilities; that they have sought to create a strategic role which has little basis in real needs; and that the expenditure levels of the authorities has been unreasonable (DoE 1983d, paras. 1.7–1.16). As a result the Government argued that:

> "The abolition of these upper-tier authorities will streamline local government in the metropolitan areas. It will remove a source of conflict and tension. It will save money, after some transitional costs. It will also provide a system which is simpler for the public to understand in that responsibility for virtually all local services will rest with a single authority" (DoE 1983d, para. 1.19).

Little detailed evidence was given for these assertions. For example, no detailed expenditure figures were given for the assertions that the authorities' expenditure levels were unreasonable or that the scheme for reorganisation would save money. The M.C.C.s therefore commissioned independent consultants to examine these expenditure issues. Their reports found that the analysis of M.C.C. expenditure in the White Paper was in many respects misleading and, in relation to the financial implications of reorganisation, that "the Government's claims for substantial savings are not supported by our analysis; indeed we conclude that there are unlikely to be any net savings as a result of the structural changes proposed by the Government and that there could be significant extra costs" (Coopers & Lybrand Assocs. 1983; 1984 p. 4).

Furthermore, in many respects the assertions were not substantiated by the proposals. Indeed the proposals seemed to indicate that while the Government rejected the idea of metropolitan authorities they still believed in the principle of metropolitan government. The reason is that, far from responsibility for metropolitan authority functions being transferred to the district or borough councils, the White Paper proposed that their functions would be largely allocated to joint boards or other countywide working arrangements between district/borough councils, central departments and other bodies. For example, over 70 per cent. by value of the M.C.C.s expenditure powers would be transferred to the police, fire and public transport joint boards and less than 20 per cent. of their services in expenditure terms would be devolved to district councils in circumstances preserving full accountability. In London joint boards would be required for fire and education but a host of special arrangements would be required for such functions as planning, waste disposal, traffic management, historic buildings and the arts.

Thus, if the metropolitan authorities have no real strategic role, why are so many of their functions being reorganised on a countywide basis? The Government's answer seems to be that the reorganisation will save money, create a simpler structure and remove a source of conflict and tension. We have already seen that the evidence suggests that the new structure is unlikely to provide a more efficient system for the planning and delivery of services. Perhaps what the Government mean about saving money is that it will be achieved by a reduction in the real level of service provision; since the White Paper proposed that the Secretary of State would control the budgets and manpower levels of the joint boards (DoE

1983d, para. 6.6) this would be within the Government's power. Also, the new managements proposed in the White Paper would establish a very complex network of interactive responsibilities and hardly create a simpler structure. This is borne out by a study of the non-financial aspects of the abolition proposals commissioned by the M.C.C.s which concluded that "the new arrangements will be considerably more complex and less accountable to the local electorate than the present structure and that it will lead to a slow, but increasingly marked, deterioration in the quality of local services provided" (PA Management Consultants 1984, p. 49). Finally, it is difficult to believe that abolition will remove conflict and tension since the metropolitan authorities were designed as vehicles for the resolution of conflict. The reforms at best will merely suppress rather than remove conflict and tension in metropolitan government; it seems even more likely that the new structure will "encourage conflict without providing any effective means of resolving it" (PA Management Consultants 1984, p. 50).

This is not to say that the existing structure of metropolitan government was ideal but rather that the defects within that structure were exploited by the Government to justify their abolition proposals. The evidence suggests that these proposals will not achieve their ostensible objectives. Instead the evidence indicates that the proposals will result in increased centralisation, increased costs, greater complexity, greater conflict, a reduced level of services and a reduction in local democratic control. It was surprising that the Government intended to embark on such a major organisational change without holding an independent inquiry which traditionally precedes such proposals. It was scarcely credible that the Government intended to implement their proposals without any serious presentation of evidence to justify them. It was entirely unacceptable that the Government, in the light of the available evidence and the complete lack of bi-partisan support for their proposals, should proceed with the speedy implementation of the reorganisation.

8.3 The Local Government (Interim Provisions) Act 1984

The complexity of the arrangements for abolition of metropolitan authorities and the reallocation of their functions was such that it could not be effected before April 1, 1986. However the complexity of the requisite legislation meant that it could not be introduced until the 1984/85 Parliamentary session. In addition to the short timescale between enactment and implementation, this timetable raised a difficult problem; elections for the metropolitan authorities were due in May 1985, eleven months before the authorities were to be abolished but in all probability prior to the enactment of the abolition legislation. There seemed three possible courses available to the Government for dealing with this problem: to allow the elections to take place; to cancel elections and allow the existing administration to continue in office for the remaining period; or to cancel elections and substitute an interim body to carry out the authority's functions for a period of transition.

Each course of action had potential drawbacks from the Government's viewpoint. If the elections took place as normal they could be turned into a referendum on the Government's proposals; given the responses reflected in public opinion polls to abolition, this had to be avoided by the Government (Forrester *et al.* 1985, p. 80). If the existing administrations were empowered to continue in office this would extend Labour control of the metropolitan authorities for a further year. If an interim body were substituted, however, the Government might either be accused of gerrymandering, since the interim body would probably be composed of representatives of the district and borough councils and this could conceivably result in it not being subject to Labour control, or alternatively it could face non-co-operation from the constituent district or borough councils.

The Secretary of State chose the last course of action, the cancellation of the May 1985 elections and the substitution of an interim body to run the authorities for the last 11 months of their existence, and in March 1984 introduced a Bill designed to give effect to these proposals. The Bill was especially controversial in three respects. First, the effect of substituting an interim body composed of appointed borough councillors would have the effect of changing political control of the GLC from Labour to Conservative. Secondly, there were doubts about the efficacy of an interim body. Finally, the Bill proposed to abolish the 1985 metropolitan authority elections before Parliament had decided on the principal issue of whether or not to abolish the authorities.

The Bill had a stormy passage through Parliament. Party discipline ensured its passage through the Commons but it survived its Second Reading in the Lords by only 20 votes. Subsequently the Lords passed an amendment to the effect that elections should not be cancelled until the main abolition Bill had been enacted. Since that Bill would not be enacted before May 1985 this entirely frustrated the substitution proposal. The Government therefore decided to accept the sense of the amendment and to reconstruct the form of the Bill around the principle of deferral.

The Local Government (Interim Provisions) Act 1984 thus provided for the suspension of the 1985 elections and the extension of the terms of office of councillors for the metropolitan authorities (s. 2). However, in an attempt to control action designed to frustrate abolition, the Secretary of State acquired powers to prescribe a quorum for the meetings of those councils (s. 3), to obtain information relating to their functions (s. 5) and to control the powers of metropolitan authorities to incur expenditure under section 137 of the Local Government Act 1972 (s. 7), to dispose of land (s. 8) and to enter into contracts generally worth in excess of £100,000 (s. 9). Furthermore, section 6(1) authorised the Secretary of State not to consider proposals for the alteration of M.C.C. structure plans or the Greater London Development Plan: see *GLC* v. *Secretary of State for the Environment* (1983) *The Times*, December 2; *R.* v. *Secretary of State for the Environment ex p. GLC* [1985] J.P.L. 543. This Act thus paved the way for the principal Bill which was introduced in that year and received the Royal Assent on July 16, 1985.

8.4 The Local Government Act 1985

8.4.1 Introduction. Section 1 of the Local Government Act 1985 provides that on April 1, 1986 the GLC and the M.C.C.s "shall cease to exist." The remaining 105 sections and 17 schedules make arrangements for the transfer of metropolitan authority functions to other bodies. Part II deals with the transfer of functions to metropolitan district councils and London borough councils. Parts III and IV deal with the transfer of functions to new authorities and Part V makes special arrangements in respect of the responsibility of metropolitan authorities for the arts, recreation and voluntary organisations. The remaining parts deal with consequential financial and administrative arrangements: staffing arrangements (Pt. VI); the establishment of residuary bodies to handle certain remaining responsibilities once the authorities are abolished (Pt. VII); financial provisions (Pt. VIII); and miscellaneous and supplementary provisions (Pt. IX).

8.4.2 Transfer of Functions to District or Borough Councils. The functions which are being transferred to district or borough councils are those concerning town and country planning (ss. 3–7; Scheds. 1–3), highways and road traffic (s. 8; Scheds. 4, 5), waste regulation and disposal (ss. 9, 10; Sched. 6), land drainage and flood prevention (s. 11; Sched. 7), responsibilities relating to the administration of justice (ss. 12–15), functions conferred by local Acts (s. 17) and building control, trading standards and various forms of licensing responsibilities (s. 16; Sched. 8).

Fairly complex arrangements are required for the transfer of town and country planning functions, because the existing legal framework reflects a two-tier allocation of responsibilities which is based on a division between strategic and detailed issues. As we have (section 6.2.2), since 1981 the district councils outside London have undertaken the vast bulk of development control functions; the Act thus generally standardises the position nationwide. The main difficulty therefore concerned development plans. The solution proposed in the Act is the creation of unitary development plans (U.D.P.s) which combine in one plan the functions of structure and local plans. This is achieved by dividing the U.D.P. into two parts; Part I is a statement formulating the authority's general policies and Part II, which must be in general conformity with Part I, their proposals for the development or other use of land in their area (Sched. 1, para. 2(2)(5)). Thereafter the procedures are similar to those for the preparation, adoption and approval of structure and local plans (Sched. 1, paras. 1–9), although for neatness of form the Secretary of State is given a general power to direct that the whole or any part of a U.D.P. be submitted to him for approval (Sched. 1, para. 7(1)). Provision is made to enable two or more local planning authorities jointly to prepare a U.D.P. (Sched. 1, para. 12). Indeed, local planning authorities in Greater London are required, before the abolition date, to establish a joint committee to consider "matters of common interest relating to the planning and development of Greater London" (s. 5). Finally, the GLC's functions related to listed buildings, conservation areas and ancient monuments are transferred, not to the borough councils, but to the Historic Buildings and Monuments Commission (s. 6, Sched. 2).

In fact, there are few functions where there is straightforward transfer of responsibility to district or borough councils. The transfer of functions, for example, is in certain aspects the occasion for centralising various responsibilities. Thus, the Secretary of State may direct that certain of the roads which were the responsibility of the GLC become that of the Department of Transport by designating them as trunk roads (Sched. 4, para. 53). The Secretary of State has acquired powers to issue and enforce guidance concerning the exercise of traffic powers (Sched. 5, para. 6). And there is a power to enable water authorities to assume responsibility for land drainage functions in the event of default by district or borough councils (Sched. 7, para. 6).

Perhaps of greater importance than those centralisation measures, however, are the reserve powers vested in the Secretary of State. Section 95 of the 1985 Act requires district and borough councils to form joint committees in each area by September 1, 1985 for the purposes of making preparations for the transfer of functions, to consider whether those functions could with advantage be discharged jointly by those councils, and to consider making schemes for providing grants to voluntary organisations (s. 48) and collecting research information on matters concerning their areas (s. 88). In addition to this provision, the Secretary of State possesses various powers of direction. Thus, the Secretary of State may at any time before the abolition date direct two or more councils to make a scheme for local valuation panels (s. 14(2)). The Secretary of State has the power to establish joint authorities for waste disposal (s. 10) and trading standards (Sched. 8, para. 15) if it appears more advantageous than the then existing arrangements. And if the Secretary of State is not satisfied with the joint arrangements which have been devised in relation to traffic control then this function may be transferred to the Secretary of State (Sched. 5, para. 10).

In general, therefore, the Act does not envisage a simple transfer of functions to district or borough councils of matters which were the responsibility of the metropolitan authorities. In respect of most of these functions the Government envisages that varying degrees of joint action will be required.

8.4.3 The New Authorities. The Act provides for the establishment of three joint authorities in each metropolitan county to undertake the M.C.C.'s functions relating to police (ss. 24, 25, 37), fire and civil defence (ss. 26, 37, 38), and passenger transport (ss. 28, 39, 40). The London Fire and Civil Defence Authority is the only joint authority established for Greater London (s. 27) since the Home Secretary is the police authority for the metropolitan police district (Metropolitan Police Act 1829, s. 1) and L.R.T. has taken over passenger transport functions (section 3.5 above).

Each joint authority shall consist of members of the constituent district or borough councils who are appointed by those councils to be members of the authority (ss. 26(3), 27(2), 28(3)). The one exception concerns the police authorities where one third of the members are magistrates (ss. 24(3), (5); 25(2)(4)). The numbers of members appointed to a joint authority by a constituent council is specified in Schedule 10 of the Act, although the Secretary of State, having regard to the number of local government electors in the areas of the councils, may by order make alterations in the numbers (s. 29). A constituent council may at any time terminate the appointment of a person appointed by it to a joint authority and appoint another in his or her place (s. 31). In making and terminating appointments, however, each constituent council must "ensure that the balance of parties for the time being prevailing in that council is reflected in the persons who are for the time being members of the authority and for whose appointment the council is responsible" (s. 33). Each constituent council must also make arrangements for enabling members of that council to put questions to members who are also members of a joint authority on the discharge of that authority's functions (s. 41).

In the White Paper the Government also proposed that the education service in inner London should be provided by a joint authority (DoE 1983d, para. 2.20). However, after consultations the Government changed its mind and announced that the "nature, scale and importance of the education service in inner London taken together justify a directly elected authority in this special case." (House of Commons 1984i). Thus the Act provides for the establishment of the Inner London Education Authority as a body corporate, with its members elected for a term of office of four years (ss. 18, 19). The Authority, however, must in each financial year consult with inner London councils about its expenditure and main policy objectives in the next financial year and if during that year it proposes to change or add to its objectives it must consult with those councils (s. 21). Furthermore, the Authority and the councils must have regard to guidance provided by the Secretary of State as to matters to be regarded as main policy objectives and generally as to consultation (s. 21(5)).

These new authorities created by the 1985 Act are subject to strict central control. They are placed on a similar financial footing to local authorities: they are entitled to block grant (s. 69), have similar borrowing powers (s. 70) and may issue precepts to the appropriate rating authorities (s. 68). However, for the first three years each new authority is deemed to have been designated for rate limitation without general principles for determining the expenditure levels being applied to them (s. 68(6)). In effect, this gives the Secretary of State a broad discretionary power to determine the expenditure level of each new authority. Also the Secretary of State is given for the first three years the power to make regulations providing for the submission to him by the authority, or for the making by him of schemes with respect to the discharge of the functions of these authorities (s. 85(1)). These schemes may apply to the number of persons employed by the authority, the authority's arrangements for obtaining any services, supplies or facilities, and the authority's organisation and arrangements for managing its affairs (s. 85(2)). The authority is under a duty to discharge its functions in accordance with such schemes (s. 85(1)).

Finally, the Secretary of State has significant reserve powers in relation to the new authorities. In the Bill the Secretary of State was to have obtained reserve powers to abolish the ILEA in 1992. This provision, however, was defeated in the House of Lords and this defeat was accepted by the Government. Consequently, the Act merely empowers the Secretary of State to undertake a review of the exercise of ILEA's functions before March 31, 1991 (s. 22). In respect of the joint authorities, however, the Secretary of State may by order transfer their functions to the district or borough councils (s. 42).

8.4.4 Transitional Arrangements. In addition to extending the functions of the Staff Commission established under section 4 of the Local Government (Interim Provisions) Act 1984 (ss. 50–56) and establishing residuary bodies to inherit outstanding GLC and M.C.C. debts, make compensation payments and administer pension funds (ss. 57–67), the Act gives the Secretary of State further powers to ensure the effective implementation of its provisions. Thus, sections 89–93 limit various powers of the metropolitan authorities by making their exercise subject to the consent of the Secretary of State. These powers include extending the controls over disposals and contracts laid down in sections 8 and 9 of the Local Government (Interim Provisions) Act 1984 (s. 93); controlling any agreement or arrangements entered into after March 21, 1985 under which the GLC and M.C.C.s assume liabilities which are not wholly discharged before the addition date (s. 92); and controlling any grant made to a local authority by a metropolitan authority or any relevant assistance given to it (s. 91). This last provision is primarily designed to control the GLC's "stress borough scheme" operated under the authority of section 136 of the Local Government Act 1972 and which has a resource redistributive effect by enabling the GLC to fund a range of projects mainly in inner city areas (McArdell 1984).

Perhaps the broadest power of the Secretary of State is that under section 101 which enables him by order to make "such incidental, consequential, transitional or supplementary provision as appears to him to be necessary or expedient ... for the general purposes or any particular purposes of this Act." This power includes the power to amend, repeal or revoke any provision of any Act passed before the abolition date (s. 101(2)(c)). Finally, the relevant authorities and their officers are under a duty to co-operate with each other and generally to exercise their functions so as to facilitate the implementation of the Act (s.97).

8.5 Conclusions

There is little in the form of the Local Government Act 1985 which might cause us to modify the assessment of the Government's reorganisation proposals outlined in the White Paper. No simple transfer of functions to district and borough councils will result; elaborate joint arrangements will be required in order effectively to exercise these functions and new authorities have been created to carry out the more important functions undertaken by the metropolitan authorities. That the actual transfer of functions to district and the borough councils is likely to prove ineffective was recognised by the House of Lords in amending the Bill to require the establishment of joint authorities to deal with highways and traffic in London and waste disposal in each of the metropolitan areas. These amendments, however, were overturned by the House of Commons. Nevertheless it is not at all clear that the joint authorities will prove effective bodies, as there are considerable doubts about the ability of such bodies efficiently to carry out their tasks and they certainly represent a weakening of local democratic accountability and a centralisation of control. The reforms undoubtedly do not constitute a streamlining of metropolitan government.

The evidence thus suggests that the Government's concern was to remove the metropolitan authorities rather than establish a simpler or more effective system of local government in the metropolitan areas. This reorganisation scheme seems quite unworkable; indeed the extent of the reserve powers conferred on the Secretary of State suggests that, to some extent this is recognised by central government. Consequently, instability is unlikely merely to be a feature of the transitional period since it is an aspect of the very nature of these reforms. The abolition of these seven metropolitan authorities is therefore unlikely to provide a permanent solution to the difficulties in providing local government services to the 18 million people who live in these areas.

Chapter 9

THE RESTRUCTURING OF CENTRAL-LOCAL GOVERNMENT RELATIONS

9.1 Central-Local Government Relations

We saw in Chapter 1 that, with the restructuring of local government functions this century, local government has increasingly performed a social welfare role. These functional changes have had a significant impact on central-local government relations in the post-war period. Central government has assumed a co-ordinating and directive role on the ground that there are critical limitations on the ability of local authorities independently to pursue redistributive policies. Indeed central government seem to have viewed local authorities, in certain circumstances, as executory agencies for national policies. Thus a high degree of central influence may be a corollary of the existence of a high proportion of redistributive functions vested in local government.

The primary role of law in central-local government relations during the post-war period has been essentially to facilitate the establishment of a constitutive structure within which central departments and local authorities could negotiate and bargain over the manner in which governmental functions would be exercised. The first function of law was therefore to cast the basic duties of local authorities in broad, and often highly subjective, terms. This maximised the formal legal autonomy of local authorities and nullified the potentially restrictive effect of the *ultra vires* doctrine. Another function of law was to provide central departments with a wide range of powers of supervision over local authorities. Also the constitutive structure created an essentially closed administrative system: third parties were vested with few formal legal rights *vis-à-vis* local authorities and central departments, the law did not establish norms regulating relations between central and local authorities, and the courts did not play an active supervisory role.

This legal structure, however, did not reflect the reality of relations between central departments and local authorities. Conventional administrative practices, rather than legal formalities, determined relations. The role of law was merely to establish a flexible structure within which central and local authorities could

186

bargain and negotiate over the manner in which these functions would be exercised (see further Rhodes 1981, Chap. 5). Furthermore, courts were felt to be inappropriate supervisory bodies for reasons of both institutional design and legal culture.

Institutional design reasons include the problems of cost, expertise and the inappropriateness of adversary procedures for dealing with disputes of a polycentric nature. Furthermore, as many studies have shown (*e.g.* Macaulay 1963; Beale and Dugdale 1975), any externally imposed settlement of a dispute between mutually interdependent bodies which must maintain continuing relations is unlikely to provide a genuine resolution of that dispute. Consequently, negotiation rather than adjudication is likely to provide a more efficient means of dispute resolution.

The issues relating to legal culture are more controversial. Nevertheless, there is a school of thought which argues that the replacement of judicial supervision of local authorities, a characteristic of the nineteenth century system, together with the administrative supervision of central departments in the twentieth century, was a progressive development since the judicial culture was a profoundly individualistic one and the courts would be biased against action organised along collectivist lines (Laski 1926; Jennings 1936; Griffith 1979; McAuslan 1983).

The role of law in central-local government relations in the postwar period has therefore been that of establishing a structure for the mediation of interests in areas (such as education, council housing and town and country planning) in which central departments and local authorities played a predominant role. This system was legitimated by its success in delivering good quality services and being able to inspire confidence that private interests were being regulated for the public good. It was effective only in so far as central and local government, at some basic level, shared a common sense of purpose.

During the 1970s the strains on this system were becoming increasingly evident. This was partly because of certain policy failures, such as high-rise system-built council housing (Dunleavy 1981) or the failure to generate confidence in the processes or products of the planning system (Dennis 1970; Davies 1972). This led to attacks on the legitimacy of the system, which was characterised as essentially a mechanism of social control (*e.g.* Cockburn 1977). But primarily it was a product of the economic crisis. The idea of mutuality of objective became severely strained since the crisis highlighted the divergence of local and central interests as service provider and financier; social needs were increasing while available revenues to finance services were diminishing. With the Conservative Government's proposed solution local-central conflict became endemic and the traditional system began to disintegrate.

As a result, the central-local relationship has been both politicised and juridified. Politicisation occurs when the idea that central and local government have a basic mutuality of objective is widely questioned, since the administrative processes and practices rest largely on consensus. Juridification arises from two sources. First, in the short-term, it results from the consequent breakdown in traditional administrative practices; the legal relationship, of minor importance traditionally, now defines the limits of central departments and local authorities' ability of independent action. Secondly, in the longer-term, it is a product of the particular form which the Conservative Government's attempted solution has taken. These trends are examined by looking to the phenomenon of politicisation in both local and central government and to the nature of these processes of juridification.

9.2 Politicisation in Local Government

The traditional pattern of central-local government relations largely went hand-in-hand with the dominance of *administrative politics* and *managerial professionalism* in local government. Administrative politics arise where officers dominate; they set the agendas and are the source of policy innovation, although of course they must be able to carry the members with them (Hill 1972, pp. 131–134). Managerial professionalism as an organisational principle draws its strength both from bureaucratic authority and professionalism and obtains its character through the operation of three principles: *functionalism*, which is the organisation of the local authority along departmental lines in accordance with its major functional responsibilities; *uniformity*, which requires that "the services of the authority are provided to a common standard and on a common pattern throughout the area of the authority"; and *hierarchy* or the top-down direction of the authority, which is viewed as a necessity of political control (Stewart 1985, pp. 99–102). The comparative lack of conflict over policies, together with the nationalisation of standards and practices through the influence of professional associations, created a climate which enabled central-local relations to be conducted through conventional administrative arrangements.

During the last 20 years the traditions of administrative politics and managerial professionalism have been challenged. Managerial professionalism has been partially challenged by the corporate approach which subverts the principle of functionalism and may contest professional prescriptions (Bains 1972; Stewart 1985, pp. 108–115). Administrative politics has been largely replaced by *ideological politics*. Ideological politics emerges when local elections are contested along party lines, with political parties submitting manifestos as a basis for electoral choice. (On the legal status of manifestos see Loughlin 1983, pp. 100–106). Once control of the local authority is won, power is allocated along party lines and party discipline is maintained (Hill 1972, pp. 211–216). In recent years, as a result of policy failures, economic crisis and the general polarisation of politics, the nature of ideological politics in local government has become more intense. This intensity has been reflected on both the right and left in politics and has certain shared characteristics:

"Both view local government in the context of its relationship to the economy. . . .Both express hostility towards the managerial power of the professional local government officer. . . . Both express a concern for greater participation by the public, though one sees it through individual consumer control in a free market and the other through an expansion of collective decision-making at the grass roots of politics. Both also desire to see local government in some way 'opened up', either to the influence of market forces or to the influence of popular political pressure" (Gyford 1985, pp. 92–93).

Nevertheless, as Gyford recognises, these superficial similarities lead to highly contrasting policies. Those of the radical right essentially echo the policies of the Conservative Government. Consequently, since developments in Labour-controlled authorities are of greater significance in examining the impact of politicisation on central-local relations, the politics of "municipal socialism" will form the primary focus for this section.

The strongholds of radical Labour politics are to be found in the major industrial cities. These cities grew with industrialisation and urbanisation in the nineteenth century and their local authorities were in the vanguard of public service provision. Today these cities are faced with problems similar to those they confronted in the nineteenth century; urban poverty, substandard housing and the need to modernise infrastructure. Today, however, expenditure in these areas cannot be justified on the ground of underwriting the process of production because these cities are experiencing *deindustrialisation* (Massey and Meegan 1978; Fothergill and Gudgin 1982; Scott 1982b) and *deurbanisation* (Young and Mills 1982). These structural changes have imposed a heavy burden on local authorities. In part this is because of the difficulty of adjusting expenditures downward in association with population declline or business loss, but mainly it is because the major cities contain higher than average proportions of groups dependent on local authority services (Loughlin 1985a, Table 1). These radical changes have contributed to fundamental changes in local politics in these areas.

The politics of municipal socialism is quite distinctive. The councillors tend to be younger, were weaned on community politics in the 1970s and often are employed in the public sector in a professional capacity (Walker 1983; Gyford 1984). Many are generally prepared to work almost full-time as councillors, as a result of informal secondment arrangements or special responsibility allowances under section 177A of the Local Government Act 1972 (Skelcher 1983). They also tend to challenge the assumption that the State is a neutral instrument of power. Consequently this form of politics is concerned to examine the role of local government in the local economy, its relationship with the communities it exists to serve and also to challenge the traditional instrumental role assigned to local government within the system of government.

Thus, an important element in their policies is an attempt to devise local economic and social strategies which complement one another. We have seen that one feature of their economic strategy is their economic development and employment policies, where the objective is not merely to bolster the market but to make strategic interventions and to obtain greater understanding of the nature of the local economy (section 6.3.3. above). These authorities have also begun to examine their role as contractor and supplier of goods and services. Some authorities are beginning to use their power of procurement to achieve socio-economic objectives; the GLC even established its own Contracts Compliance Unit (*cf.* DoE 1985c). On the supply side they have challenged the traditional hierarchical and professionalised structures of service delivery, the most widely publicised aspect of which has been the various schemes for decentralising management of services to neighbourhood offices (Fudge 1984; Wright 1984).

The policies of municipal socialism directly challenge the tradition of managerial professionalism since both the organisation and method of conduct of local authority business have been politicised. The most obvious manifestations are the appointment of staff who are known to support the politics of the majority party and the involvement of the public sector unions in local authority decision-making. Furthermore, not only has ideological politics replaced administrative politics but in some areas the nature of ideological politics is itself being transformed into a form of *bargaining politics* (Hill 1972, pp. 216–224). This has emerged in part because alongside deindustrialisation and deurbanisation has been the phenomenon of class dealignment with the result that the Labour party has, in certain areas, sought to forge alliances with community groups in order to win their support. Thus some authorities have devised special initiatives in relation to women (Goss 1984) and ethnic minorities (Ouseley 1984), have provided grant aid to a variety of community organisations and have politicised issues such as the control of police forces (Holdaway 1982; Regan 1982; Loveday 1983) and civil defence (with the establishment of "nuclear free zones").

Inevitably this form of politicisation of local government has led to a broad range of disputes. Member-officer disputes have occurred, such as the protest by Lambeth social workers over political involvement in disciplinary action over the Tyra Henry case (Boseley 1985). Member-member disputes have arisen because of political control over sub-committees resulting in the restriction of councillors' access to information: *R.* v. *Hackney L.B.C., ex p. Gamper* [1985] W.L.R. 1229. Political polarisation has resulted in a spate of inter-authority disputes: *e.g. Bromley* v. *GLC* [1983] 1 A.C. 768; *R.* v. *GLC, ex p. Royal Borough of Kensington and Chelsea* (1982) *The Times*, April 7; *R.* v. *ILEA, ex p. Westminster City Council* [1986] 1 W.LR. 28; *R.* v. *GLC, ex p. Westminster City Council* (1984) *The Times*, December 31; *R.* v. *GLC, ex p. Westminster City Council* (1985) *The Times*, January 22. And politicisation has created tensions in the local authority associations, culminating in the decision of Labour controlled authorities in London to set up a new Association of London Authorities: see *R.* v. *GLC, ex p. Bromley* (1984) *The Times*, March 27.

Thus, politicisation in local government in recent years has contributed to the destablisation of the traditional pattern of central-local government relations. Local authorities have engaged in a radical re-evaluation of their roles as employer, contractor, service provider and regulator. These developments undoubtedly have contributed to the Government's decision to set up an inquiry into the conduct of local authority business (Widdicombe 1985). The inquiry was asked to pay particular attention to the responsibilities of elected members, the respective roles of members and officers and the need to clarify the limits and conditions governing discretionary spending by local authorities, and was asked to report by March 1986. They were also asked to produce an interim report by July 1985 on the use of discretionary powers for overt political campaigning. Although this report (Widdicombe 1985) was ambivalent in its conclusions the Government introduced legislation prohibiting local authorities from publishing a very broad range of publicity material (Local Government Act 1986, Pt. II).

9.3 Politicisation in Central Government

Politicisation in central government has occurred as Governments recognised that they were unlikely to achieve their objectives through traditional administrative bargaining arrangements. They have therefore sought to use their powers to establish a hierarchical version of the central-local relationship. This is not without its difficulties, since it seeks to deny the fact that the complexities of modern government seem to require that a variety of agencies co-ordinate their activities in pursuit of certain objectives. Consequently the Government has been required to acquire powers which maximise its discretionary powers; this has led to a politicisation in the use of law as an instrument of policy. This practice has taken several forms.

First, since the Government often did not know quite how to achieve their objectives, they have acquired statutory powers which enable them to alter the rules as the results become known; this may clearly be seen in relation to the abolition of the Metropolitan Authorities (section 8.4) and the direct labour organisation legislation (section 6.3.2). Secondly, if existing statutory powers were felt to be inadequate the Government had no hesitation in promoting new legislation; here the history of local government finance since 1979 (Chap. 2) is most illustrative. Since speed was of the essence these practices had other ramifications: *e.g.* a failure to present a reasoned justification for new legislation—such as *Streamlining the Cities* as the basis for legislation to abolish the metropolitan authorities (section 8.2); inadequate consultation arrangements—see *R.* v. *Secretary of State for Social Services, ex p. A.M.A.* [1986] 1 W.L.R. 1; and active use of the guillotine in the House of Commons—the guillotine has been applied to the Education Act 1980 (twice), the Housing Act 1980 (twice), the Transport Act 1983, the Housing and Building Control Act 1984, the Rates Act 1984, the Local Government Act 1985 (twice) and the Transport Act 1985 (twice). Thirdly, the Government have had no qualms in using Parliament to overturn inconvenient judicial decisions—see *R. v. Secretary of State for Transport, ex p. GLC* [1985] 3 W.L.R. 574 and the London Regional Transport (Amendment) Act 1985.

Central government has thus been prepared to use the legal powers of the State to the full, without the restraints of conventional practices governing the conduct of relations between central departments and local authorities. The ideas of gradual and evolutionary change and of co-ordination and co-operation between the two tiers of government, as well as the sense of restraint that comes both from the acceptance of pluralism as a political value and the recognition of the limited efficacy of central direction, have all virtually disappeared. Governmental action in pursuit of their contentious view of what the public interest requires has therefore provided a good example of "political hyperactivism," a condition in which government undertakes action "before experience has generated enough understanding of our situation to allow us to act wisely" (Minogue 1978, pp. 120–121). Such action has also flouted principles of constitutionalism (Johnson 1980; Loughlin 1985b).

9.4 Juridification of Central-Local Government Relations

9.4.1 The Collapse of Traditional Arrangements.
Politicisation in both local and central government has contributed to the collapse in traditional administrative practices concerning the conduct of central-local relations. With this collapse the legal relationship between central departments and local authorities, which had previously been of minor importance, becomes critical. Local authorities have been required to examine closely the nature of their legal powers and duties because expenditure constraints cause them to re-examine the pattern of their activities and also because the law defines the parameters of their formal autonomy. Central departments are concerned about their legal powers because they outline the limits of their available power to control local authorities. In this sense, the collapse of traditional administrative arrangements results in juridification of the central-local relationship.

This process of juridification is riddled with uncertainties because it has not generally been the function of law to define powers and duties in this sphere of government with a great deal of precision. The courts have thus been prevailed upon to elucidate such basic issues as the nature of the legal relationship concerning the apportionment and payment of grants: *R. v. Secretary of State for the Environment, ex p. Brent London Borough Council* [1982] 2 W.L.R. 693; *R. v. Secretary of State for the Environment, ex p. Hackney L.B.C.* (1983) 81 L.G.R. 688; *R. v. Secretary of State for the Environment, ex p. Hammersmith and Fulham London Borough Council* (1985) *The Times*, May 18; *R. v. Secretary of State for Education, ex p. ILEA* (June 19 1985) (D.C.) (unreported). But there are other fundamental questions, such as the nature of the basic statutory duty of local authorities to provide education (section 6.3.2. above), which remain undefined. This lack of precise legal definition has been used tactically by both central departments and local authorities. Thus Liverpool City Council was able to exploit the fact that the General Rate Act 1967 does not require rating authorities to make a rate by any particular date by deferring the setting of its 1984/85 rate until July 1984 (see section 7.2.3). But this lack of precise definition has also been used by the Government, since it has the effect of leaving ultimate legal responsibility for disagreeable decisions with the local authority. This was discovered by the London Borough of Hackney when it unsuccessfully argued that expenditure targets must incorporate some concept of attainability: *R. v. Secretary of State for the Environment, ex p. Hackney L.B.C.* (1985) *The Times*, May 11.

Although the courts have generally maintained a conservative stance during this period (see section 9.4.3) the exception to this was the articulation of the fiduciary concept in the *Bromley* case, which during a critical period in 1982/83 led to a juridification of many areas of local authority policy-making. This decision also provided the catalyst for a more general trend towards politicisation in the art of briefing counsel.

Many of the legal disputes consequent on the collapse of traditional arrangements have involved challenges to the exercise of the discretionary powers of the Secretary of State. Partly these concern powers recently acquired, but many disputes have arisen merely because the Secretary of State has been prepared to use existing powers in an interventionist manner. This therefore highlights the fact that this process of juridification is inextricably linked to the phenomenon of politicisation.

9.4.2 The Reformalisation of Local Government Law. We have seen that under the traditional system of central-local government relations the role of law was to establish a closed administrative system which achieved legitimacy through its success in being able to deliver good quality services. With the collapse of this traditional system the Conservative Government have sought to re-establish a legitimate system by structuring local authority discretion through the imposition of detailed statutory procedures on local authority decision-making (*e.g.* section 3.4.3), by vesting third parties with formal legal rights (*e.g.* sections 4.5, 5.3.4), by imposing specific duties on local authorities (*e.g.* section 4.2), by incorporating notions of market rationality into local government structures (section 7.3) and by seeking to reconstitute local authorities as market support agencies (*e.g.* section 6.2).

The Government is therefore seeking to re-establish the legitimacy of the local government system by requiring it to operate within the "impartial" processes of market exchange relations and formal general rules. This attempt to structure local authority action in accordance with formal legal rules, or to achieve a reformalisation of local government law, may also result in a general process of juridification in this sphere of government. However, what must be emphasised is that this process of reformalisation in central-local government relations has been entirely one-sided. While an attempt is being made to reconstitute local authorities as rule-bound organisations, the same legislation has been extending the discretionary powers of the central government; indeed many of the new powers acquired by central government appear to have been drafted in forms consciously designed to minimise the possibility of judicial review (see, *e.g.* Housing Act 1980 s. 23; Transport Act 1983, s. 5(2); Rates Act 1984).

9.4.3 The Role of the Courts. Under the traditional arrangements we have seen that, for reasons both of institutional design and legal culture, the courts have performed a peripheral role in central-local government relations. With politicisation and juridification, however, it seems likely that adjudication will to some degree replace administrative negotiation and bargaining as a method of resolving disputes. Whether the courts are able adequately to undertake this task must therefore be examined.

In recent years efforts have been made to deal with institutional design defects. The starting point was the Order 53 procedural reforms in 1977, replacing the traditional administrative law remedies with the concept of an application for judicial review: S.I. 1977 No. 1955; see also S.I. 1980 No. 2000, Supreme Court Act 1981, s. 31. The significance of these procedural reforms has been increased by other developments. First, since *O'Reilly* v. *Mackman* [1983] 2 A.C. 237, the courts have ensured that the application for judicial review will be the preponderant procedure for public law cases. Secondly, Order 53 was followed by reforms enabling applications for judicial review to be heard by a single judge in the Queen's Bench Division. As a result the Lord Chief Justice has selected a group of judges with some specialist knowledge of administrative law to sit on all cases of judicial review. Finally, in 1981 a Practice Direction was issued enabling all cases raising public law issues to be transferred to the Crown Office list to be heard by a specialist judge: [1981] 1 W.L.R. 1296 (Blom-Cooper 1982).

These reforms, although not without their problems (Craig 1983, pp. 498–511), go some way towards meeting design defects. They attempt to establish a rational procedure which will be relatively simple and speedy and will be presided over by judges familiar with public law issues. In effect they have resulted in the establishment *de facto* of an Administrative Division of the High Court. The critical question, therefore, is whether these procedural reforms can remedy perceived defects in the legal culture.

It would appear that the dominant legal culture is still rooted in nineteenth century individualism. Elsewhere I have argued that this normativistic culture has dominated public law thinking and has been responsible for much of the formalism and inactivism which has characterised judicial review this century (Loughlin 1985c). Thus in relation to judicial review of local authority action the principles enunciated by Lord Greene M.R. in *Associated Provincial Picture Houses Ltd.* v. *Wednesbury Corporation* [1948] 1 K.B. 223 still provide the basic guidelines. Nevertheless, these principles are so general and variable that they may be used essentially as a mask to conceal the real basis for judicial decisions and it seems true to say that "the courts have been able to use the *Wednesbury* formula as a convenient rationalisation for varying policy decisions" (Elliott 1980 p. 583). Thus if a court chooses to intervene it will tend to utilise the "irrelevant considerations" aspect of that formula, whereas if it declines it will emphasise those parts of the judgement dealing with "unreasonableness." Recently this fact has been recognised by Ormrod L.J. who suggested that Lord Greene's judgement is "coming to be regarded as a proposition of law in itself" and is "indiscriminately used to express different and contradictory ideas": *Pickwell* v. *Camden L.B.C.* [1983] Q.B. 962, 1000.

It is the dominance of this normativistic legal culture which also helps to explain the way in which the House of Lords in the *Bromley* case were able to enunciate the concept of a fiduciary duty which a local authority owes to its ratepayers. This is an anachronistic and unworkable concept (Loughlin 1983, pp. 106–121). However, what must also be emphasised is the fact that the Divisional Court was able authoritatively and speedily to nullify any potentially restrictive impact of the concept. They did so by reasserting the authority of general principles of administrative law in the face of ratepayer action (*R.* v. *GLC, ex p. Royal Borough of Kensington and Chelsea* (1982) *The Times,* April 7; *British Leyland Cars* v. *Birmingham District Council* [1982] R.V.R. 92; *R.* v. *Greenwich L.B.C., ex p. Cedar Transport Group Ltd.* (1983) *The Times,* August 3) and confining the Bromley decision to its facts (*R.* v. *Merseyside County Council, ex p. G.U.S. Ltd.* (1982) 80 L.G.R. 639; *R.* v. *London Transport Executive ex p. GLC* [1983] Q.B. 484). Is this decisive action by the Divisional Court therefore to be taken as sowing the seeds for a modern administrative law jurisprudence?

This seems highly unlikely. In the central-local government context the courts have been fashioning an entirely procedural approach to judicial review. That is, they have defined their role essentially as being that of ensuring that affected authorities have a fair opportunity to present their case before a potentially adverse decision is taken by the Secretary of State: see *R.* v. *Secretary of State for the Environment ex p. Brent L.B.C.* [1982] Q.B. 593; *R.* v. *Secretary of State for the Environment ex p. Hammersmith and Fulham L.B.C.* (1985) *The Times,* May 18; *R.* v. *Secretary of State for Social Services, ex p. A.M.A.* [1986] 1 W.L.R. 1; *cf. R.* v. *Secretary of State for the Environment ex p. GLC* (1985) *The Times,* February 28. Otherwise, the courts have been unprepared to articulate norms governing central-local relations; this is highlighted most clearly in their rejection of arguments that the use of the term "principles" in statutes requires the Secretary of State to disclose the philosophy, rationale or justification for his action: *R.* v. *Secretary of State for the Environment ex p. Brent LBC* [1982] Q.B. 593, 635; *R.* v. *Secretary of State for the Environment ex p. Hackney L.B.C.* (1984) 148 L.G. Rev. 691 (D.C.); (1985) *The Times,* May 11 (C.A.). And see also *R.* v. *Secretary of State for the Environment, ex p. Nottinghamshire C.C.* [1986] 2 W.L.R. 1. Thus, although there has been some attempt to refashion the heads of judicial review under concepts of illegality, irrationality, procedural impropriety and proportionality (*Council of Civil Service Unions* v. *Minister for Civil*

Service [1984] 3 All E.R. 935, 950), this seems likely to be merely an exercise in relabelling.
This is hardly surprising. While the procedural reforms deal with certain aspects of institutional design defects they do not get to the roots of the issue; namely, that to play an effective supervisory role the courts would be required to adjudicate on complex, polycentric issues in which fact-finding processes (see *Hackney* case above) and the fashioning of relief (see *A.M.A.* case above) raise sensitive political issues. The danger is that, unless they can define a precise constitutional role, the courts would be required to play a mediating role which might challenge their independence and hence legitimacy.

The British constitutional structure militates against the courts being able to create such a role, since the government can effectively jettison any attempt at establishing norms governing conduct between intergovernmental bodies by having new rules enacted. As a result our view of adjudication is far removed from what it would become if the courts were actively to undertake a supervisory role. Thus the normativist view of adjudication is that of a bipolar, self-contained episode where the controversy is over a set of completed events and right and remedy are interdependent. This may be contrasted with the characteristics of public law litigation identified by Chayes (1976, p. 1302): the scope of the action is not exogenously given but is shaped by the parties; the party structure is not rigidly bipolar but amorphous; the fact inquiry is predictive and legislative rather than historical and adjudicative; relief is forward-looking, flexible and with important consequences for absentees; the remedy is not imposed but negotiated; its administration requires the continuing participation of the court; the judge plays an active role throughout; and the action concerns a grievance about the operation of public policy. Clearly, without a well-defined constitutional role, the courts could not undertake an active supervisory function without being presented with a fundamental challenge to their authority.

9.5 The Outlook

In the post-war period the role of law in central-local government relations has essentially been that of establishing a constitutive structure within which the interests of central departments, local authorities and affected individuals and groups could be mediated. This structure was controlled by an ambiguous partnership between central and local authorities; third parties had few formal rights and

the structure was largely legitimated by its success in the management of governmental tasks. In recent years this system has been
subject to severe strains. In fact the roots or manifestations of these
strains may be traced to all of the main forms of crisis tendencies
under advanced capitalism identified by Habermas (1975, Pt. II).
Thus, many of the strains of the system have their roots in the
economic crisis which Britain has been experiencing since the mid-
1970s. Within the political-administrative system this has manifested itself as a *rationality crisis* since the structure of central-local
government relations has collapsed in the wake of the disappear-
ance of the economic assumptions which underpinned it. However,
the system could already be said to be experiencing a relatively
independent *legitimation crisis* arising from a growing lack of
confidence by affected interests about the ability of the system
adequately to perform its functions; this was manifested by
concerns over poor management, deficiencies in service co-ordination, poor quality of service and the inability to establish a
conception of the public interest which commands confidence.
Finally, these factors have combined to produce a *motivation crisis*,
or a challenge to social integration, the most sensational manifesta-
tion of which the civil disturbances which affected British cities in
1981 and 1985 (see, *e.g.* Scarman 1981) and which have affected
significantly the climate within which many local authorities
operate.

The Conservative Government has in response attempted a fairly
radical restructuring of the system. In order to deal with the
legitimation and motivation crisis it has sought to restore legitimacy
through a process of reformalisation of local government law and
purpose and direction through the injection of notions of market
rationality into local government structures. In order to deal with
the rationality crisis it has restructed the central-local relationship in
a hierarchical form.

If the Government is successful in its restructuring attempts, then
this will have a profound effect on the status of local government
and the hypothetical local government life cycle (see section 1.6)
may prove a reality. There are, however, major difficulties with the
Government's approach. The attempt to reorganise local government on the basis of market exchange relations is fundamentally
ideological: it denies that public bodies have a different rationale to
private bodies, it asserts as an article of faith that private bodies, are
more efficient than public bodies, and it rests on an atomistic view
of individuals and an idealised view of the operation of markets.

9.5 *The Restructuring of Central-Local Government Relations*

The effect of these reforms on the functioning of the economy, the system of government and on social integration thus remain matters of controversy.

Furthermore, centralisation as a response to the rationality crisis is similarly not without its difficulties since the complexity of governmental tasks is such that a variety of agencies are required to undertake them and there are significant limitations to "top-down" central direction (Barrett and Hill 1984). Nevertheless, centralisation has been an inexorable process under the Conservative Government. The Government, for example, has been promoting agencies which can be more easily controlled to deal with particular problems previously handled by local authorities. Examples include the Housing Corporation and housing associations to meet the gap left by the decline of the private rented sector, the M.S.C. to promote Y.T.S. and N.A.F.E. schemes, U.D.C.s to regenerate inner areas, and L.R.T. to run London's public transport system. It has been using specific grants, such as improvement grants (section 4.4), education support grants (section 5.3.1) and U.D.G.s (section 6.2.3), to control innovation and to target resources towards central government priorities. And it has maintained active supervision over the implementation by local authorities of central government policies. But if the policy/action relationship is seen as a continuum and government is viewed as an exercise in learning then it seems highly likely that centralisation will provide no solution to the rationality crisis.

Finally, we should reflect on the process by which these reforms have been introduced. The process of reformalisation of law, for example, has been entirely one-sided; legislation imposing rules on local government has generally been accompanied by discretionary powers vested in the Secretary of State. And these powers have been used in a highly interventionist manner. Nevil Johnson (1980 pp. 139—140) recently identified four primary factors which have led to what he considers to be the current state of constitutional bankruptcy: the realisation that parliamentary sovereignty can be seriously misused; the misuse of the majority principle; the erosion of conventions governing institutional roles and relationships; and the politicisation of the law. These factors succinctly identify the key constitutional issues in central government's conduct in its relations with local authorities. Essentially the Government are utilising idealised versions of democracy and institutional performance in order to highlight inadequacies in local government and to justify curtailing their autonomy. This form of analysis has also been applied to other organisations such as trade unions (Simpson 1985) and the health service (see, *e.g.* S.I. 1985 No. 1067), but it has not been applied to the central government. This is a dangerous strategy; by weakening countervailing power bases and strengthening the power of the central State there is a real danger that pluralism as a political value will be jettisoned and an authoritarian regime will result. The issue for the future, therefore, is whether the trends identified are indeed part of a fundamental and inexorable process under advanced capitalism or whether these trends are contingent and are essentially the product of the package of ideologically motivated policies of a particular Government.

BIBLIOGRAPHY

AMA (1985) *Spending works: improving the economy by investing in local services* (AMA).

Adcock, B. (1984) "Regenerating Merseyside Docklands. The Merseyside Development Corporation 1981–1984" Vol. 55, no. 3 *Town Planning Review* 265.

Aldrich, R. and Leighton, P. (1985) *Education: Time for a New Act?* Bedford Way Papers 23 (Heinemann Educational Books).

Alexander, A. (1982) *The Politics of Local Government in the United Kingdom* (Longman).

Alexander, A. (1985) "Structure, centralisation and the position of local government" in M. Loughlin *et al.* (eds.) Chap. 3.

Arden, A. and Partington, M. (1983) *Housing Law* (Sweet & Maxwell).

Ascher, K. (1983) "The politics of administrative opposition–council house sales and the right to buy" Vol. 9, no. 2 *Local Government Studies* 12.

Audit Commission (1984a) *The impact on local authorities' economy efficiency and effectiveness of the block grant distribution system* (HMSO).

Audit Commission (1984b) *Bringing Council Tenants' Arrears Under Control* (HMSO).

Audit Commission (1984c) *Obtaining better value in education: aspects of non-teaching costs in secondary schools* (HMSO).

Audit Commission (1985) *Capital expenditure controls in local government in England* (HMSO).

BTURC (1983) *The Great Training Robbery* (Birmingham Trade Union Resource Centre/National Association of Teachers in Further and Higher Education).

Bacon, R. and Eltis, W. (1976) *Britain's Economic Problem: Too Few Producers* (Macmillan).

Bailey, S.J. (1982) "Do fewer pupils mean falling expenditure?" in R. Rose and E. Page (eds.) *Fiscal Stress in Cities* (Cambridge U.P.), Chap. 5.

Bailey, S. (1984) "Absurd framework" Vol. 4, no. 2 *Public Money* 6.

Bains, M. (1972) *The New Local Authorities: Management and Structure* (HMSO).

Ball, M. (1983) *Housing Policy and Economic Power* (Methuen).

Bibliography

Banfield, E.C. (1968) *The Unheavenly City. The nature and future of our urban crisis* (Little, Brown & Co).

Banham, J. (1984) "Are we being served by local government-some initial reflections" Vol. 55 *Political Quarterly* 273.

Barker, A. and Couper, M. (1984) "The art of quasi-judicial administration: the planning appeal and inquiry systems in England" Vol. 6 *Urban Law & Policy* 363.

Barlow, J. (1981) "The rationale for the control of local government expenditure for the purposes of macro-economic management" Vol. 7, no. 3 *Local Government Studies* 3.

Barnett, J. (1982) *Inside the Treasury* (A. Deutsch).

Barrett, S. and Hill, M. (1984) "Policy, bargaining and structure in implementation theory: towards an integrated perspective" Vol. 12 *Policy & Politics* 219.

Beale, H. and Dugdale, T. (1975) "Contracts between businessmen: planning and the use of contractual remedies" Vol. 2 *British Journal of Law & Society* 45.

Bennett, R.J. (1982) *Central grants to local governments: the political and economic impact of the rate support grant in England* (Cambridge U.P).

Bevan, R.G. (1980) "Cash limits" Vol. 1 no. 4 *Fiscal Studies* 26.

Binder, B.J.A. (1982) "Relations between central and local government since 1975- are the associations failing?." Vol. 8, no. 1 *Local Government Studies* 35.

Blaug, M. (1984) "Education Vouchers-it all depends on what you mean" in J. Le Grand and R. Robinson (eds.), Chap. 11.

Blom Cooper, L. (1982) "The new face of judicial review: administrative changes in Order 53" *Public Law* 250.

Blunkett, D. and Green, G. (1983) *Building from the Bottom* (Fabian Tract 491).

Board of Education (1944) *Principles of Government in Maintained Secondary Schools* Cmd. 6523 (HMSO).

Boddy, M. (1982) *Local Government and Industrial Development* (SAUS Occasional Paper 7, University of Bristol).

Boddy, M. (1984) "Local economic and employment strategies" in M. Boddy and C. Fudge (eds.), Chap. 7.

Boddy, M. and Fudge, C. (eds., 1984) *Local Socialism?* (Macmillan).

Boseley, S. (1985) "Social workers denounce council" *The Guardian* July 27.

Boyle, R. (1985) " 'Leveraging' Urban Development: a comparison of urban policy directions and programme impact in the United States and Britain" Vol. 13 *Policy & Politics* 175.

Bibliography

Boyne, G. (1984) "The privatisation of public housing" Vol. 55 *Political Quarterly* 180.

Bramley, G. (1983) "Rate-capping: do the economic and financial arguments stand up?" (mimeo, unpublished).

Bramley, G. (1984) "Grant-related expenditure and the inner city" Vol. 10, no. 3 *Local Government Studies* 15.

Bramley, G. *et al.* (1983) *Grant Related Expenditure: a review of the system.* (SAUS Working Paper 29, University of Bristol).

Bramley, G. and Evans, A. (1984) "Grant-related expenditure: an unsuitable basis for ratecapping" *Municipal Journal* February 17.

Branson, N. (1979) *Poplarism 1919–1925: George Lansbury and the councillors' revolt* (Lawrence & Wishart).

Breton, A. (1974) *The Economic Theory of Representative Government* (Macmillan).

Bridges, L. and Vielba, C. (1976) *Structure Plan Examinations in Public: A Descriptive Analysis* (Institute of Judicial Administration, University of Birmingham).

Brittan, L. (1982) "Local spending: striving for control" Vol. 2, no 2 *Public Money* 56.

Brittan, S. (1984) "The politics and economics of privatisation" Vol. 55 *Political Quarterly* 109.

Buchanan, C. (1963) *Traffic in Towns* (HMSO).

Burns, Sir W. (1980) *Review of Local Authority Assistance to Industry and Commerce* (DoE).

Buxton, R.J. (1970) *Local Government* (Penguin).

CDP (1977a) *Gilding the Ghetto* (Home Office).

CDP (1977b) *The Costs of Industrial Change* (Home Office).

CPRE (1981) *Planning-friend or foe?* (Council for the Protection of Rural England).

Carvel, J. (1985a) "40 per cent loss likely for transport" *The Guardian* January 23.

Carvel, J. (1985b) "Jenkin launches drive to aid inner cities" *The Guardian* April 19.

Chayes, A. (1976) "The role of the judge in public law litigation" Vol. 89 *Harvard Law Review* 1281.

Cockburn, C. (1977) *The Local State* (Pluto Press).

Coopers & Lybrand Associates (1981) *Service Provision and Pricing in Local Government* (HMSO).

Coopers & Lybrand Associates (1983) *Streamlining the Cities. An analysis of the Government's case for reorganising local government in the six Metropolitan Counties: first report.*

Bibliography

Coopers & Lybrand Associates (1984) *Streamlining the Cities. An analysis of the Government's proposals for reorganising local government in the six Metropolitan Counties.*

Council on Tribunals (1983) *The Annual Report of the Council on Tribunals for 1982/83.* H.C. 129 (HMSO).

Craig, P.P. (1983) *Administrative Law* (Sweet & Maxwell).

Crawford, C. and Moore, V. (1983) *"The Free Two Pence." Section 137 of the Local Government Act 1972 and Section 83 of the Local Government (Scotland) Act 1973* (CIPFA).

Cross, C.A. (1981) *Principles of Local Government Law* (Sweet & Maxwell, 6th ed.)

Cross, C. (1984) "Painting and the DLO accounts" *Local Government Chronicle* March 2, p. 250.

Cullingworth J.B. (1985) *Town and Country Planning in Britain* (Allen & Unwin, 9th ed.)

DES (1965) Circular No. 10/65 *The organisation of secondary education* (HMSO).

DES (1966) Circular No. 10/66 *School building programmes* (HMSO).

DES (1977) Circular No. 5/77 *Falling numbers and school closures* (HMSO).

DES (1980) Circular No. 2/80 *Procedure affecting proposals made under sections 12–16 of the Education Act 1980* (HMSO).

DES (1981a) Circular No. 6/81 *The school curriculum* (HMSO).

DES (1981b) Circular No. 2/81 *Falling rolls and surplus places* (HMSO).

DES (1982a) Circular No. 6/82 *The YTS: implications for the education service.* (HMSO).

DES (1982b) *Initial Government observations on the Second Report from the Education, Science and Arts Committee, Session 1981–82.* Cmnd. 8551 (HMSO).

DES (1982c) Circular No. 4/82 *Statutory proposals for secondary schools and falling rolls* (HMSO).

DES (1983) Circular No. 3/83. *The in-service teacher training grant scheme* (HMSO).

DES (1984a) *Consultation document on probation for newly appointed head teachers* (DES).

DES (1984b) *Report by Her Majesty's Inspectors on the effects of local authority expenditure policies on education provision in England-1983* (DES).

DES (1984c) *Parental Influence at School* Cmnd. 9242 (HMSO).

DES (1985a) *Education and Training for Young People* Cmnd 9482 (HMSO).

DES (1985b) *Better Schools* Cmnd. 9469 (HMSO).

DoE (1973) Circular No. 104/73 *Local Transport Grants* (HMSO).

DoE (1977a) *Local Government Finance* Cmnd. 6813 (HMSO).

DoE (1977b) *Housing Policy: A Consultative Document* Cmnd. 6851 (HMSO).

DoE (1977c) Circular No. 63/77 *Housing Strategies and Investment Programmes* (HMSO).

DoE (1977d) *Policy for the Inner Cities* Cmnd. 6845 (HMSO).

DoE (1977e) Circular No. 71/77 *Local Government and the Industrial Strategy* (HMSO).

DoE (1980a) *Local Government Finance. The Rate Support Grant Report (England) 1980* (HMSO).

DoE (1980b) Circular No. 19/80 *Action to correct overspend on housing investment programmes 1980/81* (HMSO).

DoE (1980c) Circular No. 22/80 *Development control-policy and practice* (HMSO).

DoE (1980d) Circular No. 9/80 *Land for private housebuilding* (HMSO).

DoE (1981a) *Alternatives to Domestic Rates* Cmnd. 8449 (HMSO).

DoE (1981b) Circular No. 23/81 *Local Government, Planning and Land Act 1980. Town and Country Planning: Development Plans* (HMSO).

DoE (1981c) Circular No. 38/81 *Planning and enforcement appeals* (HMSO).

DoE (1981d) Circular No. 10/81 *Local Government, Planning and Land Act 1980: Direct Labour Organisations* (HMSO).

DoE (1982a) *Housing Subsidies and Accounting Manual* (issued with DoE Circular No. 5/82) (HMSO).

DoE (1982b) Circular No. 23/82. *Local Authority Housing Project Control* (HMSO).

DoE (1982c) Circular No. 29/82. *Improvement of older housing: enveloping* (HMSO).

DoE (1983a) *Rates. Proposals for rate limitation and reform of the rating system.* Cmnd. 9008 (HMSO).

DoE (1983b) Circular No. 22/83 *Planning Gain* (HMSO).

DoE (1983c) *Urban development grant guidance notes* (DoE).

DoE (1983d) *Streamlining the Cities. Proposals for reorganising local government in London and the Metropolitan Counties* Cmnd. 9063 (HMSO).

Bibliography

DoE (1984a) Circular No. 21/84 *Housing and Building Control Act 1984* (HMSO).
DoE (1984b) Circular No. 14/84 *Green Belts* (HMSO).
DoE (1984c) Circular No. 15/84 *Land for Housing* (HMSO).
DoE (1984d) Consultation Paper *Simplified Planning Zones* (DoE).
DoE (1985a) *Home Improvement-A New Approach* Cmnd. 9513 (HMSO).
DoE (1985b) Circular No. 1/85 *The use of conditions in planning permissions* (HMSO).
DoE (1985c) Consultation Paper *Competition in the Provision of Local Authority Services* (DoE).
DoE (1986) *Paying for Local Government.* Cmnd. 9714 (HMSO).
DoT (1978) Circular No. 8/78 *Transport Act 1978: Public Transport Planning in the Non-Metropolitan Counties* (HMSO).
DoT (1982a) *Public Transport Subsidy in Cities* Cmnd. 8735 (HMSO).
DoT (1982b) *Urban public transport subsidies: an economic assessment of value for money* (DoT).
DoT (1983a) Circular No. 1/83. *Transport Act 1983* (HMSO).
DoT (1983b) *Public Transport in London* Cmnd 9004 (HMSO).
DoT (1984) *Buses* Cmnd. 9300 (HMSO).
Davies, J.G. (1972) *The Evangelistic Bureaucrat* (Tavistock).
Davies, K. (1983) *Local Government Law* (Butterworths).
Dawson, D.A. (1985) "Economic change and the changing role of local authorities" in M. Loughlin *et al.* (eds.) Chap. 2.
Dennis, N. (1970) *People and Planning* (Faber).
Dennison, S.R. (1984) *Choice in Education* (Hobart Paperback No. 19, IEA).
Department of Employment (1984) *Training for Jobs.* Cmnd. 9135 (HMSO).
Donnison, D. (1984) "The progressive potential of privatisation" in J. Le Grand and R. Robinson (eds.), Chap. 3.
Downs, A. (1957) *An Economic Theory of Democracy.* (Harper & Row).
Dunleavy, P. (1980) *Urban Political Analysis* (Macmillan).
Dunleavy, P. (1981) *The Politics of Mass Housing in Britain 1945-1975* (Oxford U.P.).
Elliott, M.J. (1980) "ACAS and judicial review" Vol. 43 *Modern Law Review* 580.
Elliott, M.J. (1981) *The role of law in central-local relations* (SSRC).
Ermisch, J. (1984) *Housing finance: who gains?* (Policy Studies Institute).

Bibliography

Evans, J.M. (1980) *de Smith's Judicial Review of Administrative Action* (Stevens 4th ed.)

Flynn, N. (1985) "Direct labour organisations" in S. Ranson, G.W. Jones and K. Walsh (eds.) *Between Centre and Periphery. The Politics of Public Policy.* (Allen & Unwin).

Flynn, N. and Walsh, K. (1982) *Managing Direct Labour Organisations* (Institute of Local Government Studies, University of Birmingham).

Flynn, N. Leach, S. and Vielba, C. (1985). *Abolition or Reform? The GLC and the Metropolitan County Councils.* (Allen & Unwin).

Forrest, R. and Murie, A. (1984) *Monitoring the Right to Buy 1980-1982* (SAUS Working Paper 40, University of Bristol).

Forrest, R. and Murie, A. (1985) *An Unreasonable Act? Central-local government conflict and the Housing Act 1980* (SAUS Study No. 1, University of Bristol).

Forrest, R. Lansley S. and Murie A, (1984) *A Foot on the Ladder? An evaluation of low cost home ownership initiatives* (SAUS Working Paper 41, University of Bristol).

Forrester, A. Lansley, S. and Pauley, R. (1985) *Beyond Our Ken. A Guide to the Battle of London* (Fourth Estate).

Foster, C.D. (1982) "Urban transport policy after the House of Lords' decision" Vol. 8, no. 3 *Local Government Studies* 105.

Foster, C., Jackman, R. and Perlman, M. (1980) *Local Government Finance in a Unitary State* (Allen & Unwin).

Forthergill, S. and Gudgin, G. (1982) *Unequal Growth* (Heinemann).

Fudge, C. (1984) "Decentralisation: socialism goes local?" in M. Boddy and C. Fudge (eds.) Chap. 8.

GLC Economic Policy Group (1983) *Jobs for a Change* (GLC).

Gauldie, E. (1974) *Cruel habitations: a history of working class housing 1780-1918* (Allen & Unwin).

Gibson, J. (1983) "Local "overspending": why the Government have only themselves to blame" Vol. 3 no. *Public Money* 19.

Gibson, M.S. and Langstaff, M.J. (1982) *An Introduction to Urban Renewal* (Hutchinson).

Glaister, S. (1984) "The allocation of urban public transport subsidy" in J. Le Grand and R. Robinson (eds.) Chap. 12.

Goss, S. (1984). "Women's initiatives in local government" in M. Boddy and C. Fudge (eds.) Chap. 5.

Gough, I. (1979) *The Political Economy of the Welfare State* (Macmillan).

Grant, M. (1979) "Britain's Community Land Act: a post mortem" Vol. 2 *Urban Law & Policy* 359.

Bibliography

Grant, M. (1984a) "Rate capping: the law and solvency." *Public Finance and Accountancy* (March), p. 19.

Grant, M. (1984b) *Rate Capping and the Law* (AMA).

Greenwood, R. (1981) "Fiscal pressure and local government in England and Wales" in C. Hood and M. Wright (eds.) *Big Government in Hard Times* (M. Robertson) Chap. 4.

Greenwood, R. (1982) "The politics of central-local relations in England and Wales 1974–1981" Vol. 5 *West European Politics* 253.

Griffith, J.A.G. (1966) *Central departments and local authorities* (Allen & Unwin).

Griffith, J.A.G. (1979) *Administrative law and the judges* (Haldane Society of Socialist Lawyers).

Gyford, J. (1984a) *Local Politics in Britain* (Croom Helm 2nd ed).

Gyford, J. (1984b) "Our changing local councillors" Vol. 68, no. 1119 *New Society* 181. May 3.

Gyford, J. (1985) "The politicisation of local government" in M. Loughlin *et al.* (eds.) Chap. 4.

H.M.Treasury (1980) *The Government's Expenditure Plans 1980-81 to 1983-84.* Cmnd. 7841 (HMSO).

Habermas, J. (1975) *Legitimation Crisis* (Beacon Press).

Hall, P. (1977) "Green fields and grey areas." *Proceedings of the Annual Conference of the Royal Town Planning Institute.*

Hall, P. (1984) "Enterprises of great pith." Vol. 53 *Town and Country Planning* 296.

Hambleton, R. (1980) *Inner Cities: Engaging the Private Sector* (SAUS Working Paper 10, University of Bristol).

Hambleton, R. (1981) "Implementing inner city policy." Vol. 9 *Policy and Politics* 51.

Hambleton, R. (1983) "Symposium on expenditure-based planning systems-developments in planning systems" Vol. 11 *Policy and Politics* 161.

Heigham, D. (1984) "Local "Overspending"." Vol. 4, no. 4 *Public Money* 12.

Hepworth, N. (1984) "Rate-capping: the reality."*The Times* January 16.

Herbert, Sir E. (1960) *Report of the Royal Commission on Local Government in Greater London* Cmnd 1164 (HMSO).

Heseltine, M. (1981) *Statement by the Secretary of State for the Environment to the Consultative Council on Local Government Finance* (June 2).

Bibliography

Hibbs, J. (1982) *Transport without Politics...?* (Hobart Paper 95, IEA).

Hill, M.J. (1972) *The Sociology of Public Administration* (Weidenfeld and Nicolson).

Hoath D.C. (1981) "The Housing Act 1980: A New Rent Act" *Journal of Social Welfare Law* 257 (Pt.I), 335 (Pt.II).

Hoath, D.C. (1982) *Council Housing* Sweet & Maxwell, 2nd ed.).

Holdaway, S. (1982) "Police accountability: a current issue" Vol. 60 *Public Administration* 60.

House of Commons (1972) Expenditure Committee, Second Report, Session 1972–73, *Urban Transport Planning.* H.C. 57 (HMSO).

House of Commons (1981a) Second Report from the Environment Committee. Session 1981–82. *Council House Sales.* H.C. 366 (HMSO).

House of Commons (1981b) Second Report from the Education, Science and Arts Committee, Session 1981–82 *The Secondary School Examinations and Curriculum* H.C. 116 (HMSO).

House of Commons (1981c) *H.C. Debates,* Vol. 998, col. 603 (February 9).

House of Commons (1982a) Second Report from the Environment Committee. Session 1981–82. *Enquiry into methods of financing local government in the context of Cmnd. 8449* H.C. 217 (HMSO).

House of Commons (1982b) Fifth Report from the Transport Committee. Session 1981–82. *Transport in London* H.C. 127 (HMSO).

House of Commons (1982c) First Report from the Environment Committee. Session 1981–82. *The private rented sector* H.C. 40 (HMSO).

House of Commons (1982d) *H.C. Deb.,* Vol. 17, cols. 465–66, Written Answers (February 11).

House of Commons (1982e) Seventh Report from the Select Committee on Education, Science and the Arts. Session 1981–82. *School Meals.* H.C. 505 (HMSO).

House of Commons, *H.C. Deb.,* Vol. 51, col. 428 (December 21, 1983).

House of Commons (1983b) Second Report from the Environment Committee. Session 1982–83. *Department of the Environment's Winter Supplementary Estimates 1982-83* H.C. 170 (HMSO).

House of Commons (1983c) Third Report from the Environment Committee. Session 1982–83. *The problems of management of*

Bibliography

urban renewal (appraisal of the recent initiatives in Merseyside) H.C. 18 (HMSO).

House of Commons (1984a) *H.C. Deb.*, Standing Committee G, col. 203. (February 7).

House of Commons (1984b) *H.C. Deb.*, Vol. 65, col. 684 (October 24).

House of Commons (1984c) *Rate Limitation Report*. H.C. 589.

House of Commons (1984d) *H.C. Deb.*, Vol. 64, col. 828 (July 24).

House of Commons (1984e) *H.C. Deb.*, Vol. 52, col. 664–666 Written Answers (January 26).

House of Commons (1984f) First Report from the Environment Committee. Session 1983–84. *Green Belt and Land for Housing* H.C. 275 (HMSO).

House of Commons (1984g) *H.C. Deb.*, Vol. 52, col. 348. Written Answers (January 20).

House of Commons (1984h) *H.C. Deb.*, Vol. 58, cols. 249–255. Written Answers (April 11).

House of Commons (1984i) *H.C. Deb.*, Vol. 57, col. 1124 (April 5).

House of Commons (1985a) Second Report from the Transport Committee. Session 1984–85. *Financing of Public Transport Services: the Buses White Paper* H.C. 38 (HMSO).

House of Commons (1985b) *H.C. Deb.*, Vol. 83, col. 863 (July 23).

House of Lords (1980) *H.L. Deb.*, Vol. 407, col. 185 (March 18).

Housing Research Group (1981) *Could local authorities be better landlords?* (City University).

Hughes, D. (1981) *Public Sector Housing Law* (Butterworths).

IEA (1978) *The Economics of Politics* (IEA).

Jackman, R. (1982) "Does central government need to control the total of local government spending?" Vol. 8, no. 3 *Local Government Studies* 75.

Jackman, R. (1984) "The Rates Bill: a measure of desperation" Vol. 55 *Political Quarterly* 161.

Jackman, R. (1985) "Local government finance" in M. Loughlin *et al.* (eds.), Chap. 7.

Jackson, P.M. (1982) "The impact of economic theories on local government finance" Vol. 8, no. 1 *Local Government Studies* 21.

Jackson, P.M., Meadows, J. and Taylor, A.P. (1982) "Urban fiscal decay in UK cities" Vol. 8, no. 5 *Local Government Studies* 23.

Jacobs, J. (1985) "UDG: the urban development grant" Vol. 13 *Policy & Politics* 191

Jenkin, P. (1984) *H.C. Deb.*, Vol. 64, Col. 335 (July 18).

Jenkin, P. (1985a) *H.C. Deb.*, Vol. 83, col. 1316 (July 25).

Jenkin, P. (1985b) *H.C. Deb.,* Vol. 80, col. 890 (June 12).

Jennings, W.I. (1936) "The courts and administrative law– the experience of English housing legislation" Vol. 49 *Harvard Law Review* 426.

Johnson, N. (1980) "Constitutional reform: some dilemmas for Conservatives" in Z. Layton-Henry (ed.) *Conservative Party Politics* (Macmillan).

Jones, G. and Stewart, J. (1982) "Rating reform" *Municipal Journal* January 22, p. 94.

Jones, R. (1985) *Local Government Audit Law* (HMSO) (2nd ed.).

Kent County Council (1978) *Education Vouchers in Kent: a feasibility study for the Education Department of Kent County Council* (Kent C.C.).

Keith-Lucas, B. (1962) "Poplarism" *Public Law* 52.

King, T. (1983) *Speech to the Conservative Party Annual Local Government Conference.* (February 19).

Kirwan, R.M. (1984) "The demise of public housing?" in J. Le Grand & R. Robinson (eds.) Chap. 9.

Laski, H.J. (1926) "Judicial review of social policy in England" Vol. 39 *Harvard Law Review* 832.

Layfield Sir, F. (1976) *Report of the Committee of Inquiry on Local Government Finance* Cmnd 6453 (HMSO).

Leach, B. (1985) "The government of the English provincial conurbations" Vol. 11, no. 1 *Local Government Studies* 17.

Leach, S. (1985) "Inner Cities" in S. Ranson, G.W. Jones and K. Walsh (eds.) *Between Centre and Periphery. The Poltics of Public Policy* (Allen & Unwin), Chap. 8.

Leather, P. (1983) "Housing (Dis?) Investment Programmes," Vol. 11, no. 2 *Policy & Politics* 215.

Leather, P. (1984) "Capital receipts and the housing programme." *Municipal Journal* February 10, p. 192.

Le Grand, J. and Robinson, R. 1984 (eds.) *Privatisation and the Welfare State* (Allen & Unwin).

Leung, H.L. *Redistribution of Land Values* Department of Land Economy, University of Cambridge Occasional Paper No. 11.

Liell, P. and Saunders, J.B. (1984) *Law of Education* (Butterworths, 9th ed.).

Loughlin, M. (1981) "Local government in the welfare corporate state" Vol. 44 *Modern Law Review* 422.

Loughlin, M. (1983) *Local government, the law and the constitution* Local Government Legal Society Trust.

Bibliography

Loughlin, M. (1985a) "Municipal socialism in a unitary state" in P. McAuslan and J. McEldowney (eds.) *Law, Legitimacy and the Consititution* (Sweet & Maxwell), Chap. 4.

Loughlin, M. (1985b) "Constitutional arguments and constitutionalist values in the debate over central-local government relations" in M. Goldsmith (ed.) *New Research in Central-Local Relations* (Gower), Chap. 8.

Loughlin, M. (1985c) "Administrative law, local government and the courts" in M. Loughlin *et al.* (ed.), Chap. 6.

Loughlin, M., Gelford, D. and Young, K. (eds.) (1985) *Half A Century of Municipal Decline 1935-1985* (Allen & Unwin).

Loveday, B. (1983) "The role of the police committee" Vol. 9, no. 1 *Local Government Studies* 39.

McArdell, C. (1984) "Grants: a discretion worth preserving." *Public Finance and Accountancy* (August), p. 26.

Macaulay, S. (1963) "Non-contractual relations in business: a preliminary study" Vol. 28 *American Sociological Review* 55.

McAuslan, P. (1983) "Administrative law, collective consumption and judicial policy" Vol. 46 *Modern Law Review* 1.

McCulloch, D. (1982) "The new housing finance system" Vol. 8, no. 3 *Local Government Studies* 97.

Macfarlane Report (1980) *Education for 16-19 Year Olds* (DES).

McKay, D.H. and Cox, A.W. (1979) *The Politics of Urban Change* (Croom Helm).

Mallaby, Sir G. (1967) *Report of the Committee on the Staffing of Local Government* (HMSO).

Mallinson, H. and Gilbert, M. (1983) "The urban development grant scheme" Vol. 268 *Estates Gazette* 970. (December 3).

Marshall, A.H. (1974) *Financial Management in Local Government* (Allen & Unwin).

Mason, C. (1984) "YTS and local education authorities: a context" Vol. 10, no. 1 *Local Government Studies* 63.

Massey, D. (1982) "Enterprise zones: a political issue" Vol. 6 no. 3 *International Journal or Urban and Regional Research* 429.

Massey, D.B. and Meegan, R.A. 1978 "Industrial restructuring versus the cities" Vol. 15 *Urban Studies* 273.

Matthews, R. (1985) "Cuts herald private sector role" *Roof* (Jan/Feb.), p. 3.

Maud, Sir J. (1967) *Report of the Committee on the Management of Local Government* (HMSO).

Mawson, J. (1981) "Changing directions in regional policy and the implications for local government" Vol. 7, no. 2 *Local Government Studies* 68.

Meredith, P. (1982) "Individual challenge to expenditure cuts in the provision of schools." *Journal of Social Welfare Law* 344.

Meredith, P. (1984) "Falling rolls and the reorganisation of schools." *Journal of Social Welfare Law* 208.

Merrett, S. (1979) *State Housing in Britain* (RKP).

Midwinter, A. (1985) "Setting the rate-Liverpool style." Vol. 11, no. 3 *Local Government Studies* 25.

Millward, R. (1982) "The comparative performance of public and private ownership" in E. Roll (ed.) *The Mixed Economy* (Macmillan).

Minister without Portfolio (1985) *Lifting the Burden* Cmnd. 9571 (HMSO).

Ministry of Housing and Local Government (1970) *Reform of Local Government in England.* Cmnd. 4276 (HMSO).

Ministry of Transport (1966) *Transport Policy* Cmnd. 3057 (HMSO).

Ministry of Transport (1967) *Public Transport and Traffic* Cmnd. 3481 (HMSO).

Minns, R. and Thornley, J. (1978) *State Shareholding. The role of local and regional authorities* (Macmillan).

Minogue, K. (1978) "On hyperactivism in British politics" in M. Cowling (ed.) *Conservative Essays* (Cassell).

Minogue, M. and O'Grady, J. (1985) "Contracting out of local authority services in Britain" Vol. 11, no. 3 *Local Government Studies* 35.

Mitchell, A. (1974) "Clay Cross" Vol. 45 *Political Quarterly* 165.

Moon, J. and Richardson, J.J. (1984) "Policy-making with a difference? The Technical and Vocational Education Initiative" Vol. 62, no. 1 *Public Administration* 23.

Morriss, P. (1983) "Should we subsidise public transport?" Vol. 54 *Political Quarterly* 392.

Munday, N. and Mallinson, H. (1983) "Urban development grant in action" *Public Finance and Accountancy* (December), p. 32.

Murie, A. (1975) *The Sale of Council Houses.* CURS Occasional Paper 35. University of Birmingham.

Murie, A. (1982) "A new era for council housing?" in J. English (ed.) *The Future of Council Housing* (Croom Helm), Chap. 2.

Murie, A. (1985) "The nationalisation of housing policy" in M. Loughlin *et al.* (eds.), Chap. 9.

Nabarro, R. (1980) "The general problem of urban wasteland" Vol. 6, no. 3 *Built Environment* 159

Bibliography

National Audit Office (1985) *Report by the Comptroller and Auditor General. Department of the Environment: Operation of the Rate Support Grant System* (HMSO).

National Consumer Council (1976) *Tenancy Agreements* (NCC).

Newton, K. (1980) *Balancing the Books* (Sage).

Newton, K. (1981) "The local financial crisis in Britain: a non-crisis which is neither local nor financial" in L.J. Sharpe (ed.) *The Local Financial Crisis in Western Europe: Myths and Realities* (Sage), Chap. 6.

Niskanen, W.A. (1973) *Bureaucracy: Servant or Master?* (IEA).

Ouseley, H. (1984) "Local authority race initiatives" in M. Boddy and C. Fudge (ed.) (1984) Chap. 6.

PA Management Consultants (1984) *The proposed abolition of the Metropolitan County Councils. A study of the non-financial aspects.*

Pliatsky, L. (1982) *Getting and Spending* (B. Blackwell).

Quarmby, D. (1984) "Transport that will leave you standing" *The Guardian* October 22.

Raynsford, N. (1984) "Housing benefit: where do we go from here?" Vol. 33, no. 4 *Housing Review* 120.

Redcliffe-Maud (1969) *Report of the Royal Commission on Local Government in England* Cmnd. 4040 (HMSO).

Regan D.E. (1977) *Local Government and Education* (Allen & Unwin).

Regan D.E. (1983) "Enhancing the role of police committees" Vol. 61 *Public Administration* 97.

Rhodes, R. (1981) *Control and Power in Central-Local Government Relations* (Gower).

Richardson, A. (1977) "Tenant participation in council house management" in R. Darke and R. Walker (eds.) *Local Government and the Public* (Leonard Hill), Chap. 12.

Robinson, R. (1984) "Radical change" Vol. 4, no. 3 *Public Money* 5.

Robson, W.A. (1935) "The outlook" in H.J. Laski, W.I. Jennings and W.A. Robson (eds.) *A Century of Municipal Progress 1835-1935* (Allen & Unwin), Chap. XIX.

Roger Tym and Partners (1984) *Monitoring Enterprise Zones: Year Three Report* (DoE).

Rogers, P.B. and Smith, C.R. (1977) "The local authority's role in economic development: the Tyne and Wear Act 1976." Vol. 11, no. 3 *Regional Studies* 153.

Rogers, R. (1980) *Crowther to Warnock. How fourteen reports tried to change children's lives* (Heinemann).

215

Bibliography

Rogers, R. (1984) "A system with too much appeal and too little choice." *The Guardian.* September 18.

Rydin, Y. (1984) "The struggle for housing land: a case of confused interests." Vol. 12 *Policy & Politics* 431.

Saunders, P. (1980) "Local government and the state." Vol. 51 *New Society* 550, March 13.

Saunders, P. (1982) "Why study central-local relations?" Vol. 8, no. 2 *Local Government Studies* 55.

Scarman, Lord (1981) *The Brixton Disorders, 10–12 April 1981* Cmnd. 8427 (HMSO).

Scott, A.J. (1982a) *The Urban Land Nexus and the State* (Pion).

Scott, A.J. (1982b) "Locational patterns and dynamics of industrial activity in the modern metropolis." Vol. 19 *Urban Studies* 111.

Scott, I. and Benlow, D. (1983) "The Struggle for Wandsworth" in S. Hastings and H. Levie (eds.) *Privatisation?* (Spokesman).

Sharpe, L.J. "Theories and values in local government" Vol. XVIII, no. 2 *Political Studies* 11.

Sharpe, L.J. (1982) "The Labour Party and the geography of inequality: a puzzle" in D. Kavanagh (ed.) *The Politics of the Labour Party* (Allen & Unwin), Chap. 6.

Sharpe, L.J. (1984) "Functional allocation in the welfare state." Vol. 10, no. 1 *Local Government Studies* 27.

Skelcher, C. (1983) "Towards salaried councillors?: the special responsibility allowances." Vol. 9, no. 3 *Local Government Studies* 30.

Simpson, B. (1985) "Labour law in Britain since 1979." Vol. 1 *Haldane Journal* 47.

Skinner, D. and Langdon, J. (1974) *The Story of Clay Cross* (Spokesman).

Smith, P. (1983a) "Local authority budgets 1983: no reduction of services." Vol. 3, no. 2 *Public Money* 47.

Smith, P. (1983b) "How targets went wrong." *Public Finance and Accountancy* (December), p. 28.

Starkie, D. (1976) *Transportation Planning, Policy and Analysis* (Pergamon).

Stewart, J. (1982) *Local Government: the conditions of local choice* (Allen & Unwin).

Stewart, J.D. (1985) "The functioning and management of local authorities" in M. Loughlin *et al.* (ed.) (1985), Chap. 5.

Stewart, M. "The inner area planning system." Vol. 11 *Policy & Politics* 203.

Bibliography

Stubbs, B. and Munday, N. (1985) "Partnerships in housing." *Public Finance and Accountancy* (March), p. 24.

Taylor, J.A. (1979) "The Consultative Council on Local Government Finance-a critical analysis of its origins and development." Vol. 5, no. 3 *Local Government Studies* 7.

Taylor Report (1977) *A New Partnership for our Schools* (HMSO).

Taylor, S. (1981) "The politics of enterprise zones" Vol. 59 *Public Administration* 421.

Travers, T. (1981) "Rate support grant 1981/82". *Local Government Chronicle* 925 (September 11.).

Travers, T. and Burgess, T. (1983) *Rates: a response to the Government's proposals for rate limitation and reform.* North East London Polytechnic Working Papers on Institutions, No. 52.

Tullock, G. (1965) *The Politics of Bureaucracy* (Public Affairs Press).

Walker, D. (1983) "Local interest and representation: the case of the 'class' interest among Labour representatives in inner London. "Vol. 1 *Government & Policy* 341.

Watt, P.A. (1982) "The control of local authority capital expenditure" Vol. 8, no. 3 *Local Government Studies* 91.

Webster, K. "Taking advantage of PWLB largesse." *Local Government Chronicle* 193 (February 17).

Whitehead, C.M.E. (1984a) "Privatisation and housing" in J. Le Grand and R. Robinson (eds.) (1984) Chap. 8.

Whitehead, C. (1984b) "Defining a role for public housing" Vol. 4, no. 2 *Public Money* 29.

Widdicombe, D. (1985) *Local Authority Publicity. Interim Report of the Committee of Inquiry into the Conduct of Local Authority Business, chaired by Mr David Widdicombe Q.C.* (HMSO).

Wright, A. (ed.) (1984) *Socialism and Decentralisation* Fabian Tract 496 (Fabian Society).

Young, K. (1984) "Governing Greater London: the background to GLC abolition and an alternative approach." Vol. 10, no. 1 *London Journal* 69.

Young, K. and Kramer, J. (1978) *Strategy and Conflict in Metropolitan Housing: the Suburbs versus the GLC, 1965–1975* (Heinemann).

Young, K. and Mills, L. (1982) "The decline of urban economies." in R. Rose and E. Page (eds.) *Fiscal Stress in Cities* (Cambridge U.P.), Chap. 4.

INDEX

Accountability, local, 34–35, 48, 49, 61, 172, 185
Administration,
    financial, 160–161
    generally, 188–189
Asset Sales, 58, 97–104, 145, 149, 167, 172
Assisted Places Scheme, 124–125
Associations of Local Authorities,
    consultation, 25, 27, 54, 106, 192, 196
    generally, 26, 156, 191
Audit,
    choice of, 161–162
    Commission, 28, 32, 33, 47, 48, 59, 129, 161–162, 165, 169
    economy, efficiency and effectiveness, 48, 161–162, 165, 169
    extraordinary, 165
    powers and duties of auditor, 161–164
    powers of the court, 162–163
Autonomy of Local Government, 1–3, 14, 35, 39, 58, 62, 92–93, 95, 135, 200

Birmingham, 71, 130, 196
Block Grant. See Grant, block.
Borrowing, 19–20, 21, 56, 104–105, 111, 113–116, 160, 166, 183
Bradford, 132
Brent, 37, 38, 45, 54, 55, 130, 186, 194, 196
Bromley, 43, 70, 77, 79, 80, 92, 108, 159, 170, 191, 194
Burns Report, 155
Bus Services,
    deregulation of, 85–92
    generally, 66–68

Camden, 163–164, 196
Capital expenditure,
    generally, 56–61
    housing, 110–113
Capital Receipts, 58, 60, 113
Capitalism, advanced, 17, 62, 201

Central Government, 14, 16, 19, 21–22, 111, 145, 154, 157
Central–Local Government Relations,
    generally, 3, 7, 37, 53–54, 66, 186–188, 198–199, 200
    juridification, 3, 188, 193–198
    politicisation, 3, 188–193
Centralisation, 1, 8, 9, 13, 58, 61, 84, 92, 110, 112, 135, 178, 185, 200
Circulars, 129, 139–141
Civil Defence, 27, 191
Clay Cross, 98, 163
Collectivism, 4–5, 14, 15, 16, 17, 56, 109, 171
Community Development Project, 143
Competition,
    in provision of services, 63, 68, 84, 86, 87, 88, 90–92, 153, 155, 159, 167–168, 172
Conservative Government, 8, 14–15, 20, 21, 24, 45, 50, 56, 68, 86, 96–97, 103, 112, 121, 127–128, 130, 144, 158, 169, 176, 189, 195
Constitutional Issues, 61–62, 193, 200–201
Consultative Council on Local Government Finance, 13–14, 25–26, 30, 125
Consumerism, 130–133, 135, 170–171, 172
Contracting Out, 159, 168, 172
Councillors, 190–192
Council on Tribunals, 131
Cumbria, 87

Damping, 24, 31
Default,
    authorities in, 164–167
    education, 120, 126
    powers, 166
Deindustrialisation. See Industrialisation.
Deregulation, 63, 85–92, 147, 171
Development. See Land Development.
Development Control, 139–141

219

Index